MISSIONS OF SHEHASTA:

A Story of World War II Bomber Aces

Missions of Shehasta:

A Story of World War II Bomber Aces

By
Lyman Austin "Ace" Clark, Jr.

Headline Books, Inc.
Terra Alta, West Virginia

Missions of Shehasta:
A Story of World War II Bomber Aces

A Headline Books, Inc. Publication
May, 1992

Library of Congress Catalog Card Number: 92-81625

For information address:
Headline Books, Inc.
P. O. Box 52
Terra Alta, WV 26764

ISBN: 0929915089

First Printing, 1992

PRINTED IN THE UNITED STATES OF AMERICA

Contents

Dedication

This book is dedicated to the brave men who served in the United States Army Air Corps during World War II, but more specifically to those who fought and those who died fighting in the Solomon Islands from New Hebrides and Guadalcanal to Rabaul on New Britain and the Island of Truk; to the Navy and Marine Pilots of the F4U Corsairs, the P-38 Lightning Pilots in the Army Air Corps and the New Zealand Fighter Pilots in their P-40 Warhawks, who provided excellent fighter cover for our bombers; to those who manned the B-24 Liberator Bombers in combat and were assigned to the 307th Bombardment Group of the 13th Air Force, United States Armed Forces in the South Pacific Area (USAFISPA), also known as the Cactus Air Force; to that special United States Navy crew of the Destroyer U.S.S. CLAXTON, DD571, who saved the life of this author after being hit over Rabaul Harbor on November 11, 1943; to the "Bomber Aces," living and dead, those forgotten crew members who served in their positions on the bombers as pilots, copilots, bombardiers, navigators, engineers, radiomen, and armorer gunners as well as career gunners, manning the turrets, the waist gunners, who faced many ordeals, destroyed many enemy planes (some five and more) without the recognition that was afforded the fighter aces; to all those brave men; and yes, to the ground support personnel who kept the planes flying and tended to our necessary needs for food, medical services and supplies; to all of these, this book is dedicated.

I also want to recognize the support and dedication of the wives, the girl friends who were always loving, faithful and forgiving in those difficult times; the brave mothers and fathers, sisters and brothers, sons and daughters and others who worked so hard back home to help keep America free, many suffering losses of loved ones during the war.

I thank those who assisted me in the completion of this book. My daughter, Connie G. Lucas, has my appreciation, especially for her efforts in typesetting and helping me to proofread my book prior to publication, and my wife, Ardith, for her understanding and encouragement. Without their help it would not have been possible. And my publishers, Robert G. and Catherine M. Teets for their excellent work in putting this all together.

Prologue

After many years, the story of combat in the B-24 "Liberators," from the islands of the South Pacific, especially Guadalcanal and the other Solomon Islands, will be told as it really happened. But writing this book posed a big problem. How can the story be told like it really was - the bravery, the fear, the love, the sex, the fun, the hate, the mistakes, the sacrifices, the prejudices, the betrayals of life, the finality of death and the unshakable belief in God, in Country and in selves? How can the down to earth and high in the sky stories, usually left out by historical writers, be told, without revealing too much about any one individual or particular members of a combat crew — experiences I have seen or been told about, sometimes in a weak moment and/ or in strict confidence?

Many of the participants are very much alive with families, pursuing the promises of the good life in this great Country which each fought for, and they are succeeding. But as young men in training, many hardly more than children, going into combat and seeking every adventure in life, expecting to live it all while life still existed, many went over the edge, squeezing it all from every minute, experiencing strange, exciting and intense feelings for the first time.

But that problem has been solved by introduction of a phantom crew who lived and fought with all the others, to act for them, even when good judgement and common sense is questionable and whose actions sometimes take the low road as well as the high roads of life in war times.

The author has made an effort to keep the contents of this book suitable for all. However, as you know, war is hell, love is wonderful and sex is sex, regardless of how it is presented. Further, when the phantom crew goes into action, the author will know, but all those who were there will know, too, and the story gets told fully as never before, with no one hurt or embarrassed, but with nothing left out.

Those great comrades in combat who served, know it is every word true, and every one of them reflected great credit upon themselves and the United States of America, with bravery and self sacrifice, above and beyond the call of duty.

So strap on your parachutes, and prepare to ride the "Liberators" in the clouds with them, while they fly to their targets and their destinies as they help sink the Rising Sun.

Crew Members:

"SHEHASTA"

*James D. "Jim" Jelley, Pilot
Norman A. "Johnny" Johnson, Co-pilot
  (left crew due to sinus trouble at high altitudes)
*Donald "Don" Taylor Co-pilot
  (replacement for Johnson)
*Ralph E. "Gene" Bruce, Bombardier
*Julius T. "Whitie" Woytowich, Navigator
**Henry E. "Hutch" Hutchings, Engineer/Top Turret Gunner
**Charles M. "Griff" Griffith, Assistant Engineer/Left Waist Gunner
**Victor J. "Vic" Meehan, Assistant Engineer/Left Waist Gunner
  (replacement for Griffith)
**Charles R. "Tommy" Thompson, Assistant Radioman/Tail Gunner
*Lyman A. "Ace" Clark, Jr., Armorer/Ball Turret Gunner
*Earl B. "Corny" Cornelius, Nose Turret Gunner
Gustave "Gus" Hosfeth, Radio Operator/Right Waist Gunner
*William "Bill" Humphrey Radio Operator/Right Waist Gunner
  (replacement for Hosfeth)

"PHANTOM LADY"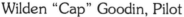
(All Pseudonyms)

Wilden "Cap" Goodin, Pilot
**Benjamin "Ben" Pudder, Co-pilot
*William "Bill" Droppelman, Bombardier
**Michael "Mike" Reeder, Navigator
*Roland "Lew" Lewis, Engineer/Top Turret Gunner
**Randolph "Pete" Peterson, Nose Turret Gunner
Joseph "Joe" Jamison, Assistant Radioman/Tail Gunner
Clifford "Cliff" Roberts, Assistant Engineer/Left Waist Gunner
  (killed in training)
Paul "Lefty" Leftowitz, Assistant Engineer/Left Waist Gunner
  (replacement for Roberts)
Phillip "Phil" Tabor, Radioman/Right Waist Gunner
***Andrew "Andy" Parker, Armorer/Ball Turret Gunner
Jack "Dave" Davison, Armorer/Ball Turret Gunner
  (replacement for Parker)

*Wounded in Action **Killed in Action ***Salvoed in Ball Turret over Kahili

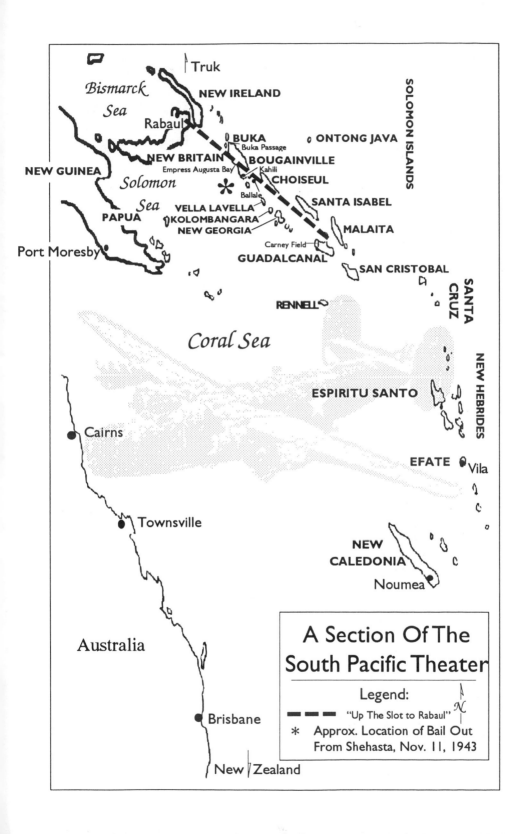

Truk

Bismarck Sea

NEW IRELAND

Rabaul

BUKA
Buka Passage
ONTONG JAVA

NEW BRITAIN
Empress Augusta Bay

BOUGAINVILLE
Kahili

SOLOMON ISLANDS

NEW GUINEA

Solomon

CHOISEUL

Ballale

SANTA ISABEL

Sea

PAPUA

VELLA LAVELLA
KOLOMBANGARA
NEW GEORGIA

MALAITA

Port Moresby

Carney Field

GUADALCANAL

SAN CRISTOBAL

SANTA CRUZ

RENNELL

Coral Sea

ESPIRITU SANTO

NEW HEBRIDES

Cairns

EFATE Vila

Townsville

NEW CALEDONIA

Noumea

Australia

A Section Of The South Pacific Theater

Legend:

N

▬ ▬ ▬ "Up The Slot to Rabaul"

Brisbane

* Approx. Location of Bail Out
From Shehasta, Nov. 11, 1943

New Zealand

MISSIONS OF SHEHASTA

Chapter 1

DREAMS OF YOUTH

Of Wings & Other Things

My interest in airplanes was very high, even as a young man. I am holding the trophy I won for the longest flight at the local airport at Jackson's Mill, Lewis County, West Virginia in 1940. This was a stick model built and propelled by rubber bands which were wound up with an egg beater or hand drill. Lightness of the model, good workmanship and a knowledge of aerodynamics were important. I won first place and later was president of the model airplane club in Weston High School in 1941.

The small patch of grassy field had been visited many times before this. It had the only allure for a young, would-be aviator for miles around, and was a part of a state park known as Jackson's Mill[1], in honor of the boyhood home of General Stonewall Jackson. It was easy to identify due to an

1. *Jackson's Mill, Lewis County, West Virginia*

old grist mill located on the small stream running through the park.

The grassy field was just large enough to handle small planes. It also served as an air mail pick-up station for the local post offices, but to me it was an opportunity to get acquainted with a real airplane close up.

I would work evenings and weekends cutting grass, or at other odd jobs, just to get enough money to take a ride in some visiting aircraft, or to take a ride with a local flyer who owned a Stenson plane. He was the air mail pilot, making flights over surrounding towns, using a grappling hook on a rope to snatch a bag of mail suspended on a line between two poles placed in the ground. The line and poles were removed after each pickup. Sometimes, I got to take them down.

This field was a place for barnstormers in the depression years, and in the later 1930's. Occasionally, some daredevil flyer, and parachute jumping partner, would show up and thrill Sunday crowds with an exhibition of aerobatics flying, ending up with a parachute jump at the end of the day. This kept the local crowds hanging around waiting for the daredevil's final feat.

But the biggest thrill for a young dreamer, like myself, was to talk to the pilots, and try to get a ride free, or for as little as possible. Because of the depression, and tight money, grass cutting or building haystacks at fifty-cents a day plus lunch, did not go far. I hoped not only to get a ride, but to also experience some acrobatic loops, stalls and spins.

As a young child of four or five, I had a curiosity about things mechanical. I can remember taking a hammer and breaking up my Big Ben pocket watch, given to me by my mother as a Christmas present, to find out what made it tick. Of course, the springs and cogs flew in all directions, and I never did get the answer to what made it tick. But I learned by way of a stick to my rear that it is best to curb a curiosity that could lead to destruction.

Growing up, I learned other lessons especially appropriate to that time in life. Due to real hard times, my father had a difficult time making ends meet. He was on the wrong political side and, as a result, working for the State, lost his job as a maintenance man. In addition to painting and making repairs, he also made pots, pans, and other metal containers used by the local mental institution[2] — the largest in the State, and whose claim to fame was being the largest hand cut stone building in the world.

I remember things were so bad during the depression, and work so scarce, we spent a few days at the county poor farm, as it was called. My brothers and I had never slept on a feather tick mattress, and occasionally one of the stiffer quills would come through and jab us somewhere. Curiosity led my brother and me to cut a hole in one corner to see what was inside. Feathers went everywhere. Fortunately, our stay was very short — and the farm manager was glad to see us go.

Later, President Franklin D. Roosevelt established the WPA (short for "We Piddle Around"), which provided some work during those depression years. Just kidding about the WPA. It really provided a much needed help to many at the time.

My father improved our situation sufficiently for all the children to continue in school and get the coveted high school diploma. We all found odd jobs selling newspapers, delivering milk, and doing farm work. My father was able to do some painting and roofing work, and finally, to work again painting the clock and steeple of the institution where he had worked previously.

When dad was working up on the steeple, he would go out on a small ledge with no railing, throw a rope up around the steeple and climb up to paint it. I would take his lunch up to him, first climbing stairs, then ladders inside the tower to the clock, then out on the ledge where he worked. But the feeling was much different from the plane rides I had taken with the pilots. This kind of height caused a mild vertigo. But after helping my father on lower buildings, I became less

---

2. *Weston State Hospital, Weston, West Virginia*

fearful of that kind of height, and it did not lessen my desire to fly.

As I grew older, I built model airplanes. They were small, of balsa wood, glue and tissue paper. But I grew familiar with the various parts of the planes and how they flew.

By the time I was in high school, it was very definite in my mind that I was going to fly, and being very poor, it was natural that the only way to do that was to enter the military and make my dream come true.

I read "G-8 and His Flying Aces," "The Lone Eagle," and every other book or magazine relating to flying I could find, preparing for that time when I could enter service.

Dad had been in the Army during World War I, and had served overseas in France fighting the Germans. He had been in battle with the 144th Machine Gun Battalion, and also served in an Aero Squadron for a time, doing repairs to the early biplanes used in combat, forming the necessary metal parts and repairing battle damage to the planes. I remember two stories which he told us boys.

One was when he was taking training at Hattiesburg, Mississippi. He said they were so short of real guns, broom sticks were used when marching. The troops were segregated at that time, and even during World War II. But there were black troops on the base, too. He told of a black man taking his physical for overseas duty. When the doctor told him to bend over and spread his cheeks, he bent over and pulled his lips as far apart as he could with his two forefingers. His cheeks were spread! But the doctor told him to spread the cheeks of his rear end, and the soldier said, "That Kaiser Bill (head of the German government) must be a powerful man to make a white man look up a black man's rear all the way over here in the United States."

My dad also told of the soldier in the trenches in France who was carrying milk pails to the fighting men in the front lines. Suddenly one pail flew out of his hand and he felt liquid running down his leg. He grabbed his leg, throwing down the other pail, and started running back toward the rear lines, yelling, "I'm shot, I'm shot!" But after running for some time, he began to realize there was no pain. Getting up enough courage to look down, he found it was only milk from the pail that had made his leg wet. The other fellows never let the poor fellow live it down. My father always denied he was the one with the milk pails, but he liked to tell the stories and laugh.

These years in growing up were not without some fun and games. Times were hard and things were tough, money was scarce, but many new learning experiences occurred. I remember one time my brothers and I went to see the Jimmy Braddock, Joe Lewis fight at the local theater. Saturday afternoon only cost us ten cents each.

The big occasion was the give-away of a pair of child size boxing gloves to the one with the lucky ticket. My brother, Bob, won. As a result, we were the most popular boys in our part of town, and we all learned how to box a little.

Being left-handed, I had some real knock down, drag out experiences that served me well later on in life. But the big lesson was—there is always someone who is ready to fight it out, to knock the chip off your shoulder — someone who is faster, smaller, larger or just better with his fists, and even with his feet, biting, brawling and scratching.

Another time, John Manley, who lived two doors from us, got a pair of child-size skis for Christmas. He let me try them, but I was too big for them and they weren't long enough.

We went "skiing" on one of the local hills. I put on John's skis and started downward in snow about three inches deep. It was my first time on skis, and once I started downhill, I couldn't stop. I ran into a barbed wire fence and was badly scratched and cut up. I learned later to sit down to stop. It was a good lesson to learn, as I've learned it is best to just sit down and keep quiet when things get out of hand with others. It's helped many times since that first episode as a young lad. Just sit down.

Not long after that, I remember George Carson and his

invitation to observe Anna Belle Roberts through a small knot hole in the back of the Roberts' privy. It was a small wooden building about one hundred feet from her house. The privy was ringed with hedge which was easy to slip through and it was hard to turn down a look at Anna Belle.

George said she invited him to look, so the rest of the boys waited to see how he made out before they also ventured a peek. George, with his eye centered over the hole, seemed intent on getting an eye full.

All of a sudden, he grabbed his face, wiped his eye, and ran back where we were waiting. He swore she had urinated on him through the hole.

At the time, we all laughed, but since then, thinking it over, I've always wondered how she was able to manage that feat, as high up as the hole was in the board. I believe George lost his nerve and used that excuse as a way out.

No one else took Anna Belle up on her offer again — that I know of — but she was regarded with mixed feelings after that.

Anna Belle did approach me once, along with Janie Malone, and asked me to go the back of the garage (a very dark area) adjacent to the local grocery store to see what it was like to feel their breasts, but I backed out and didn't go with them.

But Paul Lewis said he went, and bragged he not only felt their breasts, and they had nothing on under their clothes, but he said they let him feel other places, too. I don't know if he was just bragging or not, but I have little reason to doubt him in view of their offer to me. Later, one of them did "get into trouble," and had to leave the area before she had the baby.

Another girl was Martha Hess, whom we all named "Ivy," because she went down around the curve with Jack Parker and rolled around in the grass with him. He said that was not all he did down around the curve. Unfortunately, there was poison ivy where they were and poor Martha had a difficult time explaining to her mother how she got poison ivy on her back and behind.

I guess she had a real hard time getting it cured because she was out of school for a couple of weeks with it, and carried her nickname even longer. Later, she developed quite a "reputation" about town. But she was able to land a 4F lawyer and had two children before I returned from overseas.

In high school, one of the most ornery guys was Bill Nolan. Bill not only liked to tell jokes, he liked to play them on others, too. He was a friend and lived near me when we were growing up, but we were warned about playing with him, as you had to stay clear of some of his activities or you would get into trouble.

We walked a distance of two miles to high school together. One day Bill came to class and told some of us he had saved Mrs. Jordan's life. We asked how.

He said Mrs. Jordan was down on the river bank of the West Fork washing clothes, and forgot to put on her panties. He said she saw her reflection in the water, thought it was a boat and tried to step into it. The water was over her head and she started to drown. She yelled for help and Bill ran down and pulled her out. The girls that heard his story were red-faced, but they seemed to enjoy his stories and he always had an audience.

Another time, Bill came around and announced he had been down to Marjorie's house the night before and because it rained hard, he had to stay the night. Marjorie was quite embarrassed when Bill started to tell the story because she was very shy and not too attractive, but she was a good girl and not prepared for the likes of Bill. Then Bill explained what happened.

He said Marjorie prepared the supper that evening. They had a big mess of pickled beans, and Bill said he just loved pickled beans. Also, he said they only had one bed, and because of this, it was necessary for Bill to sleep on one side of Marjorie's dad (he was a widower) and Marjorie was on the other side.

As Bill told it, about two o'clock in the morning, the dogs

started barking and Marjorie's dad jumped up to see what was in the chicken coop. Bill said Marjorie then whispered to him, "Now's your chance, Bill."

He said, "You know what I did, don't you?" After a pause, he continued "I jumped up and ran into the kitchen and ate the rest of those pickled beans." Well, that was an example of Bill's regular entertainment.

He was great at misleading our home room teacher, a very nice lady who had never married. Bill would bring snow in his pocket and when Miss Jackson went to turn in the attendance report to the principal's office, Bill would place snow on the thermometer at the back of the room. When Miss Jackson returned, he would complain it was too cold. Miss Jackson would check the thermometer, turn the heat up, and even shiver. Soon it was much too hot for class.

Once Bill placed a lighted match too near the thermometer and blew the mercury right out the top. Another time, he put burning sulphur he had taken from the chemistry lab in the circulating air ducts, causing an odor throughout the school.

But he was to prove to be a disappointment because he claimed farming to keep him out of the service, evading the draft. He and I almost got into a scrap later when he told me, "I'd rather be a live coward than a dead hero."

His activities with the married women eventually led to his being shot by a jealous husband, so his draft dodging didn't help him dodging bullets. He never did amount to much. I guess there are a few of those types in every town.

I continued my interest in airplanes, and was the president of the model airplane club in high school. I won a few contests and a trophy for design and timed flight on a rubber powered model, given by a local sheet metal shop making parts for aircraft and training students in how to rivet, cut and weld sheet metal.

Then came Pearl Harbor on December 7th, 1941, and graduation from high school the following spring. Five of my buddies and I left to work at the Glenn L. Martin plant at

Chapter One

Middle River, Maryland.

After working four months installing de-icer boots, then bomb sight mounts on the Martin bombers, I came back home to enlist in the Army Air Corps, even though I could have been deferred from the military, working in a defense plant. Some of my buddies did stay there during the whole war. Others were like me and volunteered for service.

The irony of my volunteering was, just three days later I received a letter making me an under-aircraft model maker at Wright-Patterson Air Force Base in Ohio. My mother wrote to me in Columbus, Ohio, where I had been sent for duty.

I only stayed there three days, doing one day of Kitchen Police — KP — even before being sworn into the military.

It was the only KP I was to ever do, because I was shipped out to Jefferson Barracks, near St. Louis, Missouri for assignment and basic training. When personnel talked to me and found I wanted to fly, I was taken to see a Captain, who showed me a fifty caliber machine gun bullet and a thirty caliber one. He asked me if I would like to be flying the following week. I jumped at the chance.

I knew it would have been better to ask about pilot training, but he covered that by saying it would take months to be a pilot. He indicated I could be in the air within a week, skipping basic training, if I went in as an aerial gunner. And I would jump from private to buck sergeant in eight weeks (3 stripes!) and get flying pay each month.

But he was honest, too. He said they needed aerial gunners, because they did not last long in combat — maybe three minutes of actual combat.

But my childhood dream was being fulfilled — I was finally going to get to fly, and to perhaps die in defense of my great country! Many young men were doing it at the time, and it was the only thing to do if you were an honorable man.

Passing the physical for flight duty was a happy event.

CHAPTER 2

DUTY TO COUNTRY

Training & Temptations

My mother and father had insisted on all the children getting as much education as possible, as theirs had been limited. They wanted us to have at least a high school diploma, which we did, but college was out of the question at the time. The war offered an opportunity to obtain some additional training.

While pilots were not in demand in civilian life, aerial gunners were not wanted at all. But the Army Air Corps needed both very badly.

I was to actually learn to fly a Piper Cub and an Aeronica Champ in later life, but the thought of "flying" right away was a dream come true. Not only

At last, my dream of childhood, to have wings and fly high. This picture was taken at Las Vegas Air Base right after graduation from Aerial Gunnery School, receipt of my wings and sargeant's stripes on November 16, 1942.

would I be up in an AT-6, but there was the added bonus of attaining the rank of buck sergeant (a three striper) in only six weeks of training.

I was ecstatic with the thought! And no basic training,

either. It was almost too good to be true. I should have questioned it at the time, but the opportunity for adventure and fulfillment of a boyhood dream was too strong to delay even one moment.

The next morning I was on a train to Las Vegas Air Base, in Nevada, with no fooling around. The truck was waiting to take us to the air base at the end of our three day train trip. We were immediately processed and indoctrinated. The next day I was issued a one piece flight suit, a canvas helmet with holes for the ear phones, and started classes. We were also assigned bunks and told where the mess hall was located. That was about it.

One day later we were taken to the flight line to meet the pilots and get acquainted with the AT-6's, the plane we would initially fly and shoot from while at the base. Most of the pilots were flying Staff Sergeants, and a few Second Lieutenants — some very wild and very few with experience.

I had enlisted on September 9th, 1942, and by September 25th, 1942, I was on the flight line, ready to fly in an all metal, radial engine aircraft, with pilots who were mostly just out of pilot training themselves.

We were scheduled to go into the pressure chamber to see if we could stand high altitude flying. We were already starting the study of thirty caliber machine guns, with fifty caliber machine guns to follow, with complete assembly and naming of parts blindfolded as our final goal.

We started to become familiar with the effects of various forces on bullets, such as temperature, moisture, windage and wind drift, bullet drop (the force of gravity), bullet pattern (how much vibration when firing spread the bullets at various distances from the target), and leading the target based on its movement and direction. Skeet and trap shooting were required. How to bore sight a gun— using a vice to hold the gun while lining up the sight, then firing it to make sure of its accuracy. We began with removing new guns from storage in cosmoline, a thick grease preservative, and cleaning them piece by piece and assembling them ready for use. We learned to name each part; charging handle, the bolt, sear, trigger, cover plate, back plate, drive spring, just to name a few, and the jacket, barrel, and how to adjust head space, etc....

A part of the training was shooting shotguns, skeet and trap, plus a real challenge — moving base.

Moving base was taught by placing you in the back of a pickup truck with panels on the bed of the truck to help you stand up. The truck would then start down a road, which curved back and forth, at about forty miles an hour. A gunner was on each side of the truck with his shotgun. Along the sides of the road were small houses, square and only about three feet tall with men in the houses who shot out clay birds, high, low and in all directions. The distance between each house allowed just enough time to load and shoot.

There were twenty-five stations to shoot at the birds, and the goal, of course, was to get as many as possible. A poor showing could get you washed out of gunnery school. About eighteen hits out of twenty-five was expected. I was able to average twenty to twenty-four most of the time— even though I had never hunted as a boy since I had no gun or license— so I had no worries.

In the evenings we could practice leading targets on machines provided that shot BB's, using compressed air and moving targets. It had an unending source of air, so you could practice until all tired out. We spent hours at this only recreation provided. We couldn't leave the base until our training was completed.

The initial ride in an AT-6 training plane was designed to see if flying was really the right field for us. So it was not designed as a smooth ride. We each took along a bag, just in case, and took off facing backward. The seat was made to turn 180 degrees to the front, and had an azimuth ring to hook onto our safety belt. The safety belt was around our waist, and had straps to attach to the ring.

We also had a parachute, which had to be fitted prior to take-off. We were instructed on how to bail out over the side and count to ten slowly prior to pulling the ripcord, just to be clear of the plane. Very little was said about how to land. I guess they felt getting down came first. We did receive training later on how to land on the ground and in the ocean, which was to come in very handy later.

All of our beginning flights were take-offs with the gunner facing the tail. That first ride usually consisted of dives, spins, rolls, half rolls, loops and stalls. Some never got the loops or wing-overs, but if the pilot felt you could take it, or enjoyed the acrobatics, he would really wring you out.

If anyone got sick the first time, then a second, less eventful flight was made. Sickness on that flight was cause for washout. I made the initial flight all right, but some men were washed out after the second flight. My pilot let me face forward on take-off after the first two flights.

On our next flights, we were expected to stand up in the rear seat, load the gun belts into the guns and prepare to fire at "tow" targets. The guns were limited on how far forward and back they could be moved because some of the guys would get excited and let go, or freeze on the trigger. This could result in shooting our own — or some other — plane's rudder or wing, causing damage and usually loss of plane, pilot and aerial gunner. This action started to tell the men from the boys very quickly.

When the pilot dived down or moved in toward the tow target, our feet would leave the floor many times, causing a loss of balance. On the pull-ups, we felt as if our bodies were being driven through the floor, and our legs would buckle, pushing us back into the seat. Fortunately, after a few times I caught on, and learned how to prepare for the movements.

I had a pretty good flying Staff Sergeant to fly with, and he realized I liked the flying, so I went up with him quite a few times. The pilots were fearful of those fellows who would lose control while up in the air with a machine gun. The G forces were hard to deal with if you were scared, too.

The school cut back on some of the routine later, I understood, because the washout rate was too great. They even went to slower B-18 bomber type planes to train in as the war went on. But I trained with the hot ones, and some pilots were teed off because they weren't in combat using the fighter planes.

Aerial gunnery school was a voluntary assignment and we drew flying pay while training to fly. So that was an extra incentive.

In gunnery school, we shot various colored bullets, some yellow, some red, blue, green or black. Everyone liked black, because when we landed and counted up our hits on the tow target, any holes that showed no color were given to the guy with the black or unpainted bullets. Tracers were included in every five rounds, so we could see how we were leading on our target and if we were hitting it.

Aerial gunnery school graduates were usually assigned as tail gunners, nose gunners and ball turret gunners on B-17 Flying Fortresses or B-24 Liberators. Other crew members who were engineers, radio operators, bombardiers and navigators learned how to shoot the machine guns, operate the flexible waist guns, nose guns, and how to operate some turrets, but they did not take the same concentrated gunnery training.

I later attended armament school at Salt Lake City, Utah at the Air Base. This was invaluable training in combat.We learned about all kinds of bombs, how they were armed, and their purposes.

While in Aerial Gunnery School, one trip was most memorable because the flying Sergeant was a very good flyer and enjoyed a little sightseeing after target practice with the tow targets. He took me out over the mountainous area where a burned area with plane wreckage was visible.

He flew very low so I could get a good look at it. He informed me that was the location of the wreck that killed Carol Lombard, the wife of Clark Gable. Gable later became a waist gunner on a B-17 in the Eighth Air Force in Europe, attaining the rank of Major, which sure outranked all the aerial gunners I ever met. But, then, he was a movie star.

It was a very interesting flight.

After receiving aerial gunners' wings, and the three stripes of a buck sergeant, we were all ready to see the town of Las Vegas. We knew we would be receiving orders to join a crew in a few days and start phase training at another base, but we didn't know to what base or kind of plane we would be assigned for combat.

While going through training, I developed a very good friendship with two fellow gunners who were to figure in my future. One was Earl B. "Corny" Cornelius, the other, Andrew "Andy" Parker. Corny would wind up as a nose gunner on a crew with me, on "Shehasta," while Andy joined the crew of "Phantom Lady," as lower ball turret gunner. The three of us headed for Las Vegas on a military bus with a pass good until eight the next morning. We were all bright-eyed and bushy tailed, ready for anything.

Leaving the bus and walking down the street, we immediately faced a dilemma. Three girls approached us, all very attractive, and each handed us individual folded pieces of paper. The message, in very large and easy to read lettering said, "Come with me."

I looked at Corny and Andy, then, almost in unison, we asked, "What do you want?"

None of them would talk. This was very confusing, and we couldn't decide what to do. We had been warned back at the base about "B" girls who would try to get us drunk and roll us for our money and valuables. But the money would have been slim picking because none of us had been paid, and wouldn't be until our transfer orders were cut, transferring us to another base.

Also, we had seen the movies narrated by a young Captain named Ronald Reagan, later to become our President, who explained how we could get venereal disease from loose women on the streets. Very graphic pictures of gonorrhea, syphilis, and canker sores had provided enough fear to guarantee the use of condoms, a visit to a pro station, or total abstinence for protection. With a very serious and believable face, Captain Reagan had done his job well, and the graphic examples, shown with his narration, left little to the imagination. There was little doubt he was destined to be a great actor or politician, or both.

I had decided on abstaining, since I hadn't had the experience in high school, or in Baltimore, and had yet to get seriously involved with any one girl. The most I had observed was a visit to the vaudeville show with the rest of the guys from my home town to see a stripper. Burlesque was the right name for it, and I remember to this day her name was Annie Fong, an oriental beauty. Little was left to the imagination to see and the jokes were just as vivid. Anyway, with the prospect of going into combat soon, I didn't think it fair to have any young lady face that prospect, perhaps pregnant and alone back home.

But I might add, there was the feeling that began to develop, and discussed among ourselves, that life could be short. We were taking great risks daily since entering training to become combat aerial gunners, and the prospect of death without experiencing as much of life as possible posed an urgency to raise a little hell, and for some excitement of any kind that may come our way. In other words, many became the "Flyboys" that were pretty cocky and hell bent for trouble, and some did pursue the "B" girls for the special excitement and pleasure they could offer.

Wings, sergeant's stripes, and a confidence only a young fighting man could convey would be no match for these girls — or, so we thought — so we decided to follow them.

As I said, they did not talk, just smiled at us. In fact, they were so friendly, Corny, Andy and I felt we had run into what promised to be a very interesting evening. They each took one of us arm in arm to walk down the street. They stopped in front of a lounge and handed us each another note. It read, "Come in here with me and sit at a table with me and my friends."

We looked at each other for approval of our next act together, but moved into the lounge without delay.

Sitting at the table were three other attractive ladies and three Second Lieutenants sitting by their sides. Then one of the girls stood up. She started talking, explaining the girls had decided to have a scavenger hunt as a way of entertaining some very lonely servicemen (that was us all right) who were away from home.

We were to take a list of items and go into the neighborhood, knock on doors or whatever, to secure such items as a feather, a spoon, or a safety pin. You wouldn't dare do that in this crime and drug infested world, but at that time, all was patriotism, innocence and trust. People did not even lock their doors most of the time in the evenings. Times have changed.

The first couple returning to the club with all the items on the list was the winner. We didn't know how long it would take, but the list was quite long. We didn't know yet what the prize was, either, but each of us had our own idea what it could be, with thoughts of collecting on the way. But we were wrong.

The girl I was with was very attractive and drove a small red convertible, so I felt I had hit the jackpot already, because in 1942 that was not the usual transportation of the average young lady about town.

We had great fun collecting the items, and by the time we returned to the lounge it was about eleven o'clock that night. We were third to return, beaten by one of the girls with a Second Lieutenant. Andy had returned with his girl friend, but Corny and the other two officers and their friends had not made it back. The suggestion was made by one of the girls that we leave a note for the others and head for their respective homes. My friend wanted me to meet her parents.

Corny's friend was also a friend of the girl I was with, so they joined us shortly after our arrival at her house. Her parents were there and both were very nice, serving us soft drinks and dessert — pie and ice cream. It turned out to be a very nice and enjoyable evening, offered by some very nice and patriotic Americans, not what we had imagined in the beginning at all.

I made a date for the next evening, thinking it would be nice if we stayed in Las Vegas the rest of the war. But when we got back to base, we had received orders and were frozen on base pending shipment to Davis-Monthan Field at Tucson, Arizona. We were on a train to Tucson the next day.

Walking Tall, Feeling Proud

Above: Reproduction of the author's gunnery school diploma.

Left: Reproduction of the author's promotion papers giving him the rank of Sergeant.

CHAPTER 3

RIDING THE CLOUDS

The Partnership Begins

We were ready for assignment to crews and to begin training in the type of aircraft we would be flying into combat.

Upon arrival at Davis-Monthan Field, I had my first look at a Consolidated B-24 Liberator, also known as the "Flying Boxcar." At that time, it was much larger

Top: Me and my Sperry Lower Ball Turret. These guns were used to shoot down three Japanese planes; I brought down two more while riding in "Man-O-War." This is the business end of the twin fifties on Shehasta in June, 1943. Note the gun sight and oxygen hose through the bullet-proof glass. While riding in this position, it was easy to scan all areas of the sky for enemy planes and to observe bombing runs and hits on our targets. **Bottom:** A close-up of the turret.

than any other bomber in the American arsenal.

The Liberator had the longest range, carried the biggest bomb load, and with changes made later in its armament, was the most formidable in combat with the enemy, exceeding the B-17 Flying Fortress in firepower.

It carried a crew of ten men, and with the four, twin, fifty caliber machine guns carried in the nose, top, tail, and bottom ball turrets, plus fifty calibers in each waist window and another behind the nose turret which could be fired by the navigator and/or bombardier, it was unmatched by any fighter, except when greatly outnumbered. The secret Davis wing had tremendous lifting capabilities, even with a full bomb load.

The B-29 Superfortress had not yet entered the war in 1942-43. The B-29 and B-52 were only dreams that would become realities much later, with the B-29 an actuality before the end of World War II, when it dropped the Atomic bombs on Japan. The B-36 Bomber was still on the drawing board, too. So we were to get the big bomber, the Liberator. Immediately, we began to wonder whether we would go to Europe or Africa to fight or would we be heading for the South Pacific?

We were now to form crews, and begin "phase training," a series of three phases of approximately one month each, which tested our abilities not only on an individual basis, but also our ability to work as a crew, acting as a team, just as a football or basketball team would do in sports, except for one major difference.

This was a life or death situation, where very few who made a mistake or failed to train properly, had a second chance. Getting together, getting acquainted, learning to trust the other fellow with your life, were all a part of the first phase. The pilots and co-pilots, the bombardiers, the navigators as well as the engineers, the radio operators and the professionally trained turret gunners, often with back up jobs for others, all had a part in the ultimate success of our mission — to beat the enemy and come home alive.

Crew members had to attend school when not flying to learn more about their assigned positions on the plane. Everyone also learned alternate positions, in the event someone became ill or was injured or killed as a result of combat. So we were all kept very busy on the ground and in the air.

Our crew was formed within a week of our arrival. Luck would be with Corny and me — we were put on the same crew. Being buddies from our days at aerial gunnery school, we had already become familiar with a "Flyboy" mentality, enjoying ourselves when and where possible. Trust, a very necessary ingredient for teamwork, had already formed during our adventures in Las Vegas.

The make-up of our crew was as follows: Pilot, James D. "Jim" Jelley (from then on the crew was known as Jelley's Crew, as was custom, the crew being identified by the name of the pilot); Co-pilot, Norman A. Johnson; Bombardier, Ralph E. "Gene" Bruce; Navigator, Julius T. "Whitie" Woytowich. This completed the list of officers of the crew.

The enlisted men were: Engineer, Henry E. "Hutch" Hutchings; Assistant Engineer, William H. "Griff"Griffith; Radio Operator, Whitsett (who later left the crew during phase training); Radio Operator, Gustave "Gus" Hosfeth (replaced Whitsett and stayed on); Assistant Radio Operator, Charles R. "Tommy" Thompson; Nose Gunner, Earl B. "Corny" Cornelius; and Armorer, yours truly.

Hutch also operated the top turret, Griff the left waist gun, Tommy the tail turret, Corny the nose turret, and I was the lower ball turret operator on the crew.

The lower ball turret was considered the most dangerous and complicated to operate, and since I had aerial gunnery training, and weighed only 119 pounds, it was logical I would be the likely choice for the Sperry Lower Ball turret.

The B-24 Liberators did not yet have the lower ball turret installed. This was done later at our first overseas stop. However, I learned its operation as part of training.

Further, since I was to be the armorer, I had to become familiar with the operation of all the turrets, as well as with the minor operation of bombing systems, release, loading, etc.

So, our crew was ready to begin phase training as a very efficient and harmonious unit. That training was to separate the men from the boys from that time on into combat.

It was at the beginning of the first phase that we met the crew who would fly the "Phantom Lady." Andy Parker, who came with Corny and me from Las Vegas, was assigned as ball turret gunner on Wilden "Cap" Goodin's crew. Goodin was the pilot. Benjamin "Ben" Pudder was the Co-pilot, William "Will" Droppelman was bombardier, and Michael "Mike" Reeder was the navigator.

Roland "Lew" Lewis was engineer, and also operated the top Upper Local Turret during combat. Randolph "Pete" Peterson was nose turret gunner. Joseph "Joe" Jamison was assistant radio operator and tail gunner, and Clifford "Cliff" Roberts was the assistant engineer and left waist gunner. He was replaced by Paul "Lefty" Leftowitz during phase three training, when he flew with another crew that blew up on take-off due to an engine fire that developed just after leaving the runway. Phillip "Phil" Tabor was radio operator and right waist gunner.

Soon after starting training as a crew, we lost power on two engines on take-off and almost "bought the farm," as we would put it later. But Jelley was able to gain enough altitude to come around, line up with the runway and land.

The ground crews thought the gasoline strainers were dirty, but after another B-24 lost power on take-off, a check was run on the gasoline. They found the octane to be high test for automobiles. All planes were grounded until every one was tested for aviation octane fuel.

The planes were used for training different crews, which included pilots and other members of their crews, as well as ground maintenance personnel — all relatively inexperienced.

This contributed to many accidents, and I know that at one time, during second phase training at Alamogordo, New Mexico, it seemed more planes and crews were being lost in

training than in combat. Seven planes were lost in one
month, which was equal to our combat losses in some
months overseas.

Since flying in the Army Air Corps was strictly voluntary,
many less inclined toward adventure chose the infantry or
administrative type duty. But even that choice was always at
the risk of winding up in the trenches of a foreign land.

Little did we know we would wind up many nights in fox
holes, too, during bombing and strafing raids by the enemy.
The choices were not great.

But the men who did continue training liked the excitement and the benefits in spite of the risks. This risky life style
did make the need for some light-hearted recreation very
necessary, as some of us got pretty uptight during training.

The macho image of the "Flyboys" helped offset the
fear, too. Girls liked the higher rank and wings of an airman,
which did help to provide some compensation for the hazardous duty, in addition to that extra flight pay.

Passes were given more freely on weekends at Tucson,
and even sometimes during the week when flights were not
on the schedule at night or early in the mornings. We didn't
fly every day, but it was very regular and we were quite busy.

One of our favorite haunts in town was the Apache
Hotel, where some of Goodin's crew, as well as Jelley's crew,
stayed overnight on pass. The Blue Moon and ABC Club
were pretty active places as night spots for the servicemen
stationed at Davis-Monthan Field.

Our first passes downtown went to all members of
Jelley's and Goodin's crews, and included some of the other
crews that would go through phase training, eventually picking up a B-24 and flying overseas with us from Topeka,
Kansas. We all became good friends.

Usually the officers would team up while the enlisted
men went their own way. This changed somewhat with time,
for us. The distinctions became fuzzy and the friendships
greater, with less consideration of rank and with greater
consideration of the merits and skills of the individual.

Among other military members, Rank Had Its Privileges, and these were observed, but among ourselves, the bars and stripes mattered little, but due respect was always given in mixed groups. Of course, we all knew the value of command and rank as well as the penalty for insubordination.

It is always necessary to accomplish a mission whether in the military or in civilian life, but the penalties were much greater for a violation in the military than in civilian life, especially in a nation at war. I believe we operated like a marriage, with respect and trust the key words necessary to describe a good relationship.

On this first overnight pass, Corny, Tommy, Hutch and myself went along with Joe, Pete, Phil and Andy of Cap Goodin's crew. Corny and I went to the show "Wings of the Navy," all about aircraft carriers. We saw Pete and Joe down in front of us with two girls.

The next morning we asked them what happened — how they made out. Joe had a great story to tell.

He had gone down to the train station where he happened to meet a beautiful blond. She had a large suitcase that was giving her some trouble so he offered to carry it off the baggage platform for her. Joe had asked her where she was going and she gave the name of a local hotel. He offered to help and they took a taxi.

Joe warmed up to her quickly and even paid for the room, proceeding to make out great. Her name, he found out, was Sandy. She told Joe she was going to meet a boyfriend who was coming in from leave in California that evening. He described her in detail, as it was obvious he was very proud of her — the flowered green dress, long flowing blond hair and pretty jewelry, rings and all.

Then Joe went into great detail outlining his success with her, her great beauty, ample bosoms, curvaceous hips and long beautiful legs. His only complaint was her insistence he leave early, before her friend came in from California.

That very next morning, a story in the local newspaper told about the arrest by the FBI, along with the Military Police, of a draft dodger who had been blonde headed, wore a green flowered dress and used the alias "Sandy." Her (his) picture was in the paper along with a picture of him in men's attire.

Joe had the roughest time explaining to us what really happened with "Sandy." He didn't live it down easily, either, because all we had to do was mention the name to him and he was ready to fight.

By the time he met the enemy overseas, I know he was ready for them. Andy didn't have much better luck, but his story was much closer to us than Joe's.

Andy had gone to a local jewelry store to look at rings. A very cute clerk waited on him. As Andy told it, she was so pretty he just had to make a pass at her.

Beautiful brunette with everything in the right places, was his description. He asked her when she got off work. She told him she worked until four o'clock, but would be glad to go with him to the show later.

Her name was Wilma Wright. He took her to a restaurant for dinner and she invited him up to her small apartment at the local hotel. Andy figured he was in luck. Andy went into her combination living room and kitchenette. He didn't smoke but Wilma did.

Most of the crew members didn't smoke because of the inconvenience of being around the aircraft and gasoline fumes. Chewing gum was the best release for nervous tension. I never smoked, so did not have a problem with stopping the habit. Only three of the members of our crew smoked, so we had that in our favor, too.

But Andy did not want to seem inexperienced, so he took one when she offered them. She noticed how he held it between his thumb and forefinger and laughed, telling him to put it out. She had discovered his secret.

She moved over to the couch and laid down, elevating her right leg and looking very provocative. She wore a skirt and sweater of pink, which made it hard to distinguish from her underthings. Andy said he asked to go to the wash room and she pointed to the bedroom. This made it necessary to go past the dresser located next to the bathroom door. Wilma followed him into the bedroom. Andy looked on the dresser and saw a picture of a serviceman.

Andy asked who he was. Wilma replied, "My husband." Andy suddenly got cold chills. He realized the sergeant was the same Sergeant Wright instructing him in aerial gunnery at the base.

He couldn't get out of the apartment fast enough, even though she tried to assure him the sergeant would not get off duty for three hours and was, in fact, on a flight with a new crew.

Andy's evening was a disaster, and he was pretty uncomfortable in the presence of Sergeant Wright. Andy confided to me he didn't do too well on the range, either. We still practiced skeet and trap shooting as well as other practice in small arms, the 45 caliber pistol and M-1 Carbine. Andy didn't know when Wilma might slip about that afternoon, or get angry for some reason and spill the beans about knowing Andy.

Needless to say, he was not too eager to start another relationship without checking it out very carefully first.

It was at Tucson, I decided to go out to a ranch and ride a real western horse. Back home in the hills of West Virginia, I had helped a local farmer turn soybeans and hay in the fields. Nothing was as back breaking as turning green soybeans. I also helped build hay stacks, tramping them down, salting the hay and topping them out. The older guys would pitch the hay up to me and I had to spread it evenly until it topped off.

As a boy, I received fifty cents a day and a noon meal which usually consisted of green beans, corn and ham. Sometimes we got a dessert, such as apple pie, but not too often. But the men received a dollar a day and a noon meal. It didn't seem fair either, because I worked just as hard as they did all day.

But the really tough job was riding an old mare horse on

the side of the hill, keeping it from going down hill while the farmer, Mr. Bennett, guided a plow making furrows to plant corn and beans on the hillside. It was pretty steep, and Toby, the mare, would slip or trip and fall. I had to keep constantly alert to make sure I could jump off on the uphill side to keep from falling under the mare. I couldn't go to sleep on the job, just as on a flying mission later in combat — even for a second.

Since I felt I was an expert on riding horses — in view of my childhood experiences — I assured the rancher I could ride. But I wasn't ready for the spirited colt he saddled up and brought out for me to mount.

I had no more than hit the saddle when he reared up, even before I could get my feet in the stirrups, and took off at a gallop down the dirt road from the ranch, jumping, bucking and flat out running. When I tried to reign him in, he reared up on his hind legs. I grabbed the saddle horn (as any tender-foot would do) and held on tightly, forgetting the reigns and caring little where he went — just hoping he would stop and return to the corral.

He finally slowed to a walk and started back toward the ranch where we had started that hectic ride.

The rancher met us and pointed out I'd said I could ride. I told him the kind of riding I had done back in West Virginia. He looked very serious, then he laughed as he said, "I guess you know what horseback riding means now, son."

I replied, "I sure do, Sir, and it's not in front of a plow."

I never had much interest in horseback riding after that first real western ride. My rear end and back ached for almost a week, but I learned a good lesson. Limited experience in any subject doesn't make you an expert, and it is best to admit it before you get in over your head.

After a month in first phase, we were transferred to Clovis Air Base, Clovis, New Mexico for Phase Two training.

The second phase involved longer trips to give the pilot, co-pilot, bombardier and navigators more training in cross country flying and night flying. We flew to March Field,

California and down the Pacific coast over outlying islands such as Capistrano, in the Guadalupe Islands, though we never saw the swallows.

One flight in particular stands out. We flew some high altitude missions to test our ability to handle the high altitudes and still function as a crew at the fighting stations, waist windows, and in the turrets. It was to prove to be a true test.

We were on oxygen, flying at about 24,000 feet along the Pacific Coast. We had on the heavy, sheep's wool lined flying clothes. When we moved about, we had to carry portable oxygen bottles. Each of the turrets, and other working locations on the Liberator, had oxygen outlets to plug the masks into while doing your job.

On this mission, Corny disconnected his oxygen hose without being aware of it happening. He became somewhat dizzy and became difficult to talk with, just like a drunk person, laughing and acting up. He had somehow made his way back through the catwalk of the bomb bays, into the rear section of the plane. We called Jelley and told him Corny was in trouble.

Jelley immediately began to lose altitude, trying to get down to near 10,000 feet as soon as possible. Hutch, Tommy and I had to hold Corny down and get the oxygen mask back on him. He had removed it, not realizing the effect the lack of oxygen was having on his reasoning power.

We finally got the hose connected to his portable bottle as Jelley made a very fast descent to 15,000, to 12,000 feet. We finally got the situation under control, learning a very good lesson in the process that would serve us well in the future when flying combat at higher altitudes. Sometimes the hoses would collect moisture and freeze up, cutting off our oxygen supply. We learned to constantly monitor our gauges to make sure we had pressure and everything was working.

Clovis Base probably brought me closer to a real mistake than any other time of my military career. This one was on the ground.

Part of our crew and Goodin's crew were on pass in

town when we started a night of partying in a hotel lounge. By eleven o'clock, Mike Reeder, the navigator for Goodin's crew, had imbibed too much, and in fact, was plain drunk.

Mike was supposed to be on call after midnight as a back up to the Officer of the Day (OD), and so, even if he was not needed, he had to sign in at the base as evidence of being back on duty. If he failed to sign in, he would be considered absent without leave (AWOL), and this could result in a punishment or perhaps even a court martial.

Mike Reeder was a second lieutenant while I was only a buck sergeant, but we were about the same size and there was a little resemblance. Since I didn't drink, I was sober. Cap Goodin and Will Droppelman came up with a great idea, or so they thought. They suggested I trade uniforms with Mike and go back to base and sign in for him. I didn't like the idea, but they finally convinced me to do it.

They assured me they'd keep Mike in his room until I got back so he wouldn't get into any trouble with my uniform and ID card on him.

By the time we got to base, I was very nervous and jumpy. Just one slip would do it now.

The Military Policeman at the gate checked my pass, as well as the others' on the bus. The bus was crowded, and that was in my favor, since some of the airmen weren't feeling too much pain at near midnight. The fact I was wearing the bars of a second lieutenant, and sober, did not hurt either, and the MP corporal did not check my pass too closely.

I signed in for Mike at the orderly room of the officers' quarters and skipped out of there as fast as my legs would carry me, back to the bus station at the front entrance of the base.

Fortunately, the same corporal was checking passes on the way out, and he scarcely gave me a glance as he went back on the bus to check those getting off. I hurriedly found a seat, and was thankful for the MP's negligence — or perhaps his passing me over quickly because of my seeming friendliness toward him.

When I signed in for Mike, there were no messages and no need for Mike to report for duty. Had he been needed,

I have no idea what I would have done. In any event, I was headed back to town and damned glad of it, for by that time what I had done had really sunk in — impersonated an officer, an offense in wartime which would have resulted in severe punishment.

The fellows helped me get Mike's, or rather, my uniform off of him and put his back on him. I was glad he was still too looped up to move out of his room. Had the military police caught him, he would have been in more trouble than I would have been, being an officer.

I've reflected on that episode many times since, and have never found a more foolish act in my life. I guess I did it to prove my guts and to be a real team player. I wanted to show I could be counted on in a pinch, and to be accepted as a real part of the group. Actually, we all flirted with real trouble during that incident, one I find hard to accept, even now.

Of course, at the time, I was a hero to both crews. But after the risk of what we had done sunk in, one could almost say combat did not offer a greater challenge. But I had to wait to see about that later.

Not long after this incident, Pete Peterson, the nose gunner and Andy Parker, the ball turret gunner on Goodin's crew, went into town together. Andy told me about their trip later.

They had gone into a popular restaurant for dinner. I knew the restaurant because one of the waitresses had been real nice. She had noticed I was left-handed and set the table for me just the opposite of a right-hander, even with my water or coffee cup. Corny, Tommy and I returned, along with Hutch, on the other three weekends we were out on pass. I always left a big tip for her considerations.

Anyway, Pete and Andy sat down right across from two very attractive girls, one a gorgeous blonde and the other with hair only slightly darker. Their hair was long, reaching half way down their backs, with waves that had to be natural.

Andy described them as having great personal charm and shapes that were almost duplicates — in fact, they looked almost like twins.

Pete and Andy waited outside the restaurant after dinner. When the girls came out, they asked them what kind of entertainment was available about town. They were already somewhat familiar with the town, but it was a good line. What attractive girls could refuse to help two handsome airmen who probably flew the big bombers at Clovis Air Base, especially if the airmen had wings and stripes?

The girls were very talkative and seemed fun loving. One was named Judy, the other, Trudy. One of the first questions Pete asked was if they were twins, especially when their names were so much alike, as well as their looks. They said there were two years difference in their ages. They also told them their father was a Lieutenant Colonel at the base, working in material, the supply side of operating the field. He was on temporary duty (TDY) at the time for six weeks.

The girls told them about a skating rink on the south side of town, so Pete asked Judy if she would go skating with him. She agreed, but Trudy was not for going with Andy. She wanted to return home, where her mother was waiting, and besides, she had a friend who was to call on her later. But she asked Andy to go home with her to visit a short time and meet her mother. Andy was pleased because it might lead to something else on another evening.

Their home was a nice bungalow in the suburbs of Clovis, in an above average neighborhood. Andy was very much impressed by the girls' mother. She hardly looked old enough to have two grown daughters, and it was obvious where the girls got their good looks.

Her name was Bonnie and she made Andy feel welcome, offering him coffee or something cold to drink, including a whiskey sour or bloody mary. It was a real friendly way to greet a lonesome "Flyboy," and had portent of things to come later.

Bonnie was dressed in a very revealing dress which

looked just too close to her body to be accidental, clinging to her youthful figure which matched her daughters'. Andy found her very interesting to talk with, as she asked him all about his job, how he liked it, and if he had a girl friend in Clovis or a wife at home. Andy didn't.

Shortly thereafter, Trudy went to freshen up, and to use the telephone. Andy could hear her talking, but Bonnie kept him occupied in many ways and he couldn't hear what Trudy was saying. While asking questions, Bonnie served him a whiskey sour, bending over to show an unlimited amount of cleavage. Two children had not hurt her a bit. The firmness and sufficiency of her breasts was obvious.

Trudy suddenly came out of her room, announcing loudly that she had to leave but would be back in about two hours, and skipped through the front door and out into the evening. That left Andy with Bonnie.

It was obvious to Andy that Bonnie was lonesome, and it didn't take long to determine she would welcome some gentle moves in the right direction on his part. The difference in ages posed no insurmountable problem, and it took no time to mount the problem head on — with the enthusiasm and eagerness of a small child finding the cookie jar for the first time.

Andy said it was the first time he had gone "over the edge" to lose his innocence, but it could not have happened with a more appreciative and warmly affectionate, or experienced, seductress. She gave him a tour of all the exotic, as well as erotic, places — missing nothing in her trip around the world with him. Andy was happy with the results, later bringing up the topic often after leaving Clovis. He never entertained the idea he had been set up for a lonely woman by her beautiful daughters.

The next week, our crews were flown to Alamogordo, New Mexico, south of Clovis and only about eighty miles from El Paso, Texas and Juarez, Mexico. This was the start of Phase Three, the last and final phase prior to picking up our assigned aircraft and overseas assignments.

Training was becoming more intense and more serious. We started to use our turrets and waist guns for more air to ground practice and to drop real bombs. I used some of my time to fly the high tower (simulated plane) on which was mounted the Norden Bomb Sight, a very secretive and highly accurate sight.

Gene Bruce, our bombardier, would ride on a platform sitting in front of me while I guided the tower on a course leading to the bomb run, with simulated speed and approach to the target. Gene would then take over control of the direction of the simulated run by use of the small dials on the sight which moved the tower right or left as needed. I had to maintain the correct altitude and speed.

I enjoyed acting as the pilot, and I learned to respect Gene and his job. We agreed it would be more correct to call the crews by the name of the aircraft's assigned bombardier rather than the pilot, since the whole reason for the mission was the delivery and accurate dropping of the bombs. All other positions were important and necessary, of course, but the whole purpose of the training in piloting, navigation, engineering, communications, and gunnery was to complete a successful bombing mission.

Since I was the armorer designate, I did get the opportunity to make a few runs with the sight, just in case something happened to the bombardier. The target was placed on the cement floor, and when the bomb drop was tripped, a time lapsed for the drop of the bombs from the aircraft. The altitude and speed entered into the curved trajectory the bombs would take to reach the target. Outside elements such as wind speed were considered, the theory very similar to the effect on bullets fired from machine guns, such as bullet drop, wind drift and pattern. Chalk was dropped to mark where the bombs would hit.

Gene always asked for the bomb bay doors to be opened prior to the run — just a simulation to make sure they were not forgotten on a real bomb run. I always got uneasy on the real runs in combat because in the lower ball I could look forward and see the bombs dropping out, and I was always afraid one of the bombs would hang up in the bomb bays if they didn't release properly from the B-7 shackles to which they were attached on the bomb racks.

Of course, a release of the bombs without opening the bomb bay doors could cause a real catastrophe, too. The doors could be torn off, perhaps hitting the ball turret; or the bomb, especially the incendiary or fragmentation type, could roll around on the doors and finally explode. In fact, this did occur on one bomb run in combat. It will be explained later.

One of the jobs I had was to go out on the catwalk between the racks in the forward and aft bomb bays and pull the pins which safetied the bombs prior to getting near the target. These were in the tail fins of the bomb and had to be removed so the bombs would be armed. I always carried extra pins in case I dropped some, because occasionally a mission was aborted and it was necessary to replace them.

The pilots never liked to land with a full load of bombs and none of the crew was too keen on the idea either. So unless the weather was too bad, an alternate target was always found to drop the bombs on, even to small boats or enemy villages. We just did not go for keeping those bombs in the racks longer than we had to on a mission. Just taking off with them was risky enough with full fuel tanks and a full bomb load.

Also, after a bomb run, I would go out into the bomb bays and free any bombs that were hung up. Gene would leave the doors open and I would take a screwdriver or kick them loose from the shackle. Usually, only one side failed to release, and by tripping a catch through a small hole in the B-7 shackle, using the screwdriver would cause it to release.

Due to the small space in the bomb bay, I usually did not wear a parachute, relying only on good footing and the ropes that were strung along the catwalk. The view was one I was familiar with when looking down, since I did it all the time anyway in the ball turret.

Fortunately a hang up did not occur too often because I

checked them out pretty thoroughly before take-off, and the bombardier usually looked things over, too.

The ground crews were careful, and I cannot say too much to compliment all the ground personnel, the armorers, the mechanics and other support personnel. They always did an A-1 job on the planes.

Even though the other crew members were responsible for cleaning their guns, it was my duty to see it was done, to check out any problems and to get the maintenance crews to correct them. The engineers and radio operators always checked out their equipment, too. Also, it was important that plenty of ammunition was on board, loaded properly in the canisters in the turrets and at the waist windows. Extra boxes of ammunition were near the waist guns and turrets. We always had plenty of ammunition on the gunnery range.

All the crew, even the pilot and copilot went back to the rear of the plane and fired the waist guns while the other one piloted the plane. We flew about four hundred feet above the ground while firing at targets on the ground.

And all crew members had an opportunity to sit in the copilots seat and learn something of the controls, how they felt, just in case that was necessary. In combat anything can happen, and sometimes we needed to have some knowledge of all the positions on the plane.

During our training, we all heard about the trips taken on three day passes — to El Paso, Texas and Juarez, Mexico, just across the Rio Grande River — from other crew members who had been there. It was some eighty miles away, but offered much in the way of entertainment, which Alamogordo did not have at the time.

Before we left Alamogordo Air Base on pass, we were instructed on some of the problems associated with a visit to El Paso and Juarez. To prevent trouble, the Group Commander had made the rule that if any violations came to his attention, such as drunk and disorderly, fighting, staying overtime on pass, or other lesser disturbances, there was a special punishment awaiting: If any of the officers were involved, then all officers on that crew had to dig a six by six by six foot hole in the ground and bury the order directing their punishment. If enlisted men on the crew were involved, all six of the enlisted men on that crew had to do the same thing. It was especially tough for the officers, because there were only four of them to do the digging.

It was common knowledge certain crews were bigger hell raisers and goof-ups than others. Captain Wilden Goodin's crew had established their reputation early in training. But they were good when it came to flight performance, and they had the respect of the others. Jelley's crew had a pretty close relationship with them, so we shared in that reputation. So did some of the others who wound up in Topeka later, and went overseas with us.

When we all received a three day pass, we all headed south for El Paso. What a weekend it was, and in fact, we made two weekend trips during the month we were in training at Alamogordo. But the first was so memorable, it served to subdue us later.

We no more arrived by bus in El Paso than the action started. We rented rooms at the Hotel Hilton in El Paso. It was a large hotel for the times and first class, not the place that would ordinarily cater to flight crews about ready to fly out to foreign lands. But it was war time, and every one was patriotic, including those in business who wanted to provide the best in lodging for the serviceman.

Our crew and Goodin's crew, all registered in on the same floor, as I remember, the seventh. Corny and I were in one room, Griff Griffith and Tommy Thompson in another, while Hutch and Whitsett were in an adjoining room. The officers were in other rooms adjacent to ours. Goodin's crew teamed up as we had, and other crews that flew with us later had also checked in on the same floor.

We started out by visiting all the little shops immediately near the hotel. That evening, wine and liquor bottles passed around the rooms. Our crew was quiet compared to Goodin's crew.

Chapter Three

Ben Pudder had met a girl down on the corner across
from the Hilton and asked her to go with him to a little bar
with a Mexican band to dance. Soon they were both feeling
good, and Ben invited her up to his room for a drink.

She was a cute Spanish-Indian girl, wearing bright,
colorful yellow and rust colored clothing. Her fingernails were
long with bright orange polish that blended well with her dark
skin. She was full of energy and fast talk, with a strong Spanish accent. Her well molded and sensuous body matched a
face with soft heart shaped lips that were full and playful
when she smiled. Her eyes, large, deep brown and very
inviting, her long lashes that you could not help but notice, all
promised things to come for Ben.

It was obvious Ben felt luck was with him as he held her
close on the elevator up to the seventh floor, but he wasn't
prepared for what faced him when he reached his room.

Mike Reeder was laying on his bed in an obvious intoxi-
cated condition, and he was not about to leave their room.
Ben was having a problem with his armful of passionate
pulchritude that made it obvious to him she was more than
willing to share her charms with him.

Ben grabbed the two pillows from off the bed, picked up
a bottle of scotch, and headed for the bathroom with his
eager friend. Mike slept until four in the morning, becoming
aroused when he felt the urge to go to the bathroom.

He went into the bathroom, only to see Ben in the
bathtub spattered with blood. Mike shook him, thinking he
was dead, as he was laying on the pillows face down, his tee
shirt torn into shreds over his back. There were large
scratches up and down and across his back, blood all over
from the scratches. Mike turned Ben over, and was surprised
to see a half grin on Ben's face.

He was alive, but obviously tired and "petered" out from
his very active night, but his contented look spoke louder
than words. His companion was nowhere around, having
eased herself out past Mike while he slept. It was obvious she
only wanted what she got, because she did not bother the

37

pockets of Ben or Mike, a fate which did befall many of the fellows who were unfortunate enough to get too much to drink in the presence of a greedy bed companion.

Ben could hardly get up, and since some of the scratches had dried up, he experienced real pain removing what was left of his tee shirt. He said she was the wildest woman he had ever had the good fortune to meet, and even though he could hardly move for the pain, he never made one complaint about the evening. Ben said she was like a tiger, and the hottest female he had ever had or ever wanted to meet again, a real sex kitten, one with long claws. Fact is, we called him "Tiger Ben" for a time, in a gesture of fun, and perhaps of envy that he should have had such an evening.

Meanwhile, Will Droppelman, the bombardier and Wilden "Cap" Goodin, the pilot, had made their way out on the small platform, leading from their room onto a circular balcony with a wrought iron fence around it, provided for guests to sit on and watch the activity below on the streets. They had been hitting the bottle pretty regularly and were feeling no pain. Will was looking out over the ledge at the city and watching the people on the street below.

Suddenly, he went back into the room, grabbed two of the brown paper bags the liquor came in, and went into the bathroom. He filled both of them about half full of water, and even though they were leaking slightly, headed back to the platform. He said, "I'm going to bomb them down below."

Cap tried to get him to come back in, but Will bent out over the ledge and dropped one of the bags. It dropped onto the street, just missing a man walking below, but splashing his clothes. Will held his arm out, moving it along, and let go of the second bag full of water which made a direct hit on a lady with a package in her arms. She dropped her package and screamed loudly.

Within minutes, two Military Policemen were on the seventh floor looking for the guilty party. They knew it had to be someone in the room above the sidewalk in the front side of the hotel. Will was still high enough and happy enough to brag loudly about his good aim and expertise as a bombardier.

The MP's took him down to their office in El Paso, which was along side the civilian police station, but being an officer, they only wrote a report on him which found its way back to the Commander at Alamogordo Air Base. So the four officers had to dig a hole and bury the order directing the punishment.

The only good thing about the punishment was nothing was written on his service record, since all the evidence was buried in the hole they dug. But they found the white sands of New Mexico to be very hot, and the underneath clay and rocks very hard to dig up in the hot sun.

The second morning, we decided to go over the Rio Grande River to Juarez, Mexico. The law required that any United States currency be changed to silver dollars prior to going through customs. The officials used this means to determine how much currency was going into Mexico as a result of crossing the border. Further, we were restricted to staying within the twenty mile limit from the United States border and go no further into Mexico.

Our first stop was at the Club Conquistador. Our second was at the Lobby Number 2. Clark Gable was in the club at the time with a nice looking lady. He was stationed at Biggs Field near El Paso. At least that was the story we were told at the time.

We had a few drinks and then decided to eat. It was probably one of the longest dinners I ever attempted to eat. First a drink or two of tequila, depending on our taste buds, along with some small appetizers consisting of crackers with cheese to munch on while the other courses were being prepared. Then some soup which I believe was highly seasoned pea soup, with garbanzo beans in it. It took time for the waitresses to serve, so there was plenty of time to talk about the sights and discuss the pros and cons of each waitress. Then a small plate of various fresh celery and carrot sticks, mixed with pickles, radishes and onions, all to eat with a special dip, which was also laced with pepper and cream cheese. Then came another kind of soup which I was unable to identify, but which was very tasty and highly seasoned.

Then the waitress brought us the thickest and juiciest steak I had ever seen, sizzling on the metal plate. It was cooked medium well, and the aroma increased my appetite, even though the previous courses had curbed my hunger. As we finished our steak, and salad which accompanied the order, another set of plates containing fruits and jello desserts was served. The waitress then offered pie and coffee. I do not recall any of us availing ourselves of the pie, but all had coffee. But the biggest surprise was the cost of such a dinner — only two dollars each! After tipping the waitresses, we walked outside and started down the street.

Corny and I went into the 1-2-3 Club, but did not stay. We were interested in the rings, knives with leather sheathes, and pocketbooks to send back home. But some of the young boys along the way came up to us and asked if we would like to see a show with nude girls performing various kinds of entertainment for us. Andy Parker and Pete Peterson had joined us, but none of us seemed interested until one of the boys said his older brother would take us for a tour of the city and country side in his taxi. Andy and Pete decided to take the tour, while Corny and I continued shopping and bought presents for the folks back home. Andy and Pete had quite a story to tell when we saw them back at the hotel.

They were taken some distance into the country side, perhaps exceeding the twenty mile limit placed by the U.S. Military. They had been driven briefly around the city, but sufficiently to get them completely disoriented from the direction of the border. They were told it would cost them only one dollar to see a show with some young girls which would be a "learning experience" — forty ways to make love. The offer seemed too much for them to resist, since they had never seen anything like that in the states.

Andy and Peter finally arrived at a long, low building of rough lumber which resembled an army barracks on the air bases around the states. They went through the doorway and entered a large room that looked like a dance hall, but only took up a third of the space in the building. Two doors led to the other end of the building by way of narrow halls along the walls.

There were heavy wool G.I. issue blankets hanging from wires which separated the areas into makeshift rooms. The blankets hung almost to the floor and created a small room hardly five feet wide and eight feet long. Each of the cubicles was just large enough to hold a small metal bed, which had a thick G.I. looking mattress on it. This was the extent of privacy provided for anyone that used the room, and sounds from the adjacent cubicles could be easily heard by anyone with the time or inclination to listen.

There were four tables along the walls of the large room with young girls seated on chairs at the tables. Pete and Andy said the girls got up, came over and invited them to sit down. Pete told them he had come to see the show. Two girls took them into one of the rooms with the hanging blankets, stripped their clothes, and began the show.

Andy said the funny thing about the whole set up was the lack of lights. One of the girls carried a lighted kerosene lantern which she handed to Andy and asked him to hold up high so the light would be sufficient to see what was going on while the girls performed.

After they had seen about all there was to see, one of the girls asked them if they would like to participate in the action. Pete and Andy said they did not want to "participate," even though the girls indicated the price would be right, at two dollars each, and they were very attractive, but rather young, even for the eighteen- to twenty-year-old airmen.

Pete and Andy went outside to discuss what they had just observed and to wait for their young driver to come back and pick them up. In a few minutes, the driver returned, and they headed back to Juarez.

When they were making a turn into the city, the driver asked if they would like to visit some female friends that he knew well and who had refreshments to share with them. Andy and Pete indicated it would be fine with them, so the driver turned down a side street, finally stopping at a small adobe hacienda of typical Spanish design. It looked well kept, with many flowers hanging from the planters on the porch. The driver went in, and returned to invite Andy and Pete to come in and meet his friends.

Two very attractive girls were sitting at the dining table in very revealing dresses which were very bright in colors of green, orange and yellow flowers all over the dresses. Tequila bottles were on the table along with glasses. The driver said he had an errand to run, and would be back shortly.

It did not take long for it to be very clear to Pete and Andy the girls were available for entertainment. They had some Spanish music on a Victrola which had to be changed and rewound constantly to keep it from running down. They asked Andy and Pete to dance in a small area of the living room. Pete declined, but Andy took one of the girls into his arms, snuggled up close and began to dance.

He was with a short, well-shaped girl with a delightful smile — so he told it. She informed him her name was Marquita. The other girl was a bit taller and darker skinned, but also very young and attractive.

They finally came around to asking Pete and Andy if they would like to take them to the bedrooms. By that time, both Pete and Andy were feeling the effects of the tequila, plus the girls' winning ways, so proceeded to be led to their respective rooms. Pete said the price was right, too. These girls were much classier (to hear them tell it) than the ones in the country, but more expensive too — five dollars each.

Afterward, their taxi was waiting for the ride back to downtown, but that's when the problems developed. Andy remarked to Pete how good Marquita was in bed, how well she had performed, laughing as he told of her sexual offerings.

The driver suddenly reached up onto the dash of the car, took a long knife out of its sheath, stopped the car, turned around and said, "I no mind you have fun with my seester, but I no like you talk about her. You no talk about her, eh, Gringo?"

Andy immediately replied, "I was only complimenting your sister on how nice she was, how nice her personality was, and her beauty." Pete also assured the driver nothing improper was intended.

There was no more conversation during their trip back to the border area, and Pete and Andy were happy to arrive safely.

One other interesting note about this trip to Juarez and Mexico. Pete discovered he had lost his flight gloves that had been in his leather A-2 flight jacket. Even though we were in a warm area, we all wore our flight jackets for their macho, flyboy image. Besides, the nights were cool enough for them.

Pete and Andy went back to where the driver was parked and asked him if he had found the gloves in the taxi. He said no, but he would go back to the girls' house and see if the gloves were there. About fifteen minutes later, he returned with the gloves, which he said had been left at his sisters. Pete gave him three dollars for finding them for him. We all wondered if Andy would have gotten his gloves back from the driver, had he lost his instead, considering the close call he had with the driver.

We finally made it back to Alamogordo and settled in for some intensive training. On our second trip to El Paso, we did not go over the border, and the crews kept out of trouble, spending most of their time visiting shops and buying souvenirs. No more sex shows or street "bombings" for these crews.

Training had become pretty serious in phase three, as we had lost seven planes for various reasons, more than some squadrons were losing in combat in a month. Increasingly, to gain efficiency in our jobs, we required longer and more frequent flights. Jelley was one of the younger pilots, and we had to fly more to increase his proficiency in night (blind) flying, and the same with Julius "Whitie" Woytowich, the navigator. In fact, we were all under the gun to get more knowledgeable about our jobs.

We also had to learn more about our alternate positions, mine being the armorer. On one trip across the Grand Canyon, Whitie became ill and I helped him with the navigation. The main problem was reading the maps, which gave the elevations for the various mountains and peaks we had to fly around and over.

Since there were clouds near or over some peaks, it was very important that we knew not only where we were, but at what altitude we must fly to avoid winding up a black spot on a mountain side. It was fortunate that Whitie had explained this to me, and how it was done, so I was the one who came up front and worked in his seat.

His seat was behind the pilot. Hutch, the engineer, had a seat on the other side, behind the copilot, Norman "Johnny" Johnson. Hutch also operated the General Electric upper local top turret in combat. There were differences in the B-24 Liberator and B-17 Flying Fortress turrets and other armament.

While the B-24's we trained in did not have the lower ball turret or the nose turret, it was added to the B-24 before going into combat. This gave us top, bottom, nose, and tail turrets.

I liked the Sperry Lower Ball Turret, although getting in and out of it was more complicated than in the B-17 Flying Fortress. In the B-24 Liberator, the turret had to be lowered after take-off for operation by a hydraulic jack which was attached to the supporting center post over the turret, letting it settle to the azimuth ring upon which the turret turned a full 360 degrees. The turret had to be raised up into the fuselage after use so it would not interfere with landings and take-offs. The handle was pumped until the turret was locked in up position.

Further, the guns had to be manually turned into position facing directly to the rear of the aircraft so the 50 caliber machine guns would fit into the gunwells provided. The gunner could line them up to the rear prior to turning the master electrical switch off in the turret, but the guns had to be pointing straight down before the exit and entrance door to the turret was up into the aircraft, enabling the gunner to unfasten his safety belt and climb out. It was a very awkward position in that his back and head were almost in a suspended position looking straight down to the earth below.

When the guns were on a horizontal plane, the gunner was almost laying on his back. He could create a feeling of spinning and rocking all at the same time, and this was especially true when searching the skies for enemy aircraft.

In actual operation, two control handles were mounted in front and slightly forward of the gunner's body on each side of the sight. The handles were moved forward and back to lower and raise the turret. The triggers were on top of the control handles, and would work separately or in tandem by flipping a control switch. This was in case of injury to an arm in combat. Further, there was a dead man's switch on each control handle which had to be depressed by hand before the solenoids to the guns would work. Moving the handles left or right moved the turret around horizontally.

The biggest problem was getting out of the turret in an emergency, such as hydraulic leaks or electrical breakdown caused in combat, or for that matter at any time someone was in the turret. There was provision for such a contingency, using small handles to move the turret slowly to a position which would enable the occupant to get out. But when time was of the essence, due to loss of control of the aircraft, due to enemy action or other malfunction of engines, injured pilots or other crew members, the ball turret gunner did not have time to escape.

Due to the very confined area in the turret, only a small or skinny person was able to ride in it. A parachute harness could be worn over the heated suit, but the two types of chest packs provided, square or oblong, were pretty bulky getting in and out of the turret or while operating it. Therefore, some of the ball turret gunners did not even wear parachutes, but left them up in the plane, to quickly snap onto the rings on the harness, if lucky enough to get out of the turret. Otherwise, they could just kiss the world good-bye and say a mighty short prayer.

The most important part of the turret was the Sperry Automatic Computing Sight. It was the most accurate sight on any of the turrets, but it required a complete reliance upon the sight and not upon the gunner's judgement in combat. That's not to say he didn't use any judgement, but he had to trust the sight to be computing properly. I will explain it this way.

The sight was contained in a small square box which had a rheostat that could control the amount of light in the lines making up the sight.

A gunner controlled the turret with his left foot by pushing a lever. If a target was sighted some distance from the plane, and the gunner followed it with the sight and kept the wing-tips of the approaching aircraft within the two vertical lines, and a small circular dot in the center of the horizontal line, he could not miss. If the enemy aircraft went by on a parallel course and the gunner had the fuselage framed between the vertical lines, the sight automatically computed the direction, position and speed of the approaching aircraft and provided the necessary lead.

But the biggest problem for many ball turret gunners was the position of the turret with respect to the sight. The sight turned, but the guns and turret moved forward ahead of the position of the sight. This meant that sometimes the gunner's body would be turned, along with the turret, ahead of the target, while the sight would be on the target, making a seemingly much slower movement. Therefore, trusting the sight was difficult.

In March, 1944, after serving in combat, I became an aerial gunnery instructor on B-17 Flying Fortresses at MacDill Field, Tampa, Florida. This was the most difficult turret to teach because of a tendency of the new gunners to override the sight. I had been able to shoot down three Zeroes, two

Haps, plus four probables in combat using the Sperry Automatic Computer Sight, so I trusted it completely. I cannot speak too highly about the turret and sight.

I trust the future fighters and bombers in our arsenal of defense provide the same degree of accuracy. I am sure they do, because we had that much technology in 1943. While much has been written about the tail gunners and their position of being a choice target of fighters, especially on B-17's, and nose gunners on B-24's prior to installation of the nose turret, I believe the enemy fighters were well aware of the hazards of approaching a bomber from down under the lower ball turret with its computerized sight and with a well trained gunner at the controls.

The firepower of the B-24 Liberator was tremendous once the modifications were made, placing turrets in the nose, tail, top and bottom of the plane, as well as waist guns, too. I do not know why the B-24's did not make use of the ball turret as extensively in the European Theater as was made of it in the South Pacific. But I do know it was a great advantage for our B-24's and B-17's in combat. The B-17's made use of the turret as part of their basic defense and firepower in all theaters of war.

As you can tell, I was a true believer in our ability to deal with the enemy, regardless of the enemy or the odds. It was not long before we would test that belief in combat.

It is appropriate at this time to make a comparison of the two primary bombers in the arsenal of the United States designed to carry maximum bomb loads to the enemy targets across the greatest number of miles. Since I flew combat in the B-24 Liberator and instructed in aerial gunnery in the B-17 Flying Fortress, it is natural that I would make a comparison of the two planes. Personally, the choice goes to the B-24, even though the B-17 was the bomber that received much more news coverage in the European theater of war.

ARMAMENTS The B-24 had an advantage in armament of two turrets, with over 180 degrees of radius in nose and tail, and two turrets of 360 degrees radius (full circle in

Comparisons of America's Largest Bombers

TYPE:	B-24F	B-17F
LENGTH	66ft. 4 in.	74 ft. 9 in.
HEIGHT	17 ft. 11 in.	19 ft. 1 in.
WING SPAN	110 ft.	103 ft. 9 in.
POWER	4 Pratt & Whitney 1200 HP Radial	4 9-Cyl. 1100 HP Wrights Radial
MAX.SPEED	306 MPH plus at lower weights	280 MPH plus at lower weights
MAX.RANGE	3,000 plus miles with bomb bay fuel tanks, less bombs	3,400 plus miles with less bomb loads
CREWS	10 Man: Pilot, Co-pilot, Navigator, Bombardier, Engineer, Asst. Radioman, Asst. Engineer Nose Gunner, Tail Gunner, Lower Ball Gunner, Eng. Manned Upper Turret	9 Man: Pilot, Co-pilot, Navigator, Bombardier, Engineer, Radioman, Tail Gunner, Lower Ball Gunner, Asst. Engineer, Eng. manned Upper Turret
MAX. BOMB LOADS	8,000-10,000 lbs. internal on racks. No external bombs under wings	6,000 lbs., internal on racks. Plus could carry 4,000 lbs. under wings
MAX. GROSS WGHT.	65,000 lbs. plus, has been known to exceed 85,000 lbs.	65,000 lbs.
SERVICE CEILING	35,000 plus with turbo superchargers, paddle props and reduced loading	30,000 plus, also with high altitude configurations, superchargers

top and bottom turrets), plus elevations of 160 degrees or more in all turrets. The B-17 nose and tail guns had limited flexibility due to the limitations of the mountings and tracks of the guns.

Further, the B-24 had an advantage on bomb runs of speed due to the bomb bay doors on the B-17 opening outward, which caused drag resistance to movement forward, while the B-24 bomb bays rolled up the side of the fuselage without any drag. This could pose a problem when mixed flights of B-17's and B-24's were on missions together.

It was discovered on some very critical missions that the B-24 Squadrons should lead any strike on enemy targets, due to their superior speed while on the bomb run with bomb bay doors open. Otherwise, the B-24's would over run the B-17's, resulting in mid-air collisions, and/or faulty bomb drops over the target. As a result of this problem, it was decided the two bombers were not compatible on joint strikes to the same targets.

Both bombers were well known for their ability to take great punishment from flak and gunfire and still remain flying. The B-17, due to its design, had a much longer glide path in the event engines were lost, but the B-24 had great lifting power in its wings due to the secret Davis wing design. After the B-24 had conversions made in its nose, tail and lower ball turrets, it was quite superior and formidable in firepower against enemy planes. But the enemy soon learned of this and kept their distance, except for the more bold or kamikaze dedicated pilots.

It was easy to see why the B-24 Liberator was the proper bomber for use in the South Pacific theater of war, while the B-17 was utilized more extensively in the European theater. Of course, both served in the Pacific, and in fact, the B-17 was the only bomber in the Hawaiian Islands at the beginning of World War II with the ability to carry large bomb loads. And the B-24 was used in Africa as well as in raids on Europe.

The Poletsi Raid on the Romanian Oil Wells is well remembered as a result of the destruction to the storage tanks and to the B-24's lost on that raid. Both planes contributed greatly to the great victory which we eventually won against Germany and Japan, by destroying vital targets as well as many enemy aircraft on the ground and in the air.

A further breakdown of the firepower on each follows:

Armament Comparisons

CONSOLIDATED B-24	BOEING B-17
Nose Turret-Consolidated with 2-50 caliber machine guns, operated by career gunner	Two Nose guns on chin turret, under nose below bombardier who operated turret.
Tail Turret-Emerson or Consolidated with 2-50 caliber machine guns, Asst. Radioman	Tail guns with 2-50 caliber machine guns, career gunner
Upper Local Turret-Sperry or General Electric, with 2-50 caliber machine guns, Engineer	Sperry Upper Local Turret with 2-50 caliber machine guns, Engineer
Lower Ball Turret-Sperry (raised for take-offs and landings, lowered for combat) with 2-50 caliber machine guns, Armorer Gunner	Sperry - same guns, but fixed on azimuth ring supported by center post
Two Waist Guns, one on each side of plane operated by Asst. Eng. & Asst. Radioman or career gunner	Same armament at waist guns, one on each side of 50 caliber machine guns

It was late January, 1943, and the war was becoming more fierce. We had completed Phase Three training and were given a short ten days leave to go home. Our orders were to return to Topeka Air Base, Topeka, Kansas, where we would get our overseas assignment.

Our venturesome crews, Jelley's and Goodin's, were to stir up quite a few troubles at Topeka.

My crew went out on its first flight after having our new plane, "Shehasta" assigned and flew over a nearby farm. We dived down and came so close to the ground the slipstream and noise blew, or scared, the chickens on the ground up against a fence, killing almost two hundred of them. The chicken farmer called the Air Base and reported us — and his dead chickens. However, the name was not yet on any of the planes, and he didn't get our aircraft number.

When the Military Police came to the flight line after we landed to question us, it was appalling how our memories failed us. Other planes were operating from the field, too, so we were able to blame it on someone else.

This was just additional justification of our reputation as a wild and crazy crew which we had established in phase training at Tucson, Alamogordo and Clovis. So Goodin's crew had some competition for top goof-ups and daredevils of the sky, even before we left the States for overseas.

This is the crew that arrived in the South Pacific after we lost William Griffith (he was flying a night mission with another crew which was shot down over Ballale). The Shehasta had hit some trees on take-off at Espirto Santos and was delayed a month for repairs. We went on up to the Canal and flew missions until she was brought up by a replacement crew for Man-O-War. We took her over and she had been equipped with flame dampners for the superchargers, a rarity for B-24's at that time. So we flew some night missions because the Japs couldn't locate us as easily at night. Back Row (L-R): Charles R. Thompson, Tail Gunner (KIA), Lyman A. Clark, Jr., Armoror Gunner (Ball Turret), Henry E. Hutchings, Engineer (KIA), and Earl B. Cornelius, Nose Gunner. Front Row (L-R): Ralph E. Bruce, Bombardier, James D. Jelley, Pilot, N.A. Johnson, Co-Pilot, Julius T. Woytowich, Navigator. Johnson went to Transport flying and was replaced by Lt. Taylor after this photo was taken.

Chapter 4

PACIFIC BOUND

With "Shehasta" and "Phantom Lady"

While the leave back home in West Virginia was uneventful, my arrival at Topeka was not. Orders were waiting for Pete, Andy and me to go to Salt Lake City, Utah for some additional training prior to going overseas. It was for only one week, but since we had missed basic training and entered gunnery school directly, we had not qualified on the M-1 Carbine or 45 Caliber Pistol. Neither had we been trained in the use of the gas mask or chemical warfare. While no poison gas was being used, as had been used in World War I, there was always that possibility, and we had to be prepared for any contingency in battle.

We had been firing shotguns, thirty caliber and fifty caliber machine guns for months, but still, we had to make a trip completely out of our way to receive that additional, official training.

To test our speed and efficiency in using the gas mask, we were placed in tents and tear gas was released from canisters. We also received some additional training in various kinds of bombs — their use and their firing mechanisms. But the best part of this training was the passes given at the end for us to go into Salt Lake City.

While I was fortunate enough to meet a nice girl at a bakery, Pete and Andy hit it off with two not so nice girls. Pete told it like this, with great enthusiasm and humor.

52

They had decided, since our passes were just until midnight, they would take the very direct and bold approach — they would ask the first two females they met to come up to their hotel room with them for some drinks. It was a version of that old story of the sailor that always did well at all the ports of call when he asked every good looking girl he met to go to bed with him. His buddy said, "You must get your face slapped a lot." "Yes," the sailor replied, "but I get a lot of companionship, too." He found it to be a risk worth taking.

Andy hit the jackpot the first time, and she went up to his room to have a few drinks. He said she had on gloves that went to her elbows and a party dress, perhaps because she was looking for a party. Anyway, when she got around to removing her clothing, she kept her gloves on. Andy asked her why and had to laugh when she replied, "I feel undressed without them." But he never did get to see if she wore an engagement — or any other — ring.

But this was not the end of his story. After removing the rest of her clothing, she not only kept her gloves on, but she kept her panties on as well! And when he asked her why she did not remove the panties, her reply completely broke him up when she said, "What kind of a girl do you think I am?"

Of course he did find out what kind of girl she was, and could hardly wait to get back to Salt Lake Air Force Base to tell us about his evening with the "lady" who did "protest too much."

I had a close call that evening, too. After what had happened in Clovis, New Mexico, when I had helped out a fellow crew member by temporarily exchanging uniforms, I had tried to be a "good" soldier. But I tried one last time to take military service as a game, or a frivolous matter in its discipline.

I was walking up the right side of the street with a very attractive blonde which Pete and I had met earlier. A Second Lieutenant with nice new shiny yellow gold bars on his shoulders and a very neatly pressed uniform of an infantry officer — a ninety-day wonder if I ever saw one — was approaching us. My friend had a firm hold on my right arm, so in a very flippant manner and a very unmilitary stance, gave that ninety-day wonder a left-handed salute. Pete, who was ahead of us, did not know what I had done. My friend and I had almost crossed the street to the other side when we heard a roaring, very loud "Sergeant! Hit a brace, Sergeant!"

The Second Lieutenant rushed to me and demanded, "Give me your name, rank, serial number and unit!"

"Yes, Sir," I replied, standing in a very erect and soldierly fashion, providing him with the information. I was very embarrassed in front of my new friend, and I could see Pete out of the corner of my eye. "I'm with the Army Air Corps, Sir."

"I'll have your stripes, Sergeant!"

"Sir," I said, "I am on orders to go overseas in a couple of days and if I lose my stripes, I can't fly or go with the unit."

He looked at me, almost foaming at the mouth, and I don't know if he bought my story or not, but he then said, "I would rather not have a salute at all than to be given a left-handed salute. It's an insult."

I replied, "Yes, Sir" as sincerely as I could.

He looked at me a few more seconds, then said, "Dismissed, Sergeant," and turned very abruptly and proceeded down the street. I'm sure, after what I had done to him, he felt going overseas served me right and he didn't want to stop that, thinking it was punishment enough. He was right, too, I was to learn later.

As a result, my new "friend" couldn't come up with an excuse fast enough to drop me. Pete was also angry because his new girl friend decided to leave with her. But I think Pete was also relieved to know I would be accompanying my crew, with his, on our trip overseas.

This lesson remained with me throughout my years in military service. Even when a ranking Master Sergeant and Sergeant Major, I did not forget the first lesson of military protocol — Rank Has Its Privileges (RHIP) and one of those privileges includes respect for rank. Of course, I might add, giving respect also brings respect to the one who gives it, providing the one receiving it is a gentleman.

We then joined up with the rest of the crews at Topeka Air Base, Topeka, Kansas to be assigned planes and receive our overseas orders. One thing was certain, rumors ran rampant from the day we arrived. Being a staging area for the bomber crews, slogans regarding security were on every wall, and warnings about "a loose lip would sink a ship" were everywhere.

There were three versions of the B-24 Liberators on the field. One version was painted in a light and dark green camouflage with some brown mixed throughout, with two extra fuel tanks installed in the front bomb bay. A second version had light and dark green camouflage with only one extra fuel tank installed in the front bomb bay, and a third had a sandy brown and pink camouflage with only one extra fuel tank installed in the front bomb bay.

It was not too difficult to figure out the sandy brown and pink B-24's were going to North Africa to be operating in desert areas, the ones with one tank and various shades of green were going to the British Islands, perhaps England, and the B-24's with greens and brown with two fuel tanks in the bomb bay were heading for the long flights necessary in the Pacific area, where the islands were made up mostly of jungles, with broad expanses of water and no refueling stops along the way.

Jelley's and Goodin's crews drew the Pacific bound B-24 Liberators. Eighteen other crews with bombers were scheduled to leave with us, a total of twenty planes and two hundred airmen, ten men to a crew. We were to go to California and then to Hickam Field, Hawaii.

While at Topeka Air Base, we had many things to do to get our plane ready to move overseas. There was also a possibility some of us would head North to Alaska after going to California, but we did not give that much real consideration since we knew our men in the South Pacific were taking a beating from the Japanese planes and ships, which at the time outnumbered us. We had lost the big islands of the

55

Philippines, and the Japanese were moving South, toward Australia and New Zealand. They had already occupied many large and small islands in the Central and South Pacific. After the attack on Pearl Harbor on December 7, 1941, the Hawaiian Islands were considered to be in jeopardy from the Japanese fleet and air forces.

The Solomon Islands, including Bougainville, New Georgia and Guadalcanal were in Japanese hands and battles were raging to try and recapture them before the Japanese moved on down to the New Hebrides, New Caledonia and further to the West toward Australia by way of New Guinea where the Japanese had established a foothold.

The war in Europe was given great priority in 1942 with most planes and troops shipped to England and North Africa to contain the German offensive which, along with Italy, was making great gains on the continent of Europe. President Roosevelt and the military had some very great and difficult decisions to make as to which threat was the most serious. General Douglas MacArthur had been driven from the Philippines, our men had been ravaged in the Bataan Death March and supplies were not moving fast enough to stage a strong comeback from Australia North to retake the Philippines. MacArthur was saying, 'I shall return,' and we were to be a part of that group which was to fight to make his boast a reality.

But in Topeka, Kansas, we felt ready for any challenge. We had some more flight training to complete, and one of those flights included a trip to Biggs Field, near El Paso, Texas, with a return flight to Topeka Air Base. One of the reasons for the flight was to check out fuel transfer systems from the newly installed fuel tanks in the bomb bay to the wing tanks. Hutch, our engineer, would be pretty busy on that trip, checking everything out. It would also serve as a further check on the navigator for cross country flying as well as for our pilot, who would learn of any peculiar flight characteristics of the plane. Further, some of the flight would be at night, which would build night time for Jelley and his copilot,

Johnson.

We had begun to form friendships with some of the other crew members. Of course, some of us had gone through phase training together, so we were already friends, such as Goodin's and Jelley's crews. We were identified by the name of the pilot — "Hansen's crew," "Byrd's crew," "Jelley's crew," "Francis's crew," etc. This practice continued even during combat assignments.

Another way a crew was known was by the name and number of the assigned plane. So immediately upon receiving an assigned plane, an effort was made to decide on a name which best fit the crew or conveyed some personal preference, either of a crew member or of the crew as a whole. Sometimes a figure or favorite character would be chosen, or a beautiful girl, perhaps a movie starlet. This would result in artistic work on the plane known as "Nose Art." Occasionally, there was a message contained in the name, directed usually at the enemy.

This was naturally a subject of some thought and controversy. The crew members put forth names and one was chosen that was acceptable to the majority, the democratic way in most cases.

Jelley liked "Shehasta." He explained, "She-has-ta take us over there and she-has-ta bring us back." Some of our crew wanted to name the plane after their girl friends. Others, after cartoon characters such as "Popeye," "Olive Oyl," "Mammy Yokum," "Pistol Packin' Mama," and many others. We settled on "Shehasta."

Goodin's crew finally decided on "Phantom Lady," although Andy wanted to use the picture of a senorita and call it "Marquita." Another wanted "Rosa." It was obvious they still had memories of their trip to Juarez, Mexico.

We proceeded to paint the names of the planes, or get some of the artistic members to paint a good representation of the character or design conveying a message. This practice had been started in the past for fighters and bombers, even in World War I, so it was natural for the tradition to be carried

Nose Art

These scanned images reflect a sampling of the nose art that decorated a few of the Liberators during their time on Guadalcanal.

Shackrat

Frenisi

Little Mick

Pistol-Packin' Mama

Mammy Yokum

Man-O-War

Phantom Lady
(Pseudonym)

forward during World War II.

Shehasta was hard to illustrate. Our plane number was 324, so it was painted in large letters on the nose section. The "Phantom Lady" had a silhouette of a naked lady holding a bomb over her head and delivering it to the enemy. Other

B-24 Liberators that were to become well known in our
combat tour were, Shady Lady, Mammy Yokum, Frenisi,
Man-o-War, Pistol Packin' Mamma, Jeannie C, Shack Rat,
Quiturbitchen, Dumbo, Thumper, Topper, Rod's Rowdies,
The Rattler, Little Mick, Jeremiah, as well as many others.

Many of the planes only made a few missions before
being shot down or lost due to other reasons — weather,
mechanical trouble, and in a few cases, error by pilots or
other members of its crew. But many of the planes survived
for many missions, in rare cases over one hundred missions.
Some times this meant crew members were lost and replaced
but the plane kept flying. In others, the planes were lost, but
some members of the crews survived to be assigned to new
planes. Because of this, many of the planes later on in the
war were given the same names of planes lost, but with the
Roman numeral II following the name, i.e. Thumper II or
Quiturbitchen II.

It was not unusual to find your plane being flown by a
different crew when a pilot was grounded, or some members
were on rest leave. As a result, some of the planes had many
missions and enemy planes to their credit, some with ships
and submarines, too.

Occasionally, a crew was lucky enough to complete a
tour with more than enough missions to return to the States.
But this didn't happen too often. The odds were not with the
crew on that score, and we will be addressing that later.
Replacement crews were scarce.

While still in Topeka, an interesting incident took place
involving the "Phantom Lady" and its crew. Joe Jamison, the
tail gunner, formed a relationship with a young attractive lady
who worked at the Post Exchange (PX) on base. Joe indicated to her in conversation that the crew was flying to Biggs
Field, Texas. She said she had a brother there and would sure
like to make the trip with the crew.

Well, it wasn't long before Joe discussed with Andy and
Pete the possibility of taking her along. They knew it could
hardly be done without the cooperation of Lew Lewis, the

engineer, because he always came through the catwalk to the rear of the plane when he checked the fuel, oxygen and hydraulic lines for leaks or anything unusual. Valves were also checked for correct positioning or safety wiring where it was indicated, as well as any exposed control cables. He could not pass any unusual bundle of clothing without questioning what was there. It was winter and early spring had not yet come, so heavy wool lined leather helmets, jackets, boots and trousers were necessary to keep warm in the air, especially at higher altitudes.

After some arm twisting and promises of things to come, Lew finally agreed to look the other way, denying any knowledge of the caper.

Take-off was scheduled for 5 a.m., so it was still dark when the enlisted members of the crew caught a shuttle van out to the runway. Joe had stayed with his friend in the back of the plane during the night, bundled up in the wool clothing he had checked out of flight supply. Elizabeth (Beth) had quit work at 10 p.m. and then they had made their way to the flight line, walking as though they were going to the plane to pick up some equipment. Security was tight because it was a staging area, but access was not too difficult if you were already on base and in flying clothes.

Joe was wearing his A-2 jacket and she had on his olive drab fatigues over her own clothes. Each carried the wool lined leather clothing. The guards knew a flight was scheduled for the next morning, so their going to the plane was not too unusual. He was wearing a gunners' hat and she had on a fatigue hat which protected her face from the prying eyes of the guards.

I'm not denying it was a foolish thing for the crew of Phantom Lady to do, but when I found out about it later at Biggs Field, I couldn't say anything, considering the incident I participated in at Clovis Field.

But this situation was different because Joe wanted the benefit of Beth's charms in appreciation for what he was doing for her.

During this trip to Biggs Field, Joe made it into the "Mile High Club," which is quite an accomplishment. As flyers know, this is a distinction reserved for flyers who make out with their female friends at least one mile above the ground. Actually, Joe could have qualified for a warm up during the previous night waiting for the rest of the crew to show up. Furthermore, with all those heavy flight clothes they were bundled up in and covered up with, it was hard to dispute Joe's claim to membership in the club. As for Andy or Pete making the club, I never knew for certain and they never "laid claim" to the rewards of the trip.

The other version of qualification for membership in the "Mile High Club" was if you bailed out of an airplane at least one mile high above the earth. I claimed my membership on that basis, having bailed out in combat while in the South Pacific. Irving Parachute Company had a "Caterpillar Club" for those who bailed out using one of their parachutes, alluding to the fact the threads used to make the silk cloth and cord was originally produced by caterpillars. If you sent in your story to them, you could become a member. My parachute was one of theirs, but I did not send in my story because I wanted to retain the rights to use it in this book.

The landing at Biggs Field did pose a problem for Joe, Andy and Pete. They hung around doing chores around the turrets until the officers had gone to the operations briefing room to report on their trip.

It was daylight and Biggs Field, Texas was much warmer than Topeka, so some of the winter clothing had to be discarded in the plane. Beth, was depending on her brother to get her off base, and shortly after leaving the flight line with Joe, again shielding her face from the guards under her fatigue hat, she headed for the orderly room of her brother's unit. Joe never did know if she got off base without trouble or not, because the crew took off shortly for the return trip to Topeka. He did not stay around to meet her brother and he felt pretty lucky to pull off the trip without getting caught.

Jelley's crew, with our plane, Shehasta, landed at Biggs Field shortly after Phantom Lady, and after checking in at the operations office, we also returned to Topeka. As crews do, however, we stood around at Biggs Field and talked about the trip while waiting for the officers to return from operations as we checked the planes for any problems before the return trip. It was some days later before the rest of the crew knew what had happened. By that time we were all on our way to the Pacific.

Three other incidents happened worth mentioning at Topeka.

Ben Pudder, the copilot on Phantom Lady, almost got into trouble as a result of getting too much to drink at the officers' club. Ben was a flight officer, equivalent to a junior grade warrant officer and a status held by enlisted men who were either of long experience in their field, or very technical in their knowledge — a position in between officer and enlisted status — but carrying much respect with both categories, officers and enlisted men.

Ben bought some red fingernail polish at the Post Exchange and proceeded to the flight line. He got a ladder from along the flight line, carried it up to where the cockpit windshield was located. His intentions were good, but his condition was not.

He intended to put a small line about an inch wide all around the windshield which was supposed to cut down on glare on the windshield. His partially inebriated condition did not provide a steady hand or a steady seating arrangement while painting the anti-reflecting line around the windshield. As a result, the job started to take on an uneven effect.

In an effort to correct the mistakes he had made, the lines became wider, slowly covering more and more of the glass. In his jocose state, he then started to make unnecessary stripes across the surface. The nail polish dried quickly and soon he had a mess. To make matters worse, Ben had moved away from the ladder and he was too unsteady to make his way back to it.

He started yelling for help and soon some of the mechanics and security personnel were on the ground below trying to decide the best way to get Ben out of his predicament. If he had fallen, he could have broken an arm or leg, head or back — due to the distance to the ground — especially since he was unable to navigate safely on his own. But with some effort and using additional ladders, they were able to get Ben down without additional mishap.

Ben had to spend an entire afternoon cleaning off the windshield with acetone, and the officers of his crew had to dig another six by six by six, since Ben was classified as an officer and the rules for punishment were still in effect.

The second incident involved a subject that was of great importance to everyone, especially to Corny and me when we became involved, and that was security.

All around the base were signs warning us not to talk or discuss our destination, our mission or our strength in men or planes. The signs "A loose lip can sink a ship" and "The Enemy is Listening" were at every turn, and we were given briefings constantly on the subject. In addition to the films, which were narrated by the movie star Ronald Reagan, on venereal diseases, there were films on security, showing how the girls could loosen your tongue while loosening your tie or fly.

When Corny and I went into Topeka, we were approached by a well dressed, portly man wearing glasses. He said as a part of his contribution to the war effort, he and his wife would like to have us to his home for dinner that evening. Corny and I felt we could cope with any problem that may arise and accepted. He had an accent, as did his wife, but we weren't concerned with it. Her accent was more pronounced, and Corny and I decided they were of German origin. But one thing did begin to bother me and I let Corny know my concerns, and that was their frequent questions about the Air Base. Corny agreed we should be careful.

They offered us drinks, both soft and alcoholic in variety with our food. Our concern was increased when, after dinner, his wife took us into the nursery and showed us their two sleeping children and the room where they played. They had a boy and a girl, about ages five and six, really beautiful blonde children.

But their play room looked like a miniature arsenal. There were all kinds of war toys, including small metal tanks, planes and miniature soldiers. There was no evidence of dolls or any type of normal little boys play toys such as balls or sailboats — only guns, ships and sailors. It was weird, and under the circumstances, Corny and I decided we should leave as soon as possible. Their questions never stopped — wanting information about the planes, how many, how they were equipped, how we trained, etc.

Immediately upon returning to the base, we told the military police the address of the man, giving all the information we could remember. Shortly thereafter, we were contacted by a security officer who recorded all the information we could give him. He seemed pleased and indicated we had helped them because they were having trouble with security leaks about operations on the base.

By now, I'm sure you are convinced the bomber crews did little else than fly and chase the girls. But as I explained previously, due to the high risks involved in training and the prospect of overseas combat shortly, almost all the airmen were trying to experience as much of life as possible. It was the "Flyboys" and "B-Girls" for sure.

I never did determine what the "B" stood for when referring to the girls. If it was for Bar, Buxom, Beautiful, or Bad — but whatever, nothing relaxed the tensions that developed from the close calls in the air, as did the company of an attractive female on the ground who was pleasant to be with and interested in you and your welfare.

While some of us had friends back home and spent many leisure hours writing to them, the realities of life led to some local activities, too. Sometimes a visit to the USO (United Service Organization) or to the local church of our choice.

Some of us had begun to develop a more religious attitude, giving more thought to our souls and the hereafter. I remember quite a few discussions on the subjects of Heaven and Hell. Most of us came to the conclusion that if there was any doubt about where we might go, the preference was to Heaven, and the risk was too great to risk the other place.

So most of our men did have a belief in God, a Supreme Being, eternal in the Heavens. We started to attend church services regularly on Sunday mornings. I was a Protestant, but went to Catholic Church sometimes with Charles "Tommy" Thompson, our tail gunner, and I was glad later when we went overseas. When he was lost, it was a comfort to know he had a faith to sustain him in his time of trial.

Henry "Hutch" Hutchings, our engineer and top turret gunner, was also a regular attendee at his church and wrote his girl friend back in Georgia regularly. We were to lose him, too, as well as "Griff," our assistant engineer. Griff Griffith was a happy go lucky fellow who kept us in good spirits when things looked bad, but we not only lost him, but his replacement, too — Victor "Vic" Meehan. Both served as assistant engineers and waist gunners. Knowing all were good Christian men was a help when the difficult times came to us along the way.

The last incident worth mentioning in Topeka took place at a local hotel bar. Clifford "Cliff" Roberts, Phillip "Phil" Tabor, and Paul "Lefty" Leftowitz, all from Goodin's crew, were seated at a table sipping a few drinks. It was only two days before we were due to fly out to California and then on to Hickam Field, Hawaii. A very attractive well-dressed blonde female was seated at the bar. As Cliff later told it, she was fabulous looking in every way, with an engaging smile and outgoing personality.

Phil said, "I would give my right arm to make out with her," so Cliff asked her if she would join him and the others at the table. She told them, "Fine, I'm just waiting for my boyfriend, a local attorney."

Later, a well dressed elderly man came in and she left

65

with him in a white convertible, a very expensive car. Phil was very disappointed, but he was still wishing he had become better acquainted with her, even to "losing his right arm" for a sample of her charms.

Much later, going up the elevator to their room, the bell hop asked them if they would like a little "entertainment." Of course, he indicated, she was very attractive and reasonable, just fifteen dollars for each of them. They agreed, due to the beauty they had beheld in the bar and the working of the drinks they had consumed.

It was not long before a knock came at the door. Cliff went to answer it, but Phil was more quick to reach the door. He was surprised to see the young attractive girl they had met in the bar. She said, "So we meet again."

Phil said, "You must have the wrong room."

Her reply, with a mischievous smile was, "You did ask to be entertained, didn't you?"

"Well, yes," he replied, "but I didn't expect you." She laughed and entered the room.

Phil was really pleased, but somewhat upset, too. He had learned two lessons. You cannot be sure about someone by just looking and you should never be prepared to pay too high a price for anything until you have had some time to evaluate its worth. In this case, it was worth just forty- five dollars among them, but Phil did give his right arm later, but it was for his country, a much more noble cause.

But Phil had a story to tell, too, but his was about Cliff. Phil told how the girl laughed at Cliff because he had on his GI long john underwear, dull green in color and sufficiently warm for that time of year, but they were not conducive to the kind of entertainment they were to engage in that night. He had to interrupt his part of the entertainment to take them off, and she kidded him about being so wrapped up in his underwear that he almost missed out on the good part of the evening.

"A real fun girl" was Phil's way of describing her. They said she was with them until early morning, leaving just before daybreak, having satisfied all their desires and with some memories to take with them overseas for those long lonesome nights in the jungles of the South Pacific Islands.

One other item of some importance was the regular physical examinations given by the flight surgeons to approve all crew members for duty in flying combat. We were regularly checked, without notice, sometimes in the middle of the night, for any venereal diseases we may have contracted as a result of encounters such as the one Phil, Cliff and Lefty had just experienced.

This exam consisted of the so called "short arm" exam to determine gonorrhea or "clap" infection, and a visual exam to reveal shankers or sores, or anything else unusual. Blood tests would reveal the more serious disease of syphilis. Three shots of penicillin in the rear were the normal treatment for gonorrhea, along with sulphur drugs administered orally.

The movies and stories usually were enough to assure abstinence, or if not, then at least the use of a prophylactic provided by a visit to the base or a chemical pro-treatment from a downtown dispensary. Besides, V.D. could get you grounded or thrown off flying status, which not only meant losing flight pay but could also mean missing training or replacement if your crew was shipped out before being released from treatment. No one wanted to fail the physical exams — for any reason.

Fortunately, almost every one of the two- hundred men in twenty crews were in the move to the South Pacific, leaving in intervals which were separated by a few days to a week, on the trip to Hickam Field, Hawaii.

Our crew left the good old United States on May 19th, 1943, and spent twenty-one days at Hickam Field while the Sperry lower ball turret was installed in Shehasta. That was the turret I had been chosen to operate, or rather volunteered for, since no one else expressed any interest in that position. Further, I was the likely choice, being only 119 pounds and being the armorer with experience while in the States on that

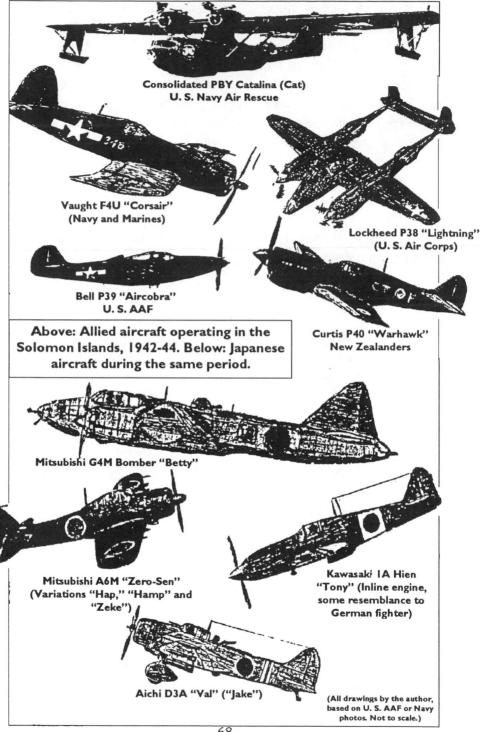

Consolidated PBY Catalina (Cat)
U. S. Navy Air Rescue

Vaught F4U "Corsair"
(Navy and Marines)

Lockheed P38 "Lightning"
(U. S. Air Corps)

Bell P39 "Aircobra"
U. S. AAF

Above: Allied aircraft operating in the Solomon Islands, 1942-44. Below: Japanese aircraft during the same period.

Curtis P40 "Warhawk"
New Zealanders

Mitsubishi G4M Bomber "Betty"

Mitsubishi A6M "Zero-Sen"
(Variations "Hap," "Hamp" and
"Zeke")

Kawasaki IA Hien
"Tony" (Inline engine,
some resemblance to
German fighter)

Aichi D3A "Val" ("Jake")

(All drawings by the author,
based on U. S. AAF or Navy
photos. Not to scale.)

68

turret, as well as the others. The nose turret was also installed and Earl "Corny" Cornelius moved into it.

The other B-24 Liberators were being converted, too. These conversions made them the most heavily armed bombers in the sky, with nose turrets, tail turrets, top turrets, ball turrets in the bottom plus guns at each waist window, all 50 caliber machine guns.

While the conversions were going on at Hickam Field, we had many things to occupy our time, on and off the base. Much of the time was spent in training. The ball turret gunners used mock-ups on platforms elevated above the hangar floors some ten feet. Our practice was in lowering the turret, raising it, manual operation (in case of hydraulic or electrical problems, either in combat or as a result of breakdown of some of the equipment) and gunnery practice using the Sperry Automatic Computing Sight. Other crew members were doing the same thing with respect to their positions on the bomber.

Aircraft identification was taught, especially with respect to the Japanese fighters, bombers and carrier based planes. Our own aircraft operating in the area were also a part of the identification taught to make sure our gunners would not shoot down our own planes by mistake. Naval vessels, both Japanese and our own were a part of identification as well, so we would be able to sight friendly and enemy vessels from remote distances with relative accuracy.

Passes were issued sparingly, but we did get to go to Honolulu to swim on Waikiki Beach and visit the Royal Hawaiian Hotel. We found some of the beaches on the other side of the island to be better for swimming due to Waikiki Beach having coral that would cut your feet if you were not extremely careful. Any cut would not heal quickly because the coral is a live organism which would grow and fester in the wound if left untreated.

But the sights were beautiful. We rented surf boards and tried our hand at surfing, too. However, it was obviously not a sport for novices. Attention had to be paid to the waves

The Royal Hawaiian Hotel in Honolulu was "the" place to be in 1942. Good food, good sun— good times— all before shipping off to the unknown destiny awaiting in the war-torn South Pacific.

and undercurrents which could sweep you out into the ocean very quickly if you were not alert to your position while surfing. I cut my feet on the coral, as did some of the others, and had to go to the dispensary on the base.

We also made a tour of the island of Oahu, which was very interesting and informative. The islands of Hawaii offered many sights and all kinds of entertainment. Some sights we visited were: Up Side Down Falls, the Blow Hole, the overlook from which we could see all of the City of Hawaii and Pearl Harbor, Diamond Head (the large mountainous cliff that overlooks the Pacific Ocean), the beautiful flower gardens and fountains leading to the temple of the Church of Jesus Christ of Latter Day Saints (Mormons), and the sugar cane fields which were very interesting.

The Up Side Down Falls was a stream of water that came down a ravine between two steep mountain cliffs. The air rushing into the ravine blew the water surface which was misty back up over the falls which created an illusion of water flowing back upward at times, hence the name "Up Side Down Falls."

The Blow Hole was a hole in the rock or coral that jetted out into the ocean. The movement of the tides had washed an area out beneath the rock and linked up with the hole in the rock. When the waves came in, pressure built up, forcing the water up into the hole, causing it to squirt up into the air some ten to thirty feet, depending upon the force of the waves incoming to shore. In more stormy times, the force was tremendous and the sound created was awesome, too.

One of the fellows from Goodin's crew, I believe it was Pete Peterson again, came back from a trip to Battle Street in downtown Honolulu with a story of his adventures. He told about the "Honolulu Twirl," about a nude girl who sat in a basket with the bottom out of it. The basket was then twirled around as it hung from a rope suspended from the ceiling above. This knotted the rope up. The rope was then released so she twirled as she came down onto a waiting table, or I believe he said bed, occupied by an expectant serviceman laying on it quite naked, too. You can imagine the result of that trip yourself. Of course, Pete could embellish any story he told with many descriptive phrases that would leave any fisherman out in the cold when it came to bragging about his big catch.

Pete didn't miss out on much that was going on at any new location he visited. Pete had told of his being on leave in New Orleans, near his home, and of meeting this beautiful girl who invited him to her room for a drink. Pete's description of the meeting — and subsequent results — were almost beyond anyone's believability.

Pete said she really gave him a rough time, had him chase her around the room, over the couch and finally, after much fun and games at his expense, gave in on the couch, only to jump up and start the routine over again. Just as he was becoming very exasperated and about to give up, she submitted to him and proceeded to show him a really good time.

After it was over she told him it was only for show. Since he had been such a nice guy and came through with flying colors, she would let him in on a little secret. She directed him to a door next to the entrance to her apartment, told him to go upstairs and join the group for the next show which could be observed through a one way mirror mounted in the ceiling.

Pete never said whether he stayed for the next one, but I'm sure he never forgot the embarrassment of his own performance, but he delighted in telling about it later.

The sights on the island were enough to keep the crews of the B-24 Liberators occupied. The crews of the Phantom Lady and Shehasta, as well as the other crews found much to see and experience. To my knowledge, only a few of our men went down to Battle Street, and Pete was the only one who admitted visiting the notorious area of clubs and prostitution. It was patrolled quite well by Military Police of the Army and Navy, and no one left the bordellos without a visit to get a "pro" at the clinic provided by our government.

Evidence was everywhere of the attack by the Japanese on Pearl Harbor and Hickam Field. Security forces were everywhere. Damaged and destroyed ships and planes were easy to see and the hangars and runways still had areas with holes where the bombing and strafing occurred on December 7th, 1941, the day of infamy and betrayal by the Japanese.

In all, I was overseas three times — Guadalcanal, Guam and Japan — during and after the wars, WW II and Korea. I had an assignment to Shori Air Force Base in Japan on a classified mission as late as 1955 and I can tell you from that experience, they had not forgotten nor forgiven us for their defeat. But it seems we have been quick to forget our own losses. Sometimes I think we won the war and lost the peace, at least financially, and in many other ways, too. My tour of duty on Guam during the Korean War at Anderson Air Force Base in 1950-52 helped to bear that out. But these are other stories which I will not attempt to cover in this book, as it is not intended as an autobiography, but an historical coverage of World War II.

Who would think that forty-eight years later the government of the United States of America would give a restitution of twenty-thousand dollars to each Japanese-American who was interned during the war because he or she was moved from his home to a detention center. Where are the twenty-thousand dollars for each American soldier who left his home and loved ones, some never to return again?

Most of the families received ten-thousand dollars of life insurance at the time of the soldier's death, and the family was lucky if they were taken care of at all after the soldier was lost or disabled for life.

To those who survived, it is a constant battle to receive any compensation or even some consideration of the physical and mental effects of that war. Many have been denied benefits because, being good soldiers, they gave all they had to give and did not seek or want help right after leaving the military. Because of that, years later they have had difficulty establishing service connected disabilities and are made to feel degraded for even asking for help.

Many are becoming derelicts and street people, rather than face the humiliation that is leveled at them by unfeeling and uncaring government employees who know nothing of the ravages of war to body and mind, with their paychecks seeming to be the only motivation that guides their actions. It is becoming progressively more difficult to receive treatment and medication for veterans while the ones who are supposed to serve them show less and less regard for the veterans.

Perhaps this part of the book is not appropriate, since it is not history but happening right now, but it is an opinion that is prevalent among ex-servicemen. All these men were and are patriots in the cause of your freedom and democracy, and the defense of the United States of America, and many have been shortchanged by unfeeling, uncaring politicians who are only interested in money, power and prestige, not in serving the citizens to the best of their abilities.

But the airmen flying our bombers and fighters, as well as the other servicemen, had no way of knowing what was in store for them in the future, after the war. All they could think of at that time was the great damage that had been inflicted at Pearl Harbor and on the runways and hangars at Hickam Field. That brought the war to each of us in a very real way and the realization that some of us would not make it back to our homes and loved ones. But each was ready and willing to make the ultimate sacrifice as Patriots.

At Hickam Field, we completed our twenty-one days of training while our planes had any additional equipment installed. Some planes left Hawaii headed for the South Pacific. Our first stop was Canton Island.

The island was so small, a soldier could see from one end of the island to the other. The coral reefs made it somewhat circular in shape, with one area long and straight enough for our bombers to land. It was used as a refueling station for aircraft, ships and submarines. The few navy and army personnel stationed on the island were almost stir crazy. One year on the island was like a year in prison.

I asked one of them what they did for entertainment and was told they watched movies, wrote home and played with themselves. I thought he was kidding (and perhaps he was) but he told me two things that made me wonder about what he had said.

One story was that they had some pigs in a pen on one end of the island which were raised for fresh meat and to feed waste garbage the gooney birds didn't eat. Two guys had been caught in the pig pen at night and were sent home for courts-martial and bad discharges. He said we could go down to the end of the island and look in the daytime, if we wanted to, but he said there was a sign on the pens, "Warning! Anyone caught in with the pigs at night will be court-martialed," the implication being that some of the men were desperate for company.

The other story concerned the gooney birds. He told me the "other" favorite sport was chasing the gooney birds, enticing them with food scraps until they were almost too heavy to fly or trying to sneak up on them and grab them before they took off. He said you have never had such an experience as putting each leg of a gooney bird in each of your side pockets and then having it try to fly away. Your imagination can provide the rest of that picture, but he was very serious when he told us.

How he kept a straight face telling the stories I don't know, but the one about the pigs left us all wondering how bad things could get where we were going. We were all united in skipping any sexual experiences offered on Canton Island. By now, we knew we were heading for the Solomon Islands, and while those stories were good for a laugh, our own possible fate in the jungles of the South Pacific was very sobering.

There were anti-aircraft guns and barricades on the Canton Island, as well as bunkers for the planes and foxholes for the men. Occasionally, Japanese submarines would sur- face and cause a stir. There sometimes were Japanese planes and ships which would appear off the shore and this always gave rise to speculation the small island may be invaded.

Our next stop was the Figi Islands for two days. This was also just a refueling stop on our next leg of the journey, New Caledonia. Our two day stop at the Figi Islands was without incident, and we began to see some of the natives of the Islands —some scantily clad.

Our guns were armed and ready to fire, which meant the daily task of cleaning guns began in earnest. We had not spotted any Japanese ships or submarines on our trip so far but as we neared New Caledonia, that possibility became more probable.

We landed at Tontuda, New Caledonia which was near Port de Gias at the western end of the island. At the other end was Noumea, the center of government, a small town which had many navy, marine and army personnel as well as allied soldiers from New Zealand, Australia, France and England. It was a French protectorate, one of their far flung islands in the Pacific Ocean.

The camp where we stayed had a guard dog training unit nearby and it was hard to sleep at night. The dogs were used for guard duty at the bunkers which protected the planes. They were also used on the islands to the north to seek out the enemy in the jungle. These dogs were vicious and I didn't envy the trainers.

The United States, as well as the other allied countries, used the area for staging assaults and for storing supplies, ammunition and fuel in their move against the islands to the north held by the Japanese. Australia and New Zealand were also used as bases to move north with troops to recapture the Islands of New Guinea and the Solomons and in their march to recapture the Philippines.

We went deer hunting in the hills above our camp. We didn't know if there would be deer, but we took our carbines and forty five pistols. The hills were steep and we could stand on one hillside and shoot across at deer running on the other side parallel with us. I shot one and Corny got one. It was like shooting ducks in a barrel, just too easy. I didn't find it a challenge and in fact, have not enjoyed deer hunting since that time.

Then we had to go all the way down into the ravine, cross a stream and climb the other side to get the deer. Then it was necessary to cut their throats to bleed them, strip their innards, which we saved for the dogs, and cut poles to drag them off the hill side. We finally got them down to camp with the help of Tommy and Hutch, who did not have as great a luck in their hunting. The cooks were happy we got them, but said they had to keep them in the freezer before we could have any to eat. We looked forward to having some before we left the Island for the New Hebrides Islands.

The next day we got a jeep out of the motor pool and headed for Noumea. The road was terrible and up steep mountains with large drop-offs on the sides, much like our own hills in West Virginia. But to add to the problems, rain kept the roads slick, muddy and in many places washed away. If it had been seasonal with ice and snow, it would have been an impossible task to reach Noumea by roads. As it was, we ran into traffic along the way, including supply trucks and jeeps.

When we finally reached Noumea, we visited some shops. There were many trinkets made by the natives for sale to the various soldiers and sailors and military from other countries that stopped there, too.

There were French speaking girls, who also spoke some English, working in the shops. Some were very attractive. They wore colorful clothes and jewelry and flowers in their hair from the tropical flower gardens in the islands, much as they did in Hawaii and the Figi Islands. But most of these girls were not Polynesian, Micronesian, or native Melanesian. Many were French, some from Australia and New Zealand. Some of the girls had the brown skin from their mixed blood, but not many of them worked in the shops.

Not long after arriving we noticed two lines of service-men on the path leading to two different buildings. One was on the right side of the hill north of the shops on main street, which was a square around a park right in the center of the shops. The harbor and ships were on the south side of the town. The other building was on the left side of the hill, which was not too steep. It was a large house easily identified by its red (or more pink) roof.

The servicemen coming from the building on the right were carrying beer cans or some other drink, and almost all of them just walked right over and got into the other line to the red roofed house on the left.

Since it was obvious they were getting drinks in the one house, we asked about the other one. We were told it was a place to satisfy your sexual desires. That was pretty hard to believe, since the movement of the line was so regular, with hardly a holdup in the line. The girls would pleasure the guys for three minutes for three dollars, the old fashioned way. Anything else was extra, but it seemed from the rapidity of the line moving that most were old fashioned in their desires.

None of our crew members availed themselves of both lines, but most did get a beer or soft drink. I could not imagine the business the girls were doing or their being able to perform so regularly, but it was explained they did get frequent breaks and had one week off out of every four, which it was not necessary to explain. It seems they did not work too long before they went back home for a rest, but they also went home very wealthy by the monetary standards of the time. Every serviceman who visited Noumea knew about the red roofed house on the hill, and even today at reunions, it is possible to get a blush when the subject is mentioned in mixed company.

I could not leave this visit without repeating the story I was told about Mrs. Eleanor Roosevelt's visit to Noumea. She had created a stir back in the United States when she visited New Zealand. A picture of her kissing a native New Zealander, a Maori, on the cheek had reached the newspapers, and many did not understand her kissing what to them was a black person at a time when integration was not yet talked about by the folks back home. Her husband, President Franklin D. Roosevelt, had sent her to visit and help the morale of the troops so far from home. But it was unthinkable for a President's wife to do such a thing at that time.

When news came she was going to visit the islands north of New Zealand and Australia, and may even come close to the combat areas in the South Pacific, many of the top military leaders did not approve. But she came to New Caledonia and visited the troops at Noumea.

This did not stop the beer drinking or partaking of the pleasures in the town. When she saw the lines, she asked what they were doing, waiting in those long lines.

The Special Service Officer, a very knowledgeable fellow, answered, "That line on the right is where the men cash their pay checks and get something to drink as they leave.

The other line to the red roofed house up there is where the men go to buy war bonds. We are very proud of our men for as you can see, they are very patriotic. Hardly any of them fail to make their contribution, even though they are putting their life on the line every day, too."

I know she must have assured the President on her return home of the patriotism and sacrifice made for the cause of freedom.

A Plane Called "Shehasta"

This is the picture taken on New Hebrides ("Buttons"), also Espiritu Santos, of our plane Shehasta with the name and number intact. This was prior to hitting trees on take-off, causing damage to the front end of the plane and landing gear and almost causing us to ditch in the ocean. The number 324 was never repainted on Shehasta prior to our final, fatal mission.

CHAPTER 5

GUADALCANAL

Chapel In The Wildwood

We left New Caledonia without getting one bite of the deer meat we had gone to so much trouble to bring back to camp.

Our take-off on the 22nd day of April, 1943, was uneventful and we flew north, landing at "Buttons," code name for Espiritu Santo, New Hebrides, now known as Vanuatu Islands. This island belonged to the French.

It was obvious when we landed we were getting into jungle vegetation. There were coconut groves and thick vegetation on the outskirts of the field. Security was tight, which signaled our entry into a combat area. We could see the tents, along with a few wooden buildings, with foxholes alongside for use by the aircrews and anyone close by when needed.

Henry E. "Hutch" Hutchings tries his hand at the waist gun on Shehasta. As Engineer, he generally used the General Electric top turret, located directly behind the pilot, co-pilot and navigator.

Our landing on steel mats made a great deal of noise, even though the matting was laid down on coral which had been bulldozed by the Seabee construction crews to a relatively level condition. The vibration of the tires along the metal runways created a bouncing effect at times, not the smooth landings we were so familiar with stateside.

Shehasta, along with Phantom Lady and five other planes, landed within a few days of one another.

Some of the other B-24s had already been there and had moved further north to Carney Field on Guadalcanal. The name used for our future location was called "Cactus," on Guadalcanal. There was also Henderson Field which had all types of aircraft there, including the 5th Bomb Group, a B-17 Flying Fortress outfit.

Many of the B-17's were being returned to the States, since the B-24 Liberator had proven to be more suitable for bombing missions over the long distances involved between the islands. The B-24 was also faster on bomb runs and the armaments were greater as a result of the conversions made in Hawaii. The Japs were already beginning to have a healthy respect for the Liberators replacing the older model B-24's and the B-17's.

It was about the time we hit Buttons that Jack Kennedy had just turned age 26 and was on the PT Boat 109, based first at Tulagi, then Russell Island, and later at Rendova. These same areas were to prove important to us, too. Of course, Kennedy was to later become our President, but his near fatal mission was on August 2, 1943 in Brackett Strait, not far from Kolombangara Island.

From the time we arrived, we had rain off and on almost every day. Sometimes it lasted for days in certain seasons, and I believe we came just in time to experience the rain season. All the islands in the Solomons were that way, which accounted for the jungles and large amounts of vegetation. The humidity was very high, too, causing everything to mildew or mold. This brought about one of our greatest problems on the South Pacific Islands— how to keep rust and corrosion from the metal parts of the turrets and especially the guns, which had to be constantly cleaned to prevent rusting and pitting of the barrels.

While some of the others moved on up to the Canal, as we referred to Guadalcanal, or Cactus, the code word for Carney Field, our crew and Goodin's crew spent most of May

1943 at Buttons flying search missions and in further training. Those search missions were conducted to locate any Japanese carriers with support ships of the Japanese Navy. Enemy submarines were frequently sighted. These we would bomb or strafe before they could submerge, and many left oil slicks indicating damage or destruction from our attacks.

We were told if we did locate the Japanese fleet with carriers, or even one carrier, it would probably result in our being shot down. We could cut and run, but the faster fighters would swarm over us, a lone aircraft, to make sure we did not carry any information with us back to our base. They would resort to suicide, if necessary to prevent such a report.

We would be able to report the enemy location and strength to our home base, if we made it back, so bombers could be dispatched to attack. Further, it just might be possible for our own fleet to cut the enemy off from a return north to their own territory.

Guadalcanal had not been secured too long by our 1st Marine Division, which had taken a beating from the Japanese Imperial Marines before the Japs abandoned the island. The 1st Marines did prevail, however, and the Japanese were not happy about that at all. They were still ranging far south of the Canal with their planes and ships, using New Georgia, Bougainville and Rabaul on New Britain as staging areas for their planes, troops and ships.

It would be our job, once we went on up to Cactus, to help take those islands, by softening them up by bombing and strafing the ships, planes and troops.

But for now we were hoping if we did sight a Jap fleet, it would be far enough away to give us a running chance, or that the skies would be stormy with sufficient clouds to hide on our return trip to our base at New Hebrides.

Being isolated many miles from any friendly forces was not a situation we looked forward to under any circumstances. These missions were of a length of eight-hundred miles out into the ocean, a turn to the right or left for two hundred miles and then a return trip to our base at New

Hebrides. The missions almost always started before daybreak and were flown at a relatively low height of three to five thousand feet. When the clouds were sparse and visibility clear, we sometimes attained a height of ten thousand feet.

We could fly with the waist windows open and did not fly high enough to necessitate the use of oxygen. Further, we were now flying in very warm air so we did not need heavy clothing.

I did not have to fly in the lower ball turret, although I did lower it after leaving our field and checked out the guns, just in case they were needed. It would not have taken but a half minute to have all of the crew at their stations in the turrets if anything was to be sighted. When we flew in cloudy or overcast skies, it was necessary to be more ready for a quick response in the event an enemy ship or plane was sighted, so we did man the turrets, test fire our guns and prepare for an immediate response.

Many times we would spot schools of fish in the ocean waves below or whales with their tattletale spouts of water. Our first thought was always of submarines. In the event they were sighted, we would immediately go down, determine if they were friendly or the enemy, and proceed to attack when necessary. I always had a good view from the lower ball turret, so from a visual sighting, I was able to identify them almost immediately.

Usually by the time we got close enough to shoot, they were already starting to submerge, leaving only the conning tower and white wake visible. If they were caught on the surface, they did have anti-aircraft guns mounted fore and aft which could be used to return fire as long as they had not started to submerge. We would bomb and strafe the sub hoping to inflict damage before we lost them. Any oil slick or churning water could signal a hit, especially if there was a large eruption of waves.

Fortunately, most of the missions were uneventful, but the long hours of flying were very tiresome. The even drone of the engines could lull us into a state of semi-contentment, but we didn't let that happen. On a few of our missions, we were unfortunate enough to lose an engine which had to be feathered, and of course this cut short those long missions.

We were starting to go to the movie shows for entertainment quite regularly. June 29th — "Man About Town," July 1st — Artie Shaw was there in person with his orchestra.

Our first bad experience was to occur at the field at Buttons on Saturday, July 3rd, 1943. I remember it clearly because the United Service Organization (USO) Group had visited us the night before, with Ray Bolger, the dancer who played the Tin Man in the "Wizard of Oz" movie and the comedian Jerry Colona, remembered for his large poppy eyes and thick black mustache. There were no females with them because the area was still considered too dangerous — a combat area. It was a great show, but little did we know what awaited us the next day.

It was our eleventh search mission and everything had been going well up to that point. We had seen only two enemy subs and no ships or planes. The subs had submerged quickly without incident.

We went out to the runway to get ready for take-off at about five o'clock in the morning. The engines were working fine, and preflight went well. I had checked the turrets and bomb bays. We had some one-hundred pounders on board as well as the usual supply of fifty caliber ammunition for the turrets and waist guns.

We were lined up on the runway and the pilot and copilot were using the check list for take-off procedure. Hutch was following along with them to make sure engines, fuel and controls were in fine working order. As we went down the runway for take-off, we lifted off without incident less than half way down the runway, gaining altitude slowly because we were fully loaded with fuel for the eighteen-hundred mile journey out into the ocean.

Suddenly we began to lose altitude, and by the time we were at the end of the runway, we were low enough to hit some trees at the end of the clearing just before leaving land, going over a small beach area and out into the ocean. We could hear a thump and jarring of Shehasta as we made contact with the trees, and as we settled further toward the coral beach, we could hear the twin rudders of the tail section scrape on the coral. But we were gaining speed, and Shehasta started to regain some altitude just as we reached the water's edge.

As I learned later, Jim Jelley and Johnny Johnson up in the cockpit were fighting to keep control of the plane. Jim had his arms tensed, pulling back on the wheel as hard as possible and Johnny was doing the same. All the engines continued to run full throttle, but it was obvious some damage had been done to the leading edge of the wing between number one and two engines. Whitey and Gene Bruce were also up front as was Hosfeth, in the area behind the pilots. I was in the back with Griffith, Tommy, and Corny.

It was never clearly established, but apparently when Jelley called for gear up after leaving the runway, Johnson must have dumped the flaps, pulling them back up into the wing and reducing the extra lift which the extra wing area of the flaps provided on take-off.

Once we hit the trees and lost altitude, coming so close to the surface of the ground, it is also probable the landing gear was already being retracted, otherwise their protrusion would have caused contact with the trees, too.

In any event, quick thinking on the part of Jelley, as well as Johnson helped to maintain control of the plane, and Shehasta started to gain altitude again. But there was a tree limb about five inches thick imbedded between the number one and two engines. This caused a loss of speed and drag to the right, making it impossible to make a left turn.

We continued to gain altitude while Jelley and Johnson attempted to align Shehasta with the runway again. This could be accomplished only by making large right turns. The fuselage had been damaged below the nose turret when the trees cut into the area.

We had settled evenly and fortunately did not drag a

wing, which would have caused the plane to do a cartwheel, and both plane and crew would have been lost.

Jelley proved himself to be a damned good pilot, as he had previously proven, and would do again later. He lined the plane up from a wide circle, estimated the exact position we would hit the end of the runway while making that wide right turn and kept the right wing elevated just high enough so as not to touch the ground, which would have caused a ground loop on touchdown. It was a landing only an "Ace" pilot could have performed, and Jelley was a "Bomber Ace" for sure. His subsequent flying accomplishments were to bear that out as our combat action progressed.

We all fastened our seat belts, put our heads down and prayed. We were right up against the bulkhead separating the bomb bays from the rear compartment. Jelly flew her in at approximately 165 MPH. Only when we touched did we discover we must have had a hydraulic line broken, because even with reverse pitch, the wheel brakes did not work. We ran off the end of the runway and the nose wheel collapsed.

We all jumped out immediately when the plane stopped and ran, as we knew it was fully loaded with fuel, but there was no fire. We were all safe, and no one was even scratched.

We were told by the operations officer that no other aircraft had survived hitting trees on take-off, and in fact, three planes had been lost previous to our accident, two going into the ocean beyond the reef. The liner "President Coolidge," had struck mines and sank off the coast in the Espiritu Santo harbor while being used as a troop carrier in the fall of 1942, but we had no desire to join her in mid '43 — but we almost did, that's for sure.

This meant the Shehasta had to be repaired. It was determined she could be put back in the air, but it would take some time. Another B-24 was warmed up, but two engines were missing fire, so we changed to another plane. We took off, still before daybreak, but we had to turn back again with number two engine out. After that landing we gave up and went back to our tents. It was just not our day.

The next day, July 4th, 1943, I read my Bible and thanked God for his protection. On July 5th, Gene Bruce was grounded with a case of dingy fever, a form of mild malaria, while we went on a search mission again. It was a policy to get a crew back up in the air as soon as possible after such an incident to overcome the deep fear that could develop as a result of a close call, or if some crew member was lost.

That evening we saw another USO show. Eddie White, Cliff Young, Gene Reaulbaine with his violin, and an orchestra from the ship U.S.S. Dixie. The next day we dug on a foxhole which we had been working on for a couple of days. We finished it on July 7th.

Our search mission on July 7th lasted eleven hours. Gene Bruce was well enough to fly with us again. We saw another movie that evening, "You Were Never Lovelier." I had seen it in the States, but the movies always seemed better over there. I guess it took us back to what it was like at home.

As I mentioned before, we went to the shows a lot. I kept a record of all the shows we attended in my diary. Fortunately, many of our activities, including combat, were kept in my diary. We were not supposed to maintain any daily records, but I believe many of the men did, but information which would have revealed our location, strength, mission objectives or losses was left out. Some sort of coding was necessary, and of course, we never took anything of identification on missions except dog tags, so nothing could be revealed except our name, rank, and serial number.

We also had a briefing on our next mission and what to expect on Guadalcanal since we were preparing to go up there. On July 8th, we just packed and went to some more briefings, gearing up for the new adventures that awaited us in combat. We saw the show "Night in New Orleans," but none of us remembered much about it as all our thoughts were on the action ahead at Guadalcanal.

On July 9th, we took a plane called Shack Rat, Number 222, up to Cactus, leaving Shehasta at Buttons for repairs.

A part of the shoreline at Guadalcanal.

We left at eight o'clock and had no difficulty on the trip north. We unloaded our baggage and prepared to dig a foxhole, the normal duty when assigned to a new tent.

The day we arrived, a crew had been shot down on Munda. The copilot and engineer had been ill and grounded, so they were not lost. The engineer moved out of the tent and we took it. This meant we did not have to build our tent or dig a foxhole. Another crew with Cobb as pilot was also lost. All of them got back later except the navigator, who was lost.

The officers also got a tent, but they had to dig a foxhole. The experience some of Goodin's crew had in digging six by sixes back in Alamogordo came in handy, I'm sure.

Just before we came to Carney our fighters, bombers and ground anti-aircraft crews had shot down 72 enemy planes to our loss of five. I guess it made the news in the States because everyone was talking about it on July 9, 1943. A guy I had known back in Tucson, Arizona was on Cobb's plane by the name of Bojanberg. I talked pretty late one night to him and two other fellows I had known back in the States by the names of Malone and Kindavater, catching up on home news.

I do not know who flew Shack Rat after we brought her up to Carney, but we flew Man-O-War for almost two months while its crew was on rest leave. Tommy had grown a goatee, but as I recall, he did not keep it long when we started the high altitude flying over enemy territory because of the oxygen masks we had to use.

Man-O-War had thirty-six missions and four Jap planes to its credit at the time we were assigned to fly it on strikes to Munda, Kahili, Ballale and Buka. Hutch, Tommy, Whitie and I, as well as Corny, Gene and Jim flew with Harold McNeese as first pilot on the missions to Kahili. Jelley flew as copilot with McNeese, then flew as first pilot with our full crew on later missions on Man-O-War.

Shehasta was finally repaired, then just about the time she was to be sent to the Canal, another plane damaged her wing which delayed her again. While still on Man-O-War, I got two Jap Zeroes from the lower ball turret while on raids to Kahili on Bougainville and the Island of Ballale, just off the southern coast, used by the Japs as a fighter base to protect Bougainville. (More on this in the next chapter.) We pulled eight missions on Man-O-War before getting Shehasta back.

We were pleased to ride with Captain Harold McNeese because he had quite a reputation already when we got to the Canal. He had pulled his crew through some tough missions, and was known to come through in a pinch.

The Commanding Officer of the 307th Bomb Group was Colonel William A. Matheny. He pulled missions right along with the rest of us, so we looked upon him as the kind of leader to have when the going was rough — and it had been rough, it was rough, and it was going to get rougher.

When Shehasta did get brought up to Cactus from Buttons, she was good as ever, but since the lower front of the fuselage had been repaired, her numbers "324" had been painted over, and they never did get repainted on the lower

89

section of the nose. But the name Shehasta still remained on the upper section.

A big change was made on Shehasta during her repairs. Flame dampers were placed over the superchargers of the engines. These screened the light emitted by the white hot superchargers from view by the anti-aircraft gunners on the ground, the only light emitted from the B-24's bright enough for the ground crews to target. Because of this, we started to pull night missions.

Normally, the altitude was radioed down by the Jap fighters who came up and flew alongside, out of range. On sufficiently dark nights we always hoped we would not be spotted until over the target. The searchlights would then be scanning the skies for us when we approached the area of the Jap fields, or other possible targets.

Living conditions at Cactus were really primitive. The steel matted Marsden runways made quite a racket on take-offs and landings, but particularly on the landings. The Seabees worked hard to clear areas to prepare for laying the runways, sometimes under very difficult circumstances, even being exposed to Japanese sniper fire from holdouts still hiding out and offering last ditch efforts of resistance.

They are to be commended for the great service and sacrifice they rendered in many areas of the South Pacific. The runways were able to support the bombers when fully loaded even in times when it was wet from the rainy season, leaving mud and coral under the matting.

The Army Engineering Companies also helped in the construction of some permanent structures like the Mess Hall, Operations Office, Photo Lab and Orderly Room. These were very rough structures, but served the purpose.

We were housed in tents back in the jungle away from the runways and bunkers housing the planes. Each tent had room for the six enlisted airmen of a crew. All the enlisted crews were housed together in one area and the officers were located in another. We settled in pretty well, the first order of business being to find or build a tent, the next a foxhole to head for in event "Washing Machine Charlie" (Jap bombers) came in to the Island. On New Hebrides and on Guadalcanal, the two things you could expect daily were small earthquakes or tremors, and the air raids.

Digging the foxhole was a very special project with each crew. They measured three or four feet deep, eight feet long and about eight feet wide — just big enough to go into bent over, then sit down on some ammunition boxes until the air raid was over. Ammo boxes also lined the walls. Tree trunks cut down back in the jungle and hauled into camp were placed over the foxhole and then packed on top with dirt.

As I mentioned, we did not have to dig our foxhole, but the officers did, this time. We were lucky, at the expense of another unfortunate crew.

The officers' facilities were not much better than the enlisted airmen, but I think they did have pillows on the bunks and facilities for shaving. We did not have pillows, so many of us used our "Mae West" life preservers. This was frowned on by the brass, and I was to learn a lesson on why later in combat. We used the valves on the Mae West to blow up one side of the preserver about half way, which made a nice soft head rest. Then when we went on a mission we would let the air out of it so we could close the valve, wear it and use the CO_2 cylinders to inflate the Mae West if it was needed on a ditching or bail out into the ocean.

We spent some time making our tents feel homey. The enlisted men built stands outside their tents from extra ammunition boxes and tree limbs. These we used for shaving. Large canvas, rubber-lined bags for water, called lister bags, were filled with water for drinking and shaving.

We went down to a small river called the Matepono, about a quarter mile from camp to swim and bathe, and to wash our clothes. On some days, I went down to write letters. I was receiving letters frequently from my friends back home and these helped to keep up my morale.

The natives were usually downstream from us, swimming, bathing and washing their clothes, too. Some were naked, but were some distance from us. We also would skinny dip at times and enjoy the swift currents that carried us along the steep banks, from which we would sometimes dive.

There were men, women and children among the na-

tives. I had the experience of meeting the chief of the tribes on Guadalcanal at that time, in 1943, a Master Sergeant Joseph Vouza. He had fought the Japanese, had been wounded and was highly regarded by our group. He helped us a great deal, but was very protective of his people, acting as the law and spokesman for them.

Sergeant Vouza had been captured by the Japanese when they occupied Guadalcanal. They had tortured him because he had a small American Flag hidden on his person when they searched him. Finally, when he wouldn't tell the Japs what they felt he knew about our troops, they cut his throat,

Jacob Vouza was given the rank of Sergeant Major (U.S. Marines) and wore the uniform and strips of that rank. He was a great asset to the American, British and French forces in the area and enjoyed great respect, especially for his bravery and leadership ability. Original 13th AAF photo in the National Archives, though this is a scanned image of a reproduction.

tied him to a tree, and left him for dead. However, he was able to get loose, make his way into the hills to his native friends and live to work against the Japs and helped to defeat them. His bravery led them to make him their Chief.

Sergeant Vouza held the rank of Sergeant Major in the U.S. Marine Corps and later was honored by the British government, receiving many medals for his valor and loyalty to our cause. He was very large and muscular, and always dressed in GI khaki uniforms with Sergeant Major Stripes on his short sleeve shirt. He looked much more powerful than the native men who followed him, and it was easy to see he was in charge when he came into our camp.

Always the women and children stayed in the background, while the men formed close behind Vouza. The women kept covered below the waist and some had their hair dyed orange, a sign they were single and eligible for

These natives lived in the jungles back in the hills of Guadalcanal. Civilization as we know it had not yet reached them, and their lifestyle was still very primitive. That changed slowly and they did visit our camp a few times with Jacob Vouza to sell grass skirts, bone and wooden combs in exchange for cigarettes or clothing. 13th AAF photo.

---

marriage. Their hair stuck out all over their heads, some as much as three or four inches.

We had been told about some of the natives on the Solomon Islands. There were many who fought constantly alongside of us, others who cooperated with the Japanese and others who were cannibals, eating anyone unfortunate enough to be captured by them.

Sergeant Vouza would come into camp and visit the

"Chapel in the Wildwood," our non-denominational church used by all to worship. When the floods came and nearly washed the chapel away, Sergeant Vouza and his men helped to restore it. They had been taught by missionaries and had a strong belief in God.

The white men had also taught them to smoke cigarettes. Even the children smoked if cigarettes were available. And the servicemen obliged them. Of course, Sergeant Vouza did not allow his people to mingle too closely with us, but he kept us informed of news from other tribes on the islands close by and visited our camp frequently.

The natives would sell us trinkets such as wooden combs they had made, bracelets, and anything else our men were interested in buying. Items of GI clothing such as shorts (cut-off trousers), shirts (long or short sleeves), and anything else they could get from us were worth the trade. But since Sergeant Vouza was in charge of the natives, he only led them down into the camps occasionally, just to barter and do some odd jobs for us. Otherwise, they stayed up in the hills far back in the jungles.

I never had an occasion to visit one of their villages, but did observe some of them from the air. The huts resembled our "Chapel in the Wildwood," the roof being of thatched type, using large jungle trees for supports and hewn logs for flooring and along the sides.

Shortly after arriving at Cactus, we did start attending church more regularly than when we were in training back in the States. The thoughts of combat and our possible death brought most of us to think of and feel the need of a Supreme Being to give us strength.

We attended services in a small chapel where we had to sit on oil barrels which were half buried and set in rows in front of the altar used by the respective chaplains of our faiths. The chaplains had a platform to preach from, upon which was suspended a large white cross. The name "CHAPEL IN THE WILDWOOD" had been placed across the front of the outside of the chapel, also in large white letters.

The chapel had been placed back some distance from the living quarters, as was the outdoor theater where we also sat on oil barrels. We did get closer to God as the risks became greater. It is true, there are no atheists in foxholes. At least, I never did meet any over there in the jungles of the South Pacific.

I'll admit, with some of us, confession, recommitment to Christ and promises made when asking for forgiveness did appear to be fleeting, but a close call usually reminded one of the need for help from a Supreme Being. The Jew, the Catholic, and the Protestant all prayed to the same God when facing death or going down into the ocean for the last time.

No Rabbi, no Priest and no Minister can give reassurance in that final moment when the parachute doesn't open, when the blood flows from the body as a result of an enemy bullet or you are trapped in a jammed turret with no means of escape, watching the fire in an engine grow larger and larger, knowing an explosion will be the ultimate finality of your life. No, it is only between you and your Savior, the trust that He will take you with Him. Some begged, some cried, some cursed the enemy, but ultimately all turned to God in that final moment.

We had rain — lots of rain most of the time. Not only was the chapel flooded, but everything else was mud and water. The mud, the dampness and mold were constant problems. Shoes had to be cleaned regularly to keep mold off of them. Clothes would smell mildewed if not washed regularly, and since the sunshine did not get through the haze of humidity enough at times, the vegetation was dense all around us.

We all immediately became familiar with the small chameleon-like lizards that crawled up and down the tent posts and all around the edge of the floor, coming out of every little crack they could fit through, quickly slithering under the bed covers or into the folds of a shirt.

Mosquito netting was tightly drawn from top to bottom
on the sides of the tent to keep the mosquitoes out, but they
were able to get in anyway. Further netting around the cots
still failed to keep them from us at night. The small lizards
were masters at the art of sneaking up on a resting mosquito
and snatching it with a long, lightning-quick jab of its tongue.
We learned the little lizards were our friends, for one less
mosquito was one less bite.

But an added and disconcerting aspect of having the
lizards was their company at night as they crawled into bed
with us and lay up close to our bodies. We could feel them
moving their creepy, crawling, cold little stomachs as they
slithered to a warm spot next to us. I was always afraid of
mashing one of them while moving around at night, and that
thought did not appeal to me at all. It never did happen and I
don't recall any of the fellows having mashed any of them.
The sun did usually come out some part of the day for a time,
but it did get cooler at night, which accounted for the extra
friendly lizards we had for company at those times.

The lizards came in all sizes, from two inches to eight
inches normally, but sometimes larger. Their big brothers and
sisters grew to lengths of five feet, and rested on the limbs of
the giant jungle trees. I always felt they must be related to the
tree iguana of Australia.

Coconut trees were prevalent throughout all the tropical
islands of the Pacific, but the lizards preferred to race along
the limbs of the tall jungle trees. Shooting the large tree
lizards became somewhat of a sport that some enjoyed, but
was frowned on by the higher-ups in charge of our Group
Operations. It could have been concern over saving ammunition was the biggest factor in their opposition to killing the
lizards.

Some of the plantation owners lived well from the sale of
coconuts and crops grown on the fringes of the jungles.
Sugar cane was another product in demand. Fishing helped
to supplement the diets of the owners and the natives, too.

Some of them had native women for wives. Some had

married venturesome ladies from their home who had joined them in the isolated lifestyle, which they seemed to enjoy. They all enjoyed a certain prestige among the natives, and it was not unusual for them to have a mistress who took care of their every need.

When the Japanese occupied many of the islands in the Solomons, the plantation owners went back into the hills and joined the natives in resisting the enemy. Some of these men were English, Australian or French and were representatives of their governments.

As a result, they became coastwatchers, helping to save allied airmen who were shot down by the Japs or sailors who had abandoned vessels plying the oceans due to accidents or Japanese attacks. Some of these coastwatchers had radios as well as small motor boats which could move from one island to another. Their friendships with the natives, as well as their familiarity with the terrain, helped them to avoid capture by the enemy.

Many of our airmen floated into inlets along the shoreline, to be met by coastwatchers or friendly natives. If it would become necessary to bail out over enemy territory, we all hoped some friendly coastwatcher or native would get to us first, aid and hide us out, and call on their tele-radio for a PBY (Dumbo Cat) Catalina Flying Boat to come at night to pick us up. Submarines from various allied countries would sometimes come in close to shore at night, too, and pick up some fortunate survivor, or survivors.

Some of the coastwatchers I heard about who helped some of our own crew members and others, were Jack Reed on Bougainville, Don S. MacFarlan on Tulagi, Martin Clemens and F. Ashton "Snowy" Rhoades in the hills of Guadalcanal in the early days of the invasion. There were also Donald G. Kennedy on New Georgia, Bill Bennett on Choiseul, Jack Keenan on Vella Lavella and Arthur Reginald Evans on Kolombangara. Mikael Forster was on San Christabal.

These men, and others like them, contributed greatly to

the defeat of the Japanese, some paying the ultimate price. We owe a great debt to all of them, and for the sacrifices that each of them made.

One thing all crews were fearful would happen was to be shot down near an island where cannibalism was practiced by the natives. No one wanted to be a souvenir on the spear of a cannibal or even worse, skinned alive, floating in a simmering pot of wild herbal stew, with the airman as the main course.

This may seem callous to refer to the situation in this way, but it was no worse than the fate awaiting those captured by the Japanese. While not practicing cannibalism, they were not human in the torture they inflicted. The Japanese Imperial Marines had already established their despicable reputation in the battle with the American First Marine Division to recapture Guadalcanal, prior to our arrival. We knew what was in store for us should we be unfortunate enough to survive bailing out or a crash landing.

The Japs would take their machetes, cut open the stomachs of the wounded American marines, and throw sand into the wound. This would preclude any hope of cleaning the wound, stitching it up or any recovery from it. It was a horrible, painful way to die.

There was no honoring the Geneva Convention provision for humane treatment of prisoners of war. Very few prisoners were taken in the early days of the war. But when the tide began to turn in favor of the American forces, their attitude did change a little, but not much where the airmen were concerned. The Japanese hated us and showed no respect for any rules of human treatment or decency, and the atrocities were beyond belief. As a result, we responded in our own vengeful way.

More Routine

On July 11th, we helped unload soft drinks and beer, which were rationed to one a day, when we had them. We later went to the river to swim. That night we were hit with an air raid by Washing Machine Charlie, but he completely missed us, dropping his bombs out in Iron Bottom Sound. The officers were still working on their foxhole, so I guess they had to scramble to find shelter.

On July 12th, we worked on putting up a latrine, then went swimming again. When we came back, all of Cobb's crew had returned from being in the drink, except the navigator. They had run out of gas and couldn't find a field close by, or any land. I talked with Bojanberg about their experience. We went to the movie, "Moonlight in Hawaii." We had another air raid that night. Whitie went on a flight to bomb Ballale. They went in at 14,000 feet.

On July 13th, I read a book, "Aphrodite, Goddess of Love and Passion." It had very interesting descriptions of the ladies of the time. We swam some more, then that evening we saw the movie, "When Johnnie Comes Marching Home Again." I answered a few letters.

On July 14th, we cleaned guns and learned to draw a map of the islands of the Solomons.

By now, you perhaps suspect we had it real easy, but don't bet on it.

On July 15th, it was routine again — drew maps, cleaned guns all morning, code practice and target shooting with carbine and forty-five pistol in the afternoon. We went swimming and that evening went to the show, "Eyes in the Night."

On July 16th, we just laid around and wrote letters in the morning. Then we got the word we were to take-off late that night to go to Kahili with Captain McNeese. We went down to the river to swim, came back and wrote some letters, then we all slept a few hours.

Hutch, Tommy, Whitie and I flew together with McNeese. But Kahili was a tough target with plenty of antiaircraft guns, searchlights, and a master beam that was plenty strong enough to reach up and find our bombers.

The Japs had plenty of fighters available to come up to meet us. They kept a steady stream of replacements coming in to Kahili, Kara and Ballale, as quickly as our fighters and bombers were able to shoot them down.

On July 17th, at two o'clock in the morning, we were over Kahili. We had been delayed on take-off because the Acorn Cross hospital had been hit in an air raid.

We went in at fifteen-thousand, which was low, but at night, we felt we could risk it. Our first run was dry, not dropping bombs. We were on oxygen, and I kept the ball turret moving all the time.

On our second run for Kahili, we were caught in the lights and the Japs started throwing ack-ack up at us. One burst off to my right, making a small puff of smoke. The night fighters did not attack us, but they got a tail gunner in the 370th Squadron. They also shot down a PBY out on a rescue mission later in the early morning hours.

Our air units on Guadalcanal were known as the Cactus Air Force. There were F4F Wildcats, P-38 Lockheed Lightnings, Bell P-39 Aircobras, Corsairs F4U's and New Zealand P-40 Warhawks on the Canal, as well as B-24 Liberators of the 13th Air Force, 307th Bomb Group and B-17 Flying Fortresses of the 5th Bomb Group. There were also some SBD Dive Bombers, and PBY Catalina "Dumbo" rescue planes.

All the current flying forces of our allies were represented, although some were pretty sparse and undisciplined, such as Major Gregory "Pappy" Boyington and his Black Sheep Squadron of F4U Corsairs that came up later. There were also some DC-3 Douglas Transports at Henderson, just north of us with the other planes. Our B-24's were on Carney Field, and not much else in the way of aircraft.

There were four squadrons in the 307th Bombardment Group (Heavy); the 370th, the 371st, the 372nd, and the 424th. Our crew was assigned to the 424th Bomb Squadron (Heavy), as was Goodin's crew and many of our friends from the phase training in the States who left Topeka about the same time for the Pacific. So we were not strangers trying to get to know each other in the middle of battle, but a close fighting force.

CHAPTER 6

ZEROES AND HEROES

The Ordeal Of Combat

What a Jap Zero looked like after our bombers and fighters met it in the air over Guadalcanal, New Georgia and Bougainville in the Solomons. Note how the trees were stripped by bombs to keep snipers from hiding in the palm leaves. All trees around airstrips were treated in this manner. American flyers were outnumbered as much as 20 to one most of the time, but with the help of the Navy F4U's, New Zealand piloted P-40's and sharp gunners on our bombers, we were able to help our soldiers, sailors and marines retake those islands and eventually return to the Phillipines.

Our crew settled in rather quickly after being assigned to the 424th Bombardment Squadron of the 307th Bombardment Group, Heavy, 13th Air Force, United States Armed Forces in the South Pacific Area (USAFISPA) at Carney Field

(Cactus), Guadalcanal, Solomon Islands. That was our official assignment and we were to continue in the 424th during our combat tour of duty.

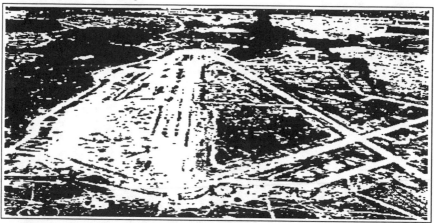

A scanned reproduction of a 13th AAF photo of Carney Field, where the Squadrons of the 307th Bomb Group (HV) and Headquarters Squadron, 370th, 371st, 372nd and 424th Bomb Squadrons took off and landed with their B-24's. Living quarters were some distance from the field and back in the jungle for as much protection as the trees and vegetation provided, serving as a natural camoflague for personnel and their equipment. The planes were also in bunkers off the runways and taxi strips, to provide some protection when the Japs came down the slot to bomb and strafe. Carney was a welcomed sight after being up to Ballale, Kahili, Buka and other targets.

In addition to our crew and Goodin's crew, there were also crews as follows flying in the 424th in July, August, September, October, and November: Price, Alexandre, McNeese, Hansen, Holmes, McCloskey, Ward, Warbon, Darr, Byrd, Ratti, Bisbee, Francis, Friend, Scott, Harpster, Marshall, Pueppke, Taylor, Edwin McConnell, Kissel, Waterman, Phillips, Vidmar, F. McConnell, and J. Binder. Some of these crews were added as of November, December 1943 and continued up into January and even later in 1944. Our pilot, Jelley, made it, too.

There were many other crews from the other squadrons that I do not have by the pilot's name, but who were flying right with us on our missions. The ones mentioned above flew on missions in the 424th per "mission sheets" provided by Edwin McConnell (please see Appendix A). The missions, the number of the planes flown on the missions and data such as target, altitude, etc., are included which helped to verify some of my own information about the missions, and in addition helped to confirm what my own diary entries indicated when writing this book.

These men were "Bomber Aces," as were their other crew members who performed their duties above and beyond the call to deliver their bombs, engage the enemy in combat when attacked, shooting many of them out of the skies and returning to home base to fight another day. Some of these crews had gone through phase training with us, while a few were replacement crews for some we lost. And we did lose a great many. A survey of the mission sheets will show some crews were dropped along the way and other new names added as the months passed. Only a few continued to appear as the missions continued up into February 1944.

Most of our missions from Guadalcanal were "Up the Slot," as the area was called where we flew north toward Bougainville. This was because the group of islands we flew over were arranged in two rows, with a body of water between them — namely the Russell Islands, Savo, New Georgia, Vella Lavella, Talagi, the Shortlands, Kolombangara, Santa Isabel, Bougainville, Buka, and further north New Britain, New Ireland and Truk.

The city of Rabaul had been a resort area before the war. There were five airfields in that vicinity. It required hours of flying to reach either Rabaul or Truk to attack airfields and shipping as well as oil and gasoline storage facilities.

As for closer targets, Kahili, with its master beam at one end and two smaller ones at the other end, posed a big problem for us. Ballale was a small triangular, almost heart-shaped island with the runway running right down the center. It was used for a fighter strip, sending planes up when enemy targets approached Bougainville from the south.

Munda had an airstrip, too, which the Japanese used for fighters. Bombers would also land there, although the strip was not very long. After it fell into our hands, later on in 1943, the airstrip was upgraded and extended to handle the B-17, B-24, and DC-3 transports as well as the amphibian PBY Flying Boats used for rescue missions.

We usually approached targets at 15- to 23,000 feet, which meant we were on oxygen. Also at that altitude, it was cold, so one piece flight suits and the leather A-2 flight jackets were necessary, as well as leather helmets, or the famous 50 mission crush hat (made to look that way by removing the supporting foam rubber inside) which took shape with the help of earphones placed over the top of the hat. All except myself. I had been issued a heated suit, since the turret was too small for bulky clothing or even a parachute. I could get the harness on, but that was all. I only weighed 119 pounds, but was almost 6 feet tall — a real skinny kid at the time.

Talking about being skinny, for a time I had the nickname "Bouky," after the Buchenwald prisoners who had been starved by the Germans, but fortunately, this changed to "Lucky" then "Ace," but most of the time, it was just "Clark," as most of us were called by our last names. If the last name could be shortened the nickname would come from it, i.e.: "Hutch" for Hutchings or "Whitie" for Woytowich.

Equipment List

I believe some additional information about our equipment is in order here.

The heated suit I was issued was made like a suit of underwear, a terrible shade of blue, almost teal green, which if you were unlucky enough to wind up in the ocean, blended right in with the water, making it difficult to spot you from a distance. It was made of a woven fabric with electric wires running all through it.

There were some light boots of the same fabric which fitted over my shoes and plugged into the receptacles in the pantlegs. An extension cord near the waist was plugged into the turret's electrical system.

I wore a helmet fitted with earphones, and a throat mike was strapped around my neck, making it possible to communicate just by pressing the intercom button on my control handle. I know what the fighter pilots, and later, the astronauts, must have felt like with all the wires and plug-in equipment they put up with on a mission. The oxygen hose had to be fitted properly to the mask which was over my nose and mouth, leaving only the eyes showing out from the helmet.

The biggest problem in using the suit was the wires, which heated up like an electric blanket. They ran under the arms and backs of my legs, and that area became too hot. It would be necessary to turn the heat down, which would let the rest of my body get cold, especially my back, which laid right up against the exit door. It was a constant problem to find a happy medium when flying at the high altitudes.

Leather gloves completed the outfit. We did wear the A-2 Flight Jackets when possible, but it was difficult for me in the ball turret. Our "Mae West" life jacket was worn over the heated suit, but before the parachute or harness, if one was used. Thank goodness, the Mae West was an orange-yellowish color which provided some visibility in the water if anyone was un-fortunate enough to have to use it.

(L-R) The author, Henry E. Hutchings, Earl B. Cornelius and Charles E. Thompson with .45 caliber pistols strapped on, except for Hutch, who was issued a Thompson sub-machine gun. Corny and Tommy also sported carbines.

We were all issued carbines and forty-five pistols, except HUTCH, the engineer, who was issued a Thompson sub-machine gun instead. I never understood why, but it was operating procedure to issue one machine gun per crew.

We were also issued steel helmets, ammunition belts, a machete, mess kits and canteens. The steel helmets weren't used much, except some of us grabbed them when we headed for a foxhole. Its biggest use was to hold water from the lister bag for shaving.

The machete was quite unique and I have not been able to locate one since coming back from Guadalcanal. It had a blade that was about 14 inches long and folded over into the handle, which was about the same length or perhaps a little longer. The blade was two inches wide and very sharp. A sheath was provided to attach to the belt.

The belt was the GI web type with small holes to attach the pistol holster, some ammo, a canteen of water, and the machete.

We were also issued a "suicide gun," as we called it, or a "sucker stick" gun. It was made of roughly machined heavy sheet metal, pressed to form a pistol grip to which was attached a short barrel, rifled to hold a .45 shell. Additional shells for it could be stored in the pistol grip by pushing a small cover off to the side. This gun used a sucker stick, a little longer in size, to push the shell casing out the back after it was fired.

I can tell you now, I never fired one and I don't know if anyone in my crew did. It was to be used as a last resort if we were unable to avoid capture. We would discuss whether to use it on a Jap or on ourselves, to save the torture we knew the Japs were capable of rendering before death. Fortunately, we did not have to make that decision, but it was close enough to suit me.

Some of the fellows were also issued the sheep wool-lined leather jacket and matching trousers with suspenders. Heavy shearling-lined boots and wool-lined leather helmets added to the high altitude protection for the waist gunners. Deerskin leather gloves lined with fur completed their outfit. Some of the fellows in the larger turrets could also use them.

Everything was open air, and with the waist windows open and the wind coming through the plane, it could really get cold up there.

I mentioned a relief tube earlier which we used in the ball turret to relieve ourselves when it couldn't be held any longer. This was a pretty uncomfortable procedure to use — sitting on the armor plate seat, trying to get it out through the fly in your trousers and heated suit (unless one was well endowed.) That point I do not want to debate at this time, but let's just say it was quite a challenge at times. And the cold didn't help, nor the leather gloves. Get the picture? So if at all possible, it was best to wait to get out of the turret.

The salt pills we were taking didn't help either, making us thirsty on missions. We didn't eat cabbage, few beans, and anything which would form gas to make us uncomfortable at high altitudes. The cooks must have had their instructions on that because we didn't have that problem on the Canal. But the mutton and horse meat we ate, along with spam, powdered eggs, and powdered milk assured most of us of not over-eating. You didn't see too many hefty guys flying on combat crews. I would say it was the chow rather than the worry of it all.

Parachutes were of various types on the bombers. Most had seat and back packs for use by all the crew except some of us riding in the nose, tail and lower ball turrets. Due to the space in the lower ball turret, my choice was to wear a harness and have a chest pack that snapped into the "O" ring type spring locked latch, or not wear one at all.

The chest packs were of two types — a square one and an even smaller one of the type used by jumpers as their emergency chute in case the main chute didn't open. The only thing was, this would be our main chute.

The chest chutes were not worn by many, at least I didn't, but it was placed in front of the armor plate on the forward part of the waist window, down between the ammunition boxes.

Usually a spare chute was in the rear section of the plane

in the event one of them was hit by enemy bullets or if one was damaged in some way. We always checked the chutes for safety wire, a recent date of packing by the packers of the chutes, to make sure the rip cord was not obstructed in any way and all other fittings properly safetied. The parachutes were taken off the planes and re-packed pretty regularly due to the high humidity, since it rained about every day. But it was up to us to protect ourselves.

We all took quinine or atabrine, a substitute for quinine which was milder, to protect against malaria, but most did get some degree of the disease. The pills made us turn yellow and our urine was yellow when we were taking them. I used to kid the others and say if we didn't watch out, we would be as yellow as those bastards we were fighting.

All the time I was on the Canal, I did not get malaria or even dingy fever, a milder form of the disease. The other crew members would kid me and say the mosquitoes would pass me by for them, because they had more meat on their bones. Of course, this flies in the face of the old saying, "the closer the bone, the better the meat."

Another dread disease was elephantitis, which involved an enlargement of the tender areas of the skin on the body and whose common form was an enlargement of the scrotum, testicles and penis. The surface of the skin became rough like that of an elephant hide, thus the name. The enlargement would grow until a victim could hardly walk. Sometimes the ears and other parts of the body were effected too, resulting in death.

We also took salt pills regularly because of the heat. This caused us to drink lots of liquids which prevented dehydration and heat stroke. It was a good thing I had a relief tube in my turret because there were many times I could not come out of the turret to use the facility behind the bomb bay doorway from the catwalk. The tube was just a small funnel with a tube going out a small hole below the guns, and quite effective.

Missions

We flew our missions in stacked elements of threes, with three elements, or a total of nine planes to a squadron. When all squadrons were flying together, we could have thirty-six planes on a full mission. But this was not always the case.

First, squadrons were alternated occasionally to provide rests from missions. Many times only two squadrons of eighteen bombers made a mission, or the missions were staggered over different parts of the day and night. We would make night missions, flying over at spaced intervals of time, and alone, not in close formation over the target. Also, some planes aborted their missions for various reasons — mechanical, or otherwise — leaving the squadrons short of a full complement of planes. Some did not even get off the ground for one reason or another. So we never knew who would be flying with us in formation.

Usually, it would be members of the same crews we were buddies with and in planes we knew well, like Frenisi #323, Mammy Yokum #221, Man-O-War #212, Shehasta #324, Phantom Lady #310, Shady Lady #212, The Topper #910, Pistol Packin' Mama, Quiturbitchen, Thumper, Rod's Rowdys #273, Tillie the Toiler, Dumbo, Shack Rat #222, and others. Man-O-War had been so named by Jim McCloskey and his crew and when we flew it, it had a picture of a red flying horse carrying a bomb on its side. As mentioned, we flew it many times before getting Shehasta back from Buttons on New Hebrides.

I will not cover every mission we were on, as a few were without too much to report. We would get in to the target and get out before the Jap fighters got up to meet us. Also at times the anti-aircraft fire was sparse and the flak not too accurate, so these were just so called "milk runs," or easy.

When the targets were active airfields or highly settled areas such as the resort city of Rabaul, or naval activity was great as at Rabaul Harbor, then things became pretty difficult to say the least. At times, our planes were outnumbered twenty to one, especially when the Japanese re-supply efforts

The Kahili Airfield was located at the south end of Bougainville and was one of the most important to the Japanese. For that reason it was well fortified with a master radar searchlight, lots of antiaircraft guns, other searchlights and plenty of fighter aircraft. Notice the pock-marked runway and surrounding area-all evidence of bomb hits. On one strike, over 100 enemy fighters were in the air to meet our bombers. As a result, losses were heavy on both sides. Scanned image from a reproduction of a 13th AAF photo.

provided re-enforcements after we had decimated their numbers. But such victories were not without a high price to our own bombers and fighters.

The Action Heats Up In July

On July 18th, we had planned on hitting Kahili with Captain McNeese. We could not see the target due to clouds, so we dropped on an alternative target, a boat in the bay. We got two hits, one on the bow and one on the stern. But those guys were pretty accurate with the ack-ack. They couldn't have been much more close without hitting us.

We bounced all over the sky it seemed. One of my guns went out, so I didn't get too many shots in. A zero went past us on a parallel heading toward another plane in the formation. Two New Zealand P-40's were after it, so I couldn't shoot. I think a P-40 finally got it.

There were nine B-24's from the 424th, and a total of twenty-seven, or three squadrons. There were thirty fighters with us, a total of nearly seventy planes went up together.

It was reported our bombers and fighters got 47 enemy planes to our five lost on that trip up to Kahili. I didn't get any, but the action was there. One tail gunner was hit, and a PBY rescue plane was brought down.

On July 19th, we didn't go bombing, but we were on

alert. My right ear had hurt during the night so I went to see Captain Groth about it. He said it was fungus of the ear, a common problem in the jungle islands. He put something in it, silver nitrate, or something like that name, and I could fly the night of the 20th.

July 20th— A Night Raid

We took off at 10 p.m., and we were over the target (Kahili) by midnight.

We were in Man-O-War, with Jelly piloting, and were in number two position of the third element. As we became more experienced and had some more missions behind us, we would move up to the second and eventually to the first element, even to the lead plane.

We had a fighter escort of about eight Curtis P-40 Warhawks flown by New Zealand pilots. Due to the long range necessary to accompany us, they flew with wing tanks which they jettisoned right before they engaged the enemy aircraft. The fuel in the wing tanks was gone by the time they were near our target and the tanks would only be extra drag.

We knew that by the same reasoning, the enemy would not follow us too far south because of our fighter cover or the chance they would run out of fuel, too. They would not get too far from their home base at Kahili, Ballale or Munda.

On this night, we were caught in the searchlights on our bomb run. We didn't feel any ack-ack, so we knew fighters were up over Kahili.

There were two of them up in front of our plane, but they shot at us from a distance, never engaging us up close. However, since it was night, we went over one at a time.

It was on this raid we lost William H. "Griff" Griffith, our Assistant Engineer. He was flying with Lt. Ward. We saw fire on one of the engines, and the plane was going down. No one escaped or returned from Ward's plane.

When we lost a plane, nothing much was said, and in fact, it was almost like it was ignored, like it didn't happen. I think we refused to face it, because we would go out on the

111

next mission and hardly think about losses on the previous raid. But I do know we thought about it in our quiet times. There was always that resolve to make them pay, those yellow bastards, to even the score.

But it is amazing, in looking at the notations in my diary years later, how little was said about the loss of a crew member. It was almost as if we shut them out of our lives, the fun we had, the close calls before the final mission. It is hard to explain to a person who has not had the experience, how a friend is gone you have had some good times with, lived in the same tent with for months, then to suddenly have to accept the fact that he was gone.

Griff's replacement stepped in, took his bunk, helped move his personal items out, and on the next mission took his place at the waist window in the turret and never asked any questions about it.

That mission, when Lt. Greig S. Ward went down, I lost another friend, Edward Kindavater, whom I had mentioned earlier and who had flown with our group going through phase training in the states.

Some other crews were hit that same mission. Shrapnel from ack-ack broke the glass in the nose turret of one plane, cutting the gunner on the nose and face rather badly. My guns were in good firing condition, so I got in a few shots but without success.

When the Japs came up to attack us, the New Zealanders engaged them in dog fights, usually before the Japs got close to us.

Two things usually happened. The Japs would fly toward us, firing as they came and the New Zealand pilots would follow them right into our formation, trusting our gunners to shoot the Jap Zeroes, Zekes, Haps or Tonys, as the case might be, since the Japs were flying many variations of fighters during the time we were assigned to bomb their air fields and shipping.

The New Zealand pilots were a very special group I found out right away. They trusted us even more than our own fighter pilots trusted each other in combat. It was sure nice to see them and they flew very close to our bombers. But I can't blame our P-38 , F4U, and P-39 pilots because some of our new crews were pretty gun happy, shooting at anything that got close to them.

I remember one report of a waist gunner shooting at an F4U Corsair, hitting the headrest behind the pilot and putting some holes in his rudder. I recall the discussion on the distrust our Marine Flyers had of getting too close to our bombers after that mission.

The fighter escort couldn't stay with us over the target because the Japs started shooting anti-aircraft guns as soon as we were in range. The Jap fighters would stay outside our range, fly along at our altitude and radio it to the anti-aircraft gunners below, so the flak would be pretty accurate. The flak would get very heavy right over the target and we could hear a slight sound if the flak was near enough, the plane would bounce around, and any flak that hit our plane would feel and sound like a hammer hitting on metal.

This first mission I had a small piece of flak hit the bottom of the ball turret, but fortunately, due to the round curve of the turret, the flak just cut a groove in the outside and bounced off. It did not come through. On the way from the bomb run, we were again engaged by the Jap Zeroes in combat.

We had dropped our bomb load in an area where enemy personnel were supposed to be housed. Being in the ball turret, it was the most advantageous position from which to observe just where the bombs hit, following them down with my eyes until they went out of sight, and again when they hit, making small puffs on the ground where they stirred up dust, smoke, and sometimes fire, depending on our success.

On briefings when we returned, the ball turret gunners usually had the best information on just where the bombs hit and what damage was inflicted.

There were many times when it was not possible to look long enough to see the results of the bomb pattern, especially if any enemy fighters were reported in the area by the nose, tail or top turret gunners. Also, the waist gunners could spot them away out to our right or left.

But again, being in the lower ball turret, the ball turret gunners could sometimes see the enemy fighters going down the runways on take-off, and some of them forming up below as they climbed to our altitude. So if they were not already in the air or somewhere in the skies above us, in clouds or preparing to dive down in a pass at us, the ball turret gunners could spot them and report where the fighters were headed.

Since I had duty as armorer, I also went out on the catwalk in the bomb bays and pulled the safety pins from the bombs to arm them. This I did as we rendezvoused with the other bombers in the group, and before getting down into the ball turret. Of course, the turret then had to be lowered down out of the fuselage to rest on the azimuth ring upon which the turret turned full circle, 360 degrees.

I always kept extra pins in my pocket in case any were dropped, because sometimes it was necessary to reinsert them, just in case it was necessary to land with the live bomb on board. I was always glad to know all had been released and dropped from the B-7 shackles which held the bombs in place in the bomb bays until the bombardier tripped them from his position up in the nose of the bomber.

As with other missions, Gene Bruce, our bombardier, either pushed the "salvo" button, releasing the bombs all at once, or the "in train" button, spreading them out to cover a greater area. The bomb bay doors were closed immediately after release of the bombs, which did increase our speed slightly and cut down on the noise and vibrations caused by the wind.

After the bomb run, Jelley started evasive action along with the other airplanes in the formation, either by banking off to the right or left and maintaining the same air speed, or at times cutting back on the air speed to throw the anti-aircraft gunners off, quickly losing altitude at the same time.

Sometimes the same action was taken by the entire

squadron, but at times we were split up by one of the planes taking a hit over the target or being damaged by an enemy fighter, causing it to drop back out of formation. If possible, we would try to protect the ones in trouble from Jap fighters who would come in for the kill. The other bombers would regroup into a tight formation around the damaged bomber as much as possible without jeopardizing themselves or other bombers in the formation.

When the planes took evasive action, it was a time of great fear for those not in the cockpit because we never knew if it was done on purpose by Jelley or due to our taking a hit. This was especially true at night when blinded by the searchlights from below engulfing the lower ball turret. In the turrets, especially the lower ball, it was almost impossible to get out and put a parachute on in the event G-forces had developed, making it difficult to control your own movements and impossible to guide yourself to a particular location in the bomber, i.e. the camera hatch, waist window or even an open bomb bay, to make the jump.

In the lower ball turret it was possible to bail out, providing you had a small emergency chest pack parachute on, by releasing your safety belt which went behind your back, reaching up and pushing the entrance hatch door open which sometimes resulted in the door snapping off from the force of the wind bending it backward, then kicking hard against the bottom of the turret with your feet.

The guns had to be as close to the fuselage as possible, then, placing your body below the azimuth ring and the door clear of the ring when it opened, you could tumble out of the turret backward. This was the only turret you could do this with, since the nose, tail and upper local turrets had entrances only back into the fuselage.

You could only make such an escape if you had time before a dive became too steep to control your movements. This was true of all the crew.

Two types of damage precluded any escape — a collapsed wing which would flip the plane almost immediately out of control, or an explosion which either caused the bomber to disintegrate or spin to a certain end for most, or all of the crew members. Sometimes a miracle would happen and one or more of the crew members would be thrown clear, perhaps out a waist window or escape hatch up front.

On our way from the target at Kahili, we were attacked by about sixty fighters. They must have come from airfields at, or further up on Bougainville, because I do not believe that many fighters could have taken off from Kahili. We had three squadrons of bombers, twenty-seven if all made it after rendezvous over the Russell Islands before heading up the slot to Bougainville.

We lost three bombers on that raid, either to flak or fighters. But the Japs lost fourteen of their fighters and we did hit the target which was the purpose of our mission. But I knew from the first mission that the odds were not good, and we were greatly outnumbered.

It was a rough introduction to what was ahead in the early days in July 1943, until our unfortunate encounter over Rabaul in November 1943. I had never expected anything like that, even though we knew from the losses and replacements coming in that things were bad — but seeing is believing.

We had left Topeka, Kansas with a contingent of twenty B-24 Liberator Bombers with crews of ten men each, or a total of two hundred flying crewmen. I'm sure others were coming from other air bases in the United States because replacements came in for those lost every week or two. But the longer I was around and saw how many were gone from the original group, the more I knew the odds were becoming greater against those who were left. But the replacement crews did not know, just as we did not know, the truth when we first arrived on Guadalcanal.

A tour of a bomber crew was supposed to end at twenty-five missions, but usually it was more before the replacements would come, unless your crew was one that was shot down by flak or fighters, or lost due to mechanical problems, and yes, sometimes due to pilot or navigational errors, resulting in wounds, injuries or a stay with a coast-watcher until rescued. Then you just might be lucky enough to go home.

Fortunately, we did not suffer any wounds on that first Kahili mission and Man-O-War suffered little damage. It seemed the Jap fighters concentrated on the bombers that went over first and then moved back to attack any damaged stragglers. While our crew got some shots at the fighters, we did not shoot any down. We were just happy to get in and out without damage or any losses on our plane. On our first mission we had it pretty good, even though a great many fighters were in the air.

Normally, we would maintain radio silence, not using our intercommunications systems unless attacked by fighters or some malfunction of the aircraft occurred. If the bomb run came off without hitch, the pilot would break silence to assure us everything was all right. We were always on alert for the unexpected, such as a fighter coming from out of a cloud or diving from above into the formation.

The clock system was used for locating enemy planes, with the front of the bomber being twelve o'clock, nine o'clock being off our left wing, three o'clock off our right wing and six o'clock at the tail end of the plane. The fighters would either approach high or low of the horizontal division. If on a level with the wings, or parallel, then high or low was not indicated, only if above or below the path of the bomber.

Two of the Jap fighters, both Zeroes, came in at 3 o'clock high, but when they dived from about two thousand feet overhead, they came down far ahead of us where the 371st Squadron planes were located. When they got close enough, we would all start shooting, but usually they would break off before coming down low and then go back up to climb for another dive.

It was not long before we realized we could not antici-pate what the Jap pilots would do next when they ap-proached our bombers. Some of them, when hit, would take a kamikaze action and make a death dive for the bombers, shooting all the way in, realizing with all the gunners shooting at them they would surely die, but hoping to take an American bomber with them. But most of the Jap fighters either lost altitude fast and were unable to approach us before losing control or the plane would explode before reaching our planes.

Some of the New Zealand P-40's were still in combat some distance below the 307th Bomb Group, when we headed home. They had engaged the Japs in combat before they got up to us. I could watch them in dog fights from my ball turret, having a ring side seat, from on high you might say, and happy we had the New Zealanders along on the mission.

One Liberator had a feathered prop on one engine and we reduced speed so it could keep up with us. We always lost altitude after leaving the target, getting below twelve-thousand feet so we could get off oxygen and into the warmer air. This permitted us to move around a bit, especially those not in turrets.

On the way home to the Canal, a leak developed in the hydraulic lines of my turret and sprayed fluid all over me and the interior of the turret. I don't believe we were hit and I did not check it out after we landed, but I did report it to the ground crew prior to going for briefing at the operations shack.

More Raids, And Farewell To A Friend

On July 22nd, we went on a daylight mission to bomb shipping. Tommy had mild dingy fever, but recovered so he could go with us today. We had 12 bombers in the formation, and about 60 fighters. We were out in full force to go up the slot. We were not attacked by Jap fighters and we came back all right. We did not get any fighters, but our bombs may have hit a heavy cruiser, setting fire to it. A TBF reportedly hit a flat top on the same strike.

Hydraulic fluid leaked from my lines again in the ball turret, but my guns worked perfectly. We returned, went to interrogation, cleaned our guns and wrote some letters home.

July 23rd, we were on alert again. Some of us packed Griff Griffith's clothes to move them out. He was one swell guy. We didn't know who the replacement would be, but hoped he would be someone as easy to like as Griff. We went down to the river to swim, then went to a show that night — "Here We Go Again," with Charlie McCarthy the dummy, and Edgar Bergen.

On July 24th we were on alert from midnight to dawn, but didn't have to fly. Today is my 20th birthday.

We all sat around writing letters. We went out to have a crew picture made. Too bad Griff could not be in it. Corny, Hutch, Tommy, Jelley, Bruce, Johnson, Whitie and myself were there. Everyone seemed in a good mood, in spite of the loss of Griff. We went to the show, "Million Dollar Baby."

July 25th

At 2 o'clock in the morning we got up to make a strike on Munda, New Georgia. We were to bomb and strafe troops at the airfield. We were set to hit at about dawn, trying to soften up the Japanese Imperial Marines for our own troops to go in and take the airfield. The Japs hold everything north of New Georgia.

The battleships and cruisers of the U.S. Navy laid off shore and shelled the airfield to soften it up for us and the troops who would land later. We could see the big guns of the

The Munda airfield was bombed and taken away from the enemy in late 1943. It was another step closer to re-taking the Philippines. As with most island airfields, this one bordered the ocean, making landings and take-offs precarious. Scanned image of reproduced 13th AAF photo.

ships firing as we approached the field. The Japs were dug in pretty well.

The bombers of the 307th Bomb Group (HV) came in really low, less than one thousand feet, carrying every type of bomb in our arsenals — fragmentation, one-hundred-pounders, and the heavier 500-pounders.

Being in the lower ball turret, I had a front row seat, so to speak, a right up front view of the action, at sea, in the air and on the ground.

The little Nipponese bastards were dug into the coral along the runway, and further back, in crevices or caves dug into the hillsides. We could see them firing from their foxholes and when the bombs or shells came too close, they would jump up and start running, in all different directions. Some would stop long enough to try and shoot up into the air at us, but it was a much easier task for us to shoot at them when they weren't moving. My tracers would follow them as they ran, kicking up dust behind them until I would catch up to them.

One thing about it, the computing sight did not help too much on this strike, so it was necessary to follow the trail of the bullets as they struck the ground, directing the fire as it found the little bastards running, or when they had stopped to shoot up at our bombers. It was like shooting ducks in a pond or fish in a barrel, as my dad would say.

Some would throw down their guns and throw up their hands as if to signal they gave up, but usually that was too late, and quite frankly, it wouldn't have made any difference anyway. We wanted them all dead. I could see the bombs hitting from the bombers that went in before us, and by the time we hit them, and the Navy was through with them, they were all shook up. But, as I said, they were really dug in, and as we went back around to make another pass, I concentrated on the ones in the caves in the hillsides.

The waist gunners, the nose and tail turret gunners all had a field day, as did all the ball turret gunners. The ball turret gunners had a choice of anything on the ground in every direction, so our canisters were empty when we returned to Carney Field on Guadalcanal.

As mentioned previously, some of the gun barrels weren't in too good a condition from the continuous firing we were able to do as we passed over the airstrip. The Japs were falling like flies and it was hard to restrain my trigger fingers long enough to allow the barrels to cool so they wouldn't jam the shells in the breech and explode or split the barrels.

After we left the target for a turn-around and return to make another run on them, the Navy ships started pounding them again. Jelley told us everything was go for a long run down the runway.

I emptied my guns, as no Jap planes were in sight and the trip back to Guadalcanal would be a relatively short one.

It was the most satisfying mission of the war for our crew as well as the others who flew with us on the mission. After the beating the Japs took on the field and in their foxholes, the ground troops should not have had too much resistance when they landed later. Since our Navy controlled the seas, reinforcements from the islands to the north that were enemy held could not have been too successful. The Navy kept pounding Munda prior to the invasion by our forces.

We lost one plane this mission, Lt. Weyse's crew, but it wasn't official for another week. This strike qualified Tommy and me for the Air Medal, and we were becoming experienced at combat missions, too.

Later That Day...

On returning to base we wrote letters, and then went out to clean guns. This was a necessary job after every mission which we were very tired of already.

Once in a while, when firing the guns, a link would break, causing the belt feed to malfunction. The bullet had to be removed to free the broken link so the belt could be reinserted into the gun and recharged. This did not happen often and I rarely had a malfunction in combat. I believe this was due to checking the guns part by part when cleaning them and loading the canisters with the belts properly placed so they would feed freely.

The old saying, "an ounce of prevention is worth a pound of cure" was very appropriate in this instance. It could mean life or death, not only to myself, but to our whole crew. I did have one gun to malfunction on my second mission, but that was the only time I can remember.

When cleaning guns, all the crew members assigned to turrets or waist guns cleaned their own, and even though I was the armorer, it was easy to monitor the cleaning because everyone was aware of his responsibility not only to himself, but to every other member of the crew.

We would clean out the empty ammunition boxes, put new belts of ammo in them, clean the guns, check the barrels for damage as well as the turrets. Then the next day we went out to the flight line to clean them again, as the guns sweated after having been fired, and if left, would pit the barrels. So our job wasn't finished after going on a mission until the plane had been checked over by each crew member, even though we knew the ground crews would check everything, too.

I received six letters today.

When we wrote home, the censors would cut them up and put them on V-Mail. This was a small reproduc-

One thing we did not like to do was cleaning the guns. But it was the most important duty after briefing on the mission. Note Hutch (right) and Corny using the ammo boxes as a table. We had to bend our backs, but we cleaned them well. Our lives depended on it.

tion of the letter which limited how much we could write in one letter, but also prevented one from being as personal as one would like to be, for we always felt the censors had a field day reading some of our mail.

I recall how I was able to get a message past them to my mother, giving her a clue as to my whereabouts, and she confirmed when I returned to the States she got the message and determined my location.

In one of my letters I mentioned a little boy by the name of Henderson, asking her if he had gone to the service yet. Well, that little Henderson boy was hardly old enough to get in first grade when I joined the service, so she caught on I was near Henderson Field, Guadalcanal in the Pacific. Not bad for outsmarting the censors.

I'm sure other servicemen did the same thing. It was like a game we played. Of course, we never gave the enemy anything they could figure out, if our own intelligence could not tell they were being duped.

One thing that happened occasionally that would have a telling effect on a buddy or some other crew member was the "Dear John" letter, telling him his wife or girl friend had found someone else to spend time with, even sleep with, while he was out in the jungles defending her and her 4F friend. Some even wrote they were pregnant. All kinds of excuses, none of them valid, were given by the unfaithful. Some of the 4F bastards back home were fat-catting on the allotment money the G.I.'s sent home to their families.

Mike Reeder, the navigator on the Phantom Lady, received a letter like that from his girl friend back in Kansas. He almost went off his rocker. He wanted to take every mission, hoping to get shot down, to end it all. This was not good because it placed other crew members in some jeopardy, too. It was some time before he accepted it, but based on his actions, I know he did not ever completely forgive and forget, as I can fully understand and I'm sure, you can too. He had played it pretty fair all through phase training, usually drowning his loneliness in a few drinks.

Even though they were not married, he had sent her money (they even had a joint bank account) and she had bought furniture, rented an apartment which Mike paid for, the whole way, which Mike was taken for before the letter.

Mike kept going up north to Kahili, Rabaul and Truk, staying past his tour, after the other older crew members had gone back to the States. In fact, he finally did get it, riding with a new crew that needed a navigator on a night mission. This was after most of Goodin's crew and our crew left the Canal.

Only one thing was worse than a "Dear John" letter — to receive information from a brother, mother or some other member of the family telling the G.I. his wife or girl friend was pregnant or had married, because she did not have the nerve or consideration (it was obvious she was no good anyway) to tell him herself.

Some guys even took them back when they went home, making allowances for human weakness and the separations of war. When the sages say "war is hell," they do not always make reference to the loss of life and limb in combat, for there is also an emotional scarring that lasts for years — sometimes a lifetime. Physical wounds inflicted by the enemy will heal over sometimes, but wounds to the feelings, the heart, are forever.

The Aftermath of the Strike

After the softening up by the Navy and Air Corps, it was not too long before New Georgia was in friendly hands. We needed it for a refueling base when making the planned missions to come up to Rabaul on New Britain and to the Island of Truk, even further north. The ultimate goal was to get into position to retake the Philippines, a primary goal of General Douglas MacArthur. It also meant we did not need to worry so much about fighters meeting us early from southern Bougainville, on our way up to Buka and beyond. But Bougainville was as strong as ever, since the Japs still held the Shortland Islands, Treasury Island and Ballale.

It would take a few weeks to completely secure the island, repair the airfield and extend the runways to handle our large B-24 Liberators for refueling prior to the long flights up north. These flights would be accomplished for some time without the benefit of our fighters, due to their limited range. Wiping up the Jap holdouts would take some time, too, and continued even after the airfield was serviceable for bombers.

Our U.S. Navy was extending patrols, too, up to Empress Augusta Bay area of Bougainville, and beyond, trying to cut off shipping coming down to Bougainville and other islands of the Solomons.

After the satisfaction of the Munda mission, we were all anxious for our next missions to Buka Passage, and beyond. We were still operating from Carney Field, straight north to Bougainville. The Japs were still getting their fighters down to Ballale, Kahili, Kieta and Bonis, so we always flew about twenty miles off the coast of Bougainville when headed north to Buka. There were some seaplanes at a base in Buka Passage, and they carried torpedoes between the pontoons, which the Japs used to dive-bomb and try to torpedo our cruisers, destroyers and any submarines which they sighted. So we had the job to neutralize as much of the area as possible.

As I said, when we got Shehasta back,

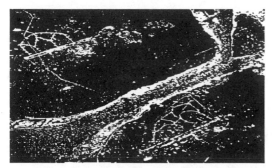

The airstrips at Buka and Buka Passage, located at the northern end of Bougainville, were vital targets. The narrow passage between the airstrips contained boats that we sighted in on sometimes as alternative targets. It was over this passage that one of our bombers was hit, the crew had to bail out and many of our men were shot in their parachutes as a result. It was that terrible act which fueled our hatred of the enemy and which gave us the incentive to fight and die in order to sink the Rising Sun.

she had flame dampeners newly installed over the super-chargers. We were to go on more night missions as a result, going over the targets individually, at intervals. I hated them every time we had to pull one, especially over Kahili.

I don't know if the Japs were superstitious or not, but they did get to know our planes by their names, I'm sure. The names and numbers were large enough to read from a distance, and when the same planes were around for a long time, the Japs must have learned to respect the crews that manned them.

Byrd's crew in Frenisi, #323 was well known. Downey, Ladd, Ira Jackson and the rest flew along side of us. So was Moeller's crew when they flew Frenisi, because the Japs knew the planes. They knew which planes had experience behind them.

Jelley's crew on Shehasta #324 and prior to that while flying Man-O-War, was getting known as was others. We were the survivors, because as planes were lost and replacements came up, the old names were still there.

Ratti's crew, with Salvadore Fatigato and Herman Schultz, was around for a long time. Gregory's crew of the 370th Squadron in Dumbo, John Rodwick's crew in Rod's Rowdies #273, George Hansen's crew from the 370th Squadron, Jerry Bourgeois' crew, Harper's crew in The Rattler #925, Wilden "Cap" Goodin's crew in the Phantom Lady #310— Pistol Packin Mama, Mammy Yokum, and many others lasted for some time.

Camp Life Anything But Routine

Attendance at the "Church in the Wildwood" was always large on Sunday morning, with almost all the barrels used for sitting occupied. Services were staggered for the Protestant, Catholic and Jewish faiths. Since the Japs did not share our belief in Christ and Sunday worship, everyone was still on alert, and it was not unusual to have a visit from "Washing Machine Charlie" on Sunday morning.

The same thing applied to our outdoor theater, which

also had oil barrel seating, with a few boards up near the screen, utilized by the top brass. Tommy Thompson always sat on the outer edge of the theater so he could get a head start to the nearest foxhole. The pictures were usually old and had been screened so they would be morale boosters — light comedy mostly.

Some of the guys who went to Auckland, New Zealand on rest leave would bring back short wave radios. We could pick up "Tokyo Rose," and she would not help any of those fellows who received "Dear John" letters, or any of us for that matter who had loved ones in the States.

She had a steady line of propaganda, i.e. she would play such songs as "Silver Threads Among the Gold," all about growing old and then say, "All you Americans serving in the South Pacific are growing old while your girl friends and wives are enjoying themselves back home."

It was also very unnerving when she would sometimes talk about the next missions we were going on "up the slot." She would sometimes even name the planes, probably the nose art helped her with that information, and would refer to the various flying groups, including the 307th Bomb Group.

She would brag about the planes we had lost, even mentioning that those who bailed out were dealt with as they deserved. We would really get angry when we heard that because we knew what she meant when she laughingly referred to their fate in that manner. It just made us meaner.

The one time I recall she made us very angry was a day after a strike we participated in at Buka Passage, located at the northern end of Bougainville. During the mission we were engaged by Japanese fighters. One of our bombers was damaged and the crew members who were able had bailed out.

The Jap Zeroes and Haps dived down and strafed our men in their parachutes. This was not all, because they would fly right over the parachutes, very close, causing some of them to collapse, firing as they approached. I saw two chutes collapse, engulfing the crewmen in the cords and silk canopy.

It was enough to make one sick and angry at the same time.

I had a very clear view of this horrible act by the Japanese from my turret. Then to hear "Tokyo Rose" brag about it in such a manner only contributed to our desire to give them as good as they gave on our subsequent missions, should the opportunity arise. We could hardly wait.

The Japs still held Vella Lavella, Kolombangara, Santa Isabel, Choiseul, Shortland, Treasury, Ballale, and Bougainville with Buka, New Britain, New Ireland, and Truk Islands to the north of us.

Fighter cover really came in handy all the way up the slot to Buka. We had not attempted any missions beyond that point, pending the capture of the airstrip at Munda, which enabled us to refuel for the long trip to Rabaul and Truk. But the Navy task force was keeping the sea lanes pretty clear and our bombs were cutting off the Jap supply lanes to the islands slowly, one by one, once Guadalcanal was secure for the Americans and we had fighter bases at the Russell Islands.

Our goal was to secure New Guinea and eventually the Philippines. Ground troops were moving slowly northward, retaking the islands after the Jap supply lines were cut and our Naval and Air Forces gained superiority. All the islands mentioned above that were in enemy hands became targets for our bombers and fighters at one time or another, many becoming alternate targets when weather or some other difficulty arose, preventing us from hitting our primary targets.

It was very frustrating to bomb Ballale, for example, sometimes with three squadrons at a time, trying to render the Jap fighter strip useless. But we could not knock it out for long, and it would continue to be in service for months. The Japs would repair our damage at night and be ready for take-off the next day.

On numerous missions we would destroy up to a hundred Jap planes on the ground and in the air, only to have new ones meet us the next day. I don't know where they came from!

On July 26th, we were up at 4 o'clock to fly another strike over Kahili at 22,500 feet and drop frag bombs. The fragmentation bombs were in bundles, wired together with a small 22 caliber shell that was tripped to cut the wires as they fell, letting the bombs fall freely over a wide area. They were made with serrated iron, as in a hand grenade, wrapped around the exploding charge which scattered the small pieces of shrapnel over a large area when they hit the ground.

A small propeller on flat twisted wire would unwind as the bombs fell, arming the bombs before they hit the terrain below us.

I never really like to drop them. The frag bombs, incendiaries and delayed action bombs always worried me, especially since I was the one who pulled the pins to arm some of them before they were dropped. Any of them could give us trouble if it hung up in our bomb bays.

The strike was uneventful this time. We returned to the Canal and cleaned guns, as well as completed our other usual chores.

July 27th and 28th were uneventful, too, but my right ear was sore again from fungus. We saw the movie, "Priorities on Parade," and sat in the rain all during its showing which resulted in my being grounded on July 29th. But we didn't fly anyway because of the weather.

I used hot packs, which Captain Groth had provided, to make the swelling go down, going to the dispensary four times.

On July 30th we did not fly again since it rained hard all day. Instead, I drew some pictures — a hobby and talent which had surfaced while I was a young child, and which I enjoyed very much.

I also traded off my carbine to a marine commander. He gave me a .45 which had been used to kill Japs in its place. The commander was due to return to the States and then on to Europe, and he didn't want to take it with him.

On July 31st, we still didn't fly. I saw the doctor again and was returned to flying status as my ear was almost well. I

Pilot James D. "Jim" Jelley (left) and Co-pilot Norman A. "Johnny" Johnson, look back from the cockpit to show their pleasure with serving on the best crew in the South Pacific.

drew more pictures and cleaned more guns. We knew we were due up on another mission the next day.

On August 1st, we all prepared to take-off for Kahili at 11 a.m. We had about twenty-four bombers with us. We hit the target dead center, and we really smashed the north end of the runway, blowing up quite a few planes on the ground. The fighters did not attack, but the ack-ack was pretty close. All in all, a very successful mission.

Norman A. "Johnny" Johnson, our co-pilot, was grounded indefinitely due to painful sinuses when he was at high altitudes. He expected to be transferred to a transport group that did not fly at high altitudes.

On August 2nd, we were to go to Webster Cove for a strike on shipping, but Shehasta had a mechanical problem and we did not get off. We came back and I went swimming and got a hair cut, then went to the show, "Slightly Dangerous" with Lana Turner and Robert Young — a real love story that brought back memories of home.

August 3rd we were grounded because we had no co-pilot. It was quite rainy, besides.

Gus Hosfeth put in for a transfer to ground duty as an instructor in radio. He was our radio operator, but the close call we had at Buttons — when we hit the trees on take-off — took its toll on Gus, and I can very well understand, considering the report of the operations officer that we were the first and only survivors of a crash on take-off. Up until that time, there had been five crashes.

On August 4th, Johnny, our co-pilot, was placed back on flying status even though he still had sinus troubles, so we were scheduled back in the air for the next mission. I went to turret school, went swimming, wrote letters and saw the show, "Time to Kill" — a heck of a title for us right now.

On August 5th we laid around until 11 a.m., then took off for a raid on Rekada Bay on St. Isabel Island. We hit the target. There was no fighter interception — a milk run. We saw the show that night, "White Cargo."

On August 7th we did not fly due to bad weather. We cleaned guns all morning, including the guns in my lower ball turret. We went to the show, "They Got Me Covered" — a comedy which I had seen before in Buttons or the States.

As you can see, our only night entertainment was movies, and occasionally watching the night fighters and searchlights follow "Washing Machine Charlie" when he flew over to bomb Guadalcanal. Watching the explosions of the ack-ack guns, hearing the shrapnel fall with its whistling sound (and hoping it would not be a bomb) would help break the monotony of an otherwise uneventful evening. Diving for a foxhole when

The Chapel was nearly destroyed by a flood, but with the help of the natives, it was rebuilt. 13th AAF photo.

131

the enemy came too close always livened up things. It was always nice to see one of the Jap bombers go down in flames.

But I knew how they must feel, when caught in our searchlights, because we had been in the same situation, with the flak, the fighters, the tracers lacing the night when the enemy attacked us, and worst of all, being blinded by the searchlights, not knowing what was out there coming in with guns blazing.

On August 8th, the weather was bad again so we did not fly, but went to church. The Chapel in the Wildwood was being dedicated after being almost destroyed by the rains back in the spring. The natives were there, including Master Sergeant Joseph Vouza, the native chief, and his followers, since they had helped to rebuild it.

On August 9th, while on a mission north, we developed an oil leak and returned to base, with no strike credit. The show that night was "Who Done It?," a comedy. We sure did get enough of the comedy performers. I guess the top brass felt it was good for morale. But we were issued our "Jap suicide pistol" today, which I had described previously. We also received some tracer bullets for signaling in case we wound up on an island and needed help.

On August 11th, we went up the slot toward Kahili, but the weather was so bad we couldn't see the target, so we returned to base. We went to the show, "Footlight Serenade," which wasn't bad.

By now you know all it did was rain and all we did was go to the movies, write letters and clean guns, with an occasional mission to break the monotony. But things were about to change for us.

August 12

On August 12th we had an interesting day. We took off at 9 a.m. for Kahili. We got over the target all right, ack-ack was close, but no planes were shot down, that is, no bombers. We were number three in the first element, so we were first over the target.

After leaving the target, three Zeroes made a pass at our plane and then went on back to the other elements behind us. We didn't get hit, although it was pretty close. Seven of them attacked the bomber on our right, shooting its rudder full of holes. They also knocked out the engine of number two plane, but it was not lost.

The planes in the third element behind us got two Zeroes and there may have been more. I saw our fighter escort engage the Zeroes behind and below our plane as we left the target. Our fighters did everything that could be done with a plane I believe, and shot down two of the Zeroes. I never saw any of our fighters in smoke or flames.

From the report when we got back, our bombers got twenty Jap planes on the runway at Kahili, and we hit an ammunition dump, causing smoke and fire to come up from the explosions on the ground. When we got back, the Japs returned the favor with an air raid that night which lasted about half an hour.

August 13—A Hard Lesson In Killing

On August 13th we went swimming, then took off at 4 p.m. for Ballale.

We were in tight formation over the Jap airfield. When we hit it, it was just dusk, but turned dark quickly.

After dropping the bombs on the target, the formation split up and we headed for some clouds. As we came out of

Air War

From an original drawing by the author.

the clouds, I saw tracers coming up from below and at about five o'clock. I let go with a burst of about twenty rounds and the tracers stopped. It could have been another B-24 shooting at us, but it was too dark to see.

About that time, I saw tracers coming from the front of the plane at about two o'clock low. They were night fighters and shooting bigger stuff than our 50 calibers. They must have had 20mm shells, because the tracers were larger than their 7.7's.

Corny shot at them first and I whirled around and shot about 30 rounds at them. The shooting stopped. But another one made a pass at us from down below, at about 11:30 o'clock. He must have dived from far out and came up out in front of the bomber. Corny and I opened up on him.

He kept on shooting and we kept our guns going, too. I shot almost a hundred rounds, or so it seemed, in quick bursts, really laying it on when he didn't turn away. I raked him as he passed under the belly of our plane, and he started flaming as he went earthward to his god.

One thing at night, you could see your tracers easily, and if a Jap flamed or exploded, you could not miss it, so it was easy to confirm.

This was my first kill! It could just as easily have been me, left wounded, bleeding or lifeless in my ball turret, to be pulled out by my buddies later.

I was so busy because more fighters were attacking, but as we left the target and there were no more fighters around us, I realized what had happened.

I began to feel cold sweat on my hands, forehead, face, and I could feel it running down my back, the result of fear and excitement.

I felt the need to use the relief tube, reached for it, feeling cold all over.

So, this was what it was like to take another man's life. It was really impersonal as I didn't know the enemy I had killed. There is a great difference in being on a bomber as opposed to being a fighter pilot who can evade an enemy fighter, or even turn and run if the odds get too great. But we couldn't, and we wouldn't. As a team everyone had to stay the course, at their stations, not let the other members of the crew down. But that didn't mean we weren't scared when the flak and the enemy fighters were waiting for us over the target.

Another truth came home to me, too. This wasn't like playing "chicken," where the one losing his nerve may lose his life, and where you knew the participants personally, the hurt you did to them and their loved ones.

All these things turned over in my mind as we headed back to Guadalcanal. But once we landed, there was no big celebration, just a pat on the back from your buddies, a trip to the briefing room for confirmation and credit for the kill. But there was always the report of those not so fortunate as you, who were lost, wounded or killed and perhaps a good buddy you had shared great times with in the States. This we never got over, but just put it out of our minds.

Another reason was because, tomorrow could be different, and you could be the one with pain, dying or with your body damaged for life. Hate and revenge was to become a motivation more intense as our losses increased.

I never wanted to write about this, but it is the **real stuff**, the result of war. No wonder men in combat developed claustrophobia from confinement in a turret or plane from which you could not escape or run away, resulting later in life in cold sweats, bad dreams and delayed stress syndrome. Few ever completely escaped it.

No, I did not look forward to the next strike or kill and the fear that went with it. Some could not face it, and I could sure understand that, but they did not want to be cowardly, let their crew down, or let their country down. This is why military men who have been in combat seek comradeship with each other in military organizations after the wars, for there is an unspoken understanding, without the verbal expression that helps to heal the soul and mind.

Friendly Fire

That night as we arrived back at the base, a Colonel flew

in over our field while it was blacked out, due to an air raid,

and the guys manning the anti-aircraft hit his plane with ack-ack, damaging one engine and the landing gear. He landed later on one wheel and with three engines, tearing the plane up pretty badly and injuring some of the crew, but all walked away from it.

A Liberator brought down by "friendly fire." 13th AAF photo.

We waited until it was all clear and then landed, being the first in after the Colonel. You just did not fly in during a red alert without waiting for clearance.

August 14th

August 14th, Hutch, Corny and Jelley went swimming with me down at the river. We had been pretty lucky by none of us getting the so called "jungle rot." My own greatest problem, of course, was with fungus of the ear, which was similar, and related to, the jungle rot.

I had a pretty hard time getting pictures developed at the photo shop which had been set up to process pictures taken by the cameras mounted on some of the planes when we went on missions. I had taken some pictures, so I picked them up at the shop and put them in my album that afternoon.

That night, the Japs came over two or three times, and it was about two o'clock before the all-clear and we could get some sleep. We will fly tomorrow. We always do after being up half the night because of Washing Machine Charlie visiting us.

August 16th, we did go on a trip, which would have been Buka, but a prop governor went out on one of the engines, so we came back and went to bed, after losing sleep all night. We slept much of the day, then went to a show,

"Life Begins at 8:30." We had an air raid alert, but no bombs were dropped. Our foxhole caved in and we had to cover it up. We had been having just too much rain, so we put more logs over it. We played cards, which was a favorite pastime of some of the crew members.

On August 17th, we had another air raid at 3 a.m., but the Japs didn't drop any of their bombs near us. In the morning, we cleaned guns.

On August 18th, a Wednesday, we got up and cleaned guns again. I read a book titled, "Josslyn's Wife," which I enjoyed. We went to the show, "Lady of Burlesque," but left early because of rain. The next day we dug a foxhole for us to urinate in, and even Jelley helped us dig it. Later we went to the river to swim.

On the 20th of August, we were supposed to go to Kahili, but didn't because of the weather. As you can tell, we sure had bum weather for flying quite a lot of the time. We saw the movie, "A Night to Remember," and I read the book,

One of the few recreational activities we had on Guadalcanal was volleyball, near our tents and near our foxholes. We usually played Byrd's crew—and lost. (1) Norman Johnson, (2) James Jelley, (3) Julius Woytowich, (4) Ralph Bruce, (5) Charles Thompson, (6) Earl Cornelius, (7) Henry Hutchings, (8) the author, (9) William H. Griffith. We had already lost our Assistant Radioman, which left a nine-man crew. From a 13th AAF photo.

"Guardian of the Trails."

On the 21st, we got our group pictures back from the photo lab — they were good. We saw the show, "Cowboy in Manhattan," and wrote some letters. August 22nd was about the same, only the show was "Margin For Error."

August 23rd we played volleyball with Byrd's crew. We only had eight members since we lost Griffith and Hosfeth. Byrd's crew beat us four out of five, which is about the way it always went when we played them. We played volleyball quite a lot for recreation when not digging foxholes or cleaning guns.

We bought some grass skirts from the natives. What big feet the natives have, I guess due to not wearing shoes. We went to the show, "Tarzan's Triumph."

August 24th we were supposed to go to Buttons but no orders were issued, so we just waited. We finally got orders to take a mission to Kahili instead. As the weather was bad, we flew over Rekada Bay as the alternate target.

I talked to a guy I knew from Middle River, Maryland, when we had worked for Glenn L. Martin Company prior to entering the service.

You will note that I covered a few days very quickly because nothing happened of any consequence on the missions we made up north to New Georgia and Bougainville, but I wanted to cover it. On August 25th we didn't fly, but we were beat again by Byrd's crew in volleyball.

The Action Heats Up—Again

August 26th we finally had some real action! It was comparable to the July 25th mission over Munda, but more dangerous.

We did not take-off until the late evening. Three squadrons of bombers were scheduled to make a strike on Ballale off the southern end of Bougainville, to try to knock the fighter strip out.

But we did not render it useless and it would continue to be a thorn in our side for some time after this mission. The

Japs would repair our damage at night and be ready for take-off the next day — a real difficult and frustrating problem for the top brass, and for us as we had to go back again and again, pounding them with everything we had.

Many of the planes dropped out on the way up to Ballale due to mechanical or other problems. As a result we only had five planes from the 424th Squadron go over the target that night. The other squadrons also had a reduced number to make the mission.

We arrived over the target just about dusk at 23,500 feet, and there was quite a bit of cloud cover which we had to fly through, but fortunately the runway below was clear on our bomb run. But the Jap Zeroes and Haps were in the air already, and I could see them coming up from two different directions, gaining altitude fast.

The Japs usually stayed clear until they had exceeded our altitude, going quite a distance above our formations. This gave them an opportunity to dive down at increased speed and to choose an angle of attack.

I do not feel we were sitting ducks, as the reference is sometimes made to a slower moving aircraft, because our armament and tight formations created firepower that was unequaled by any of the fighters we opposed. Much is made

Ballale— an island south of Bougainville that elements of the 307th Bomb Group pounded from their B-24's and B-17's in '42 and '43. From a 13th AAF photo.

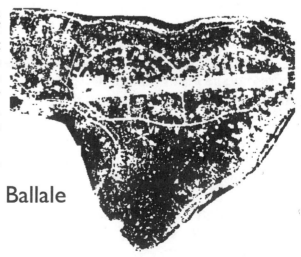

Ballale

of the Fighter "Aces" who would go and seek out the enemy, meeting them on their own terms and matching flying skills, as well as gunnery skills. By doing this, the fighters were able to pursue their goals of destroying the enemy planes.

But as a member of a bomber crew, it was much more difficult to become a "Bomber Ace" because two things had to happen which the pilots, bombardiers, navigators as well as the other crew members, including the trained gunners at the waist windows and in the turrets, could not control. The bombers had to wait for the enemy to attack before getting an opportunity to shoot the fighters down.

Secondly, the gunners had to be exceptionally accurate to take advantage of the split second opportunities presented when attacked by those enemy fighters. Many times, too, the bombers were operating under very serious handicaps; i.e., they could not deviate from their course when on a bomb run, regardless of any interference, because that was the whole purpose of the mission, to hit the target, and then to return to home base.

Another problem was difficulty with the bomber, such as mechanical or enemy-inflicted damage such as ack-ack. The enemy fighters just waited to take advantage of a bomber in trouble, that may be a straggler, without the support of the other bombers in a formation.

So to become a "Bomber Ace," a gunner had to make every opportunity and every second count. Sometimes I think he had to have some bad luck, too.

If he had the support and back-up of gunners on the other bombers in formation, it was sometimes difficult to determine who got the enemy fighter, as many gunners could get a few shots in when a fighter attacked. But those unfortunate enough to be a straggler or to have difficulty resulting in a one bomber defense had no difficulty getting credit.

On this particular mission there was no doubt about who got who. A photographer was along and covered it quite well.

Some of the Zeroes, Zekes, and Haps may have come from Kahili on Bougainville, or one of the other fields further north at Kieta or Buka. But there was little flak from the antiaircraft guns. Instead, the Jap aircraft really started coming after us. The worst part was the clouds.

The first thing I saw was a Jap fighter coming right up under our bomber, Man-O-War. I was lucky to be pointed at four o'clock low and saw him coming with the tracers already getting close.

As he bellied up in a loop, I caught him flat out and started shooting. Since he was already in a loop, he just went over as I raked him and I saw part of his tail section fly off. It looked like a part of his stabilizer. He dived and continued to dive toward the ocean below. Two New Zealand P-40's that were flying far below followed him down as he went into the ocean and exploded, but they did not reach him before he hit the water.

A record of that kill was mentioned in Samuel Walker's book, "Up the Slot," in which he mentioned Jelley's crew in Man-O-War, and the ball turret gunner getting a Zero. Corny in the nose turret was also mentioned as getting another Zero as it came in directly from the front. But you could hardly describe us as rookies, as we had a few missions as well as some Jap fighters to our credit already.

The method for bomber gunners to get credit for their kills was for the other crew members and other planes flying in formation with them to report the kills. Since so many gunners sometimes shot at the same enemy fighter, sometimes it was hard to confirm who made the kill, who delivered the fatal burst, or if it was shared, in which case, it was reported as a probable for one or two, rather than one getting all the credit.

However, as a lower ball turret gunner, I usually didn't get much help when an enemy fighter dived down out of range and then came up directly under the plane. None of the other gunners could sight in on him. Corny and I shared three probables during our tour, when he got shots from the nose turret, and Tommy and I shared one probable when a Hap dived down and came in at six o'clock, doing a barrel roll, then passing under the bomber, right under my turret, giving me an opportunity to get two good bursts into him.

This mission was a real test because when we entered the clouds there was nothing to do but spread out to prevent a possible collision, but this meant we were much more vulnerable to the enemy fighters. Each bomber was on its own.

Besides, everyone was trigger happy, and some of the inexperienced gunners were shooting the first thing they saw that looked like it could shoot back. One tail gunner was hit by a waist gunner from another squadron, because the waist gunner shot first and never waited to identify his target.

With all the fighters in the sky, it was really a nerve-racking mission.

Andy Parker, ball turret gunner on Goodin's crew in the Phantom Lady had his turret hit and a 9mm exploding type shell came through the side of his turret, landed at his feet, rolled around on the thick bullet proof (?) glass used for sighting, but did not explode.

We usually did a full 360-degree turn in our turrets and raised and lowered our guns as a gesture everything was all right. He had signaled me he was all right after we got away from Ballale and the fighters, so I didn't know his turret had been hit.

Our crew was flying in number 2 position in the second element of the 424th Bomb Squadron. Phantom Lady was in number 3 position on the opposite side, flying in the third element, bringing up the rear. We were flying a reduced formation as we began to close up again after the clouds had been left behind, giving us a more clear view of the aircraft around us.

I talked to Andy when we got back and he was really upset. He was convinced he was going to get it on the next mission because of his close call. We were all scared and shook up after that mission, but he was more upset than usual, and he would dwell on it, sometimes almost in tears, and at other times seeming to accept a fate he felt awaited him, in an almost fatalistic attitude.

I was also excited about my kill and reported it to the intelligence officer on our briefing. It was confirmed and the photographer who went along on the mission had taken a picture of it, too. Corny had one, and we shared a probable. Not bad for one mission.

Tommy Thompson shared a probable, too, for his action in the tail turret, for getting in some shots at a Zero that had come in over the top, with Hutch, in the top turret also firing on the fighter. But the Jap Zero didn't start his death dive until he was leaving at six o'clock high, going down over Hutch and down past Tommy. Man-O-War had a good day.

The Japs were using 7.7 mm bullets and either 20mm shells or 9mm piercing or explosive shells. Their 7.7mm bullets were not very large, but they sure could spray an area with them, with machine guns lining the wings of their fighters. The Japs didn't have a lot of armor plate on them, but they had lots of guns and could get up some good speed, especially in dives from above.

While their 7.7mm's weren't as large as the 50 calibers we had, they would make us take notice when the tracers and fire were coming from the barrels of their fighters. In the evenings and at night, they really looked like fireworks, a sight one could enjoy were it not for the death-dealing message they were delivering to us.

We lost only one B-24 Liberator on that mission, but it was a pretty confused mission, because the Japs had at least 50 fighters in the air and we had no fighter cover up at our altitude, though I did see F4Us and P-40's below in combat.

I forgot to mention that after the last Jap was going away at six o'clock, the one Tommy got a shot or two in on, one of my guns jammed. I felt lucky no more fighters came in at me. Also, some fluid leaked out of the hydraulic lines again. I didn't know if it was the same old leak or a new one from the combat we had on the mission. I didn't feel anything hit my turret, and none of the armorers told me it had been hit after we landed and they checked for the leak.

We had gotten two new crewmen, an assistant engineer and a radio man, with a possibility of permanent assignment with us. As a waist gunner, one of them put two holes in one of our rudders. But we hoped they would do better in the future, since some of the fellows would rather not fly with us. We were getting a reputation as a pretty wild crew, willing to take chances to get some of the little Jap bastards responsible for getting Griff and some of our other buddies.

R&R Rumors

We were constantly told we were to go back to Buttons, and some rest in New Zealand, but we were sweating out some replacement crews who were supposed to come up from down on New Hebrides to man our bomber while we were in New Zealand.

On August 27th, we packed our bags to go to Buttons. But instead of leaving, Corny and I went out to the line to clean guns. We found they had already been cleaned by another crew so we went swimming instead. We went to the show, "Lucky Jordan."

August 28— Another Hot Battle!

On August 28th, our next mission was to Kahili, and was not much better than the last. It started before daylight and we were over the target by 10 a.m., the skies were clear and the Japs were out in full force.

We had New Zealanders with us as fighter cover in their P-40's.

One pilot would match our air speed and move back and forth right under Man-O-War. I could point my guns earthward and see him right under me, not more than fifty feet below. He would look up and wave, then do a side slip, move over under some of the other planes, then back again. I almost felt like I knew the guy.

This pilot accompanied us, along with his buddies on about 12 different missions. I don't know if he was lost later or rotated back to New Zealand. He was around when we

144

flew Man-O-War and later when we got Shehasta back from Buttons. While on rest leave in Auckland, I tried to find out who he was, but was unable to learn where his fighter group was stationed. But he had guts, as did all those fellows who flew fighter protection for us.

The reason I am mentioning this now is because on that Kahili mission, the Japanese fighters were up in strength. I had counted about seventeen P-40's coming up with us. It was later that the Japs had a full contingent of fighters, 110-120, and we had all our squadrons up, too.

There were some Marine F4U's up the slot with the P-40's, too. In fact, it was on that mission that a waist gunner on a B-24 Liberator in one of the other squadrons got excited and shot at one of the F4U Corsairs, damaging part of the Corsair's right wing. It was reported he just missed the pilot, making a hit right behind the headrest. The Marine Corsairs did not get too close after that, but the New Zealand P-40's still flew just off our wings and just below us.

That New Zealander who kept close to me was some-what responsible for my kill on that mission. Some of the New Zealanders would come right into our formations, the squadrons being somewhat separated at times, when a Jap fighter would get on their tails and they could not shake him.

Hutch had spotted about six Zeroes at ten o'clock high in a dogfight with some P-40's. We had just left the target and the flak had let up. But the fighters were already at it off to the left and higher up. Our own altitude was not too high, at about 16,000 feet, and we were losing altitude fast. The skies were clear with hardly a cloud — perfect for combat.

It was said that a gunner usually only lived a total of three minutes average in combat, but that is a long time when an experienced gunner only got to fire a few 10 to 20 second bursts at the enemy, perhaps two or three times on a combat mission, unless the bomber was in trouble.

Then, if they were not shot down, they might empty their ammunition boxes or canisters. And I've seen the bar-rels of 50 caliber machine guns that actually melted down and were bent from shooting too long, some even split like they had burst, exploding in the breech from overheating.

Some guys would get scared and freeze on the triggers instead of shooting short bursts, which was the usual and most effective method before the fighter was out of range. When barrels were damaged that usually meant an inexperience gunner was at fault.

My Sperry Automatic Computing Sight on Man-O-War, as well as on Shehasta were pretty accurate and at 400 feet would make a bullet pattern of less than 10 feet circumference. So a five burst of 10 to 20 rounds each would almost guarantee a hit if you were using the sight correctly and remained calm when tracking an enemy plane coming up your gun barrels, or that's how it seemed sometimes.

But back to the P-40. He had the Zero on his tail and couldn't shake him, so he went into a dive from 10 o'clock high and some 700 yards in front of us, a little far for us to shoot effectively and accurately. But the P-40 came out of his dive about 800 yards below us. I had them both spotted.

I sighted in on the Zero, who was some distance behind the P-40 after the dives, but he was coming up fast. The New Zealander headed back up under our plane and the Jap followed, almost coming straight up on his nose. The New Zealand pilot did a loop while starting a wing-over, which carried him close to my turret, but gave him an opportunity to go back into the dive right-side-up again. It was the best piece of flying I had seen up close.

The Jap followed almost up to our plane and flipped over, too, but not before he started the loop up very close to us, shooting all the way. I started to shoot just as soon as the New Zealander veered off to the left in his wing-over, leaving the Jap Zero in prime position for me to get some clear shots at him. His bottom was in a position that I could not miss and I raked him from front to back. I could see a part of the cowling on his radial engine tear off. He was so close I could almost count the rivets on the bottom of his plane.

Still on his back, he started the wing-over, then all of a

146

sudden a puff of white smoke came trailing from his engine, but then the smoke turned black and flames spouted from his engine.

He just kept going down, slowly beginning to spin. He went on down and hit the water before he exploded, disappearing without a trace.

The New Zealander was long gone below us, but I did not see where he went because I was so busy.

Corny called out on the intercom for a Jap Zeke at two o'clock high, and I could hear the guns going up front which meant Corny and Hutch were shooting. So I swung around to keep an eye out should he dive at us, coming down below, but instead he chose to dive and come right in at us from the front, passing right over us, and I did not see him.

But Corny got off some good bursts at him from the nose turret, as did Hutch in the upper local turret. Corny scored a hit along with Hutch because the Zeke turned to the left away from Man-O-War and headed back toward Kahili, losing altitude and smoking.

We were having a rough mission, with plenty of planes in the air, but fortunately, as we tightened up again with the formation, the Japs seemed to have had enough and headed back toward Bougainville. Corny and Hutch got a probable credit for their encounter with the Jap Zeke, too.

We had a good mission and considering all the action, we were lucky to only lose two B-24 Liberators out of the twenty-five to twenty-seven that had made the bomb run over Kahili. It was a real forceful strike and damage was done.

Kahili was damaged we knew, especially since some Beatty Bombers had been reported in bunkers near the runway by the intelligence reports. I saw at least four distinct fires on the ground after the bomb run, so we did some real good on that mission. Of course, our loss of the B-24's had its price, and I don't know how many P-40's may have been lost. But we made them pay in Zeroes and Haps, too.

Our fighter kills included Corny and Hutch's one, my own kill, and the rest of the group had a reported eleven more kills. That meant we got more than our share on that mission.

Also, I'm sure the New Zealand flyers in their P-40's and the Marines in their F4U's, gave a good accounting of themselves, too. It was one of the most active missions I was to see at Kahili and Ballale.

But once again, bad news from Andy Parker on Cap Goodin's crew flying Phantom Lady. He reported his ball turret was hit again. We were flying number 3 position of the second element, while Phantom Lady was in number 2 position, over the target. We had changed positions on that mission. Even though Andy's turret was just slightly damaged, he once again indicated to me his feeling that his luck was running out. I tried to reassure him that it could have been any of us.

In fact, on another mission in August 1943, the nightmare had happened to another friend, a fellow named Carl Holmes. His turret was hit, dislodged, and he was salvoed in a terrible death. That was one reason Andy and I, as well as other ball turret gunners, were beginning to get hyper about that location.

You might say the lower ball turret gunners were a special breed, not too many could fly that position, but I liked it in a special way for its accuracy when used right and for the unobstructed view of the enemy on bombing and strafing missions.

Ready for Some R&R

We had already lost eight of the original twenty B-24 Liberators that had left Topeka, Kansas with us, coming in from the States at intervals as soon as conversions were made in our armaments at Hickam Field, Hawaii, so we all had about the same amount of time on Guadalcanal in late August 1943. A few of the crew members who had made water landings as a result of mechanical trouble or being shot down in combat did survive and came back to fly again, or rotated back to the States due to injuries or combat fatigue.

We were looking forward to the good food and female companionship which we missed so much on Guadalcanal.

After a mission we always looked forward to chow time. Ha! Ha! What a treat! For breakfast we would have powdered eggs with dehydrated potatoes. Sometimes the eggs were dipped in Spam, the favorite meat of the day —and almost every day. We could always look forward to Spam in some form at least two times a day and sometimes three.

The alternative was mutton or lamb chops fresh from New Zealand or Australia, or perhaps it was horse meat, sweet, dark red in color and course, stringy like, or even kangaroo meat. Who knows? We had conversations on that subject occasionally. I did not care for any of it too much, due to the greasy taste. Canned beef was sometimes on the menu, I think right out of the "C" rations. Believe it or not, every one of us almost liked it, especially when Spam had been served for days without letup, in every conceivable form.

Few guys in the 307th Bombardment Group on Guadalcanal went through a tour of duty without eating whatever it was.

The only bright part of our eating was the baker. He was really a whiz at fixing pies and desserts, and the best morale builder on the Canal besides mail call. He could take some institutional-sized cans of sour cherries, apples or peaches and make the best pies or turnovers you could ever find in the States. The crusts would melt in your mouth.

The only problem was, he and his bakers had to sift the flour to get the meal worms out of it. The heat and humidity would hatch them out, and a close examination would reveal movement of the small worms as well as a small dark end which I presume was the head of each one. But they wouldn't hurt us and neither did they effect the taste. I'm sure they didn't get them all out because the worms or eggs were throughout the flour.

I recall a few years later when I was on Guam during the Korean War, the same thing was a problem due to the heat and humidity.

The brightest part of the day was when he fixed pies, cookies or cobbler. He was truly the greatest morale builder on Guadalcanal. The salty spam, watery dehydrated potatoes, the mealy powdered eggs would all go down with a piece of pie to look forward to afterwards.

We also had powdered milk which was not always mixed well and would have passed for chalk or whitewash when it wasn't blended with the water properly.

Another pleasure we had some of the time was one Coca Cola a day, or some small can of fruit drink, i.e., orange, grape or pineapple. It is really amazing what pleasure can be had of such a small thing as a drink, other than the water out of the chlorinated lister bag. I believe those cans were the smallest made in the States, or so it seemed when you could empty them with only two gulps. Beer, when it was available, was rationed to one can a day.

The big reward for the flying crews was two ounces of hospital brandy for each mission, the ones when enemy forces were encountered. Some would take it when they got back to settle their nerves. The flight surgeon authorized it at the squadron dispensary. Major Groth was the flight surgeon and I sometimes think he was lenient with those who had a bad mission or lost a close buddy, because it was obvious they needed it, medically speaking. But others would save it up, the two ounces, until they saved enough to get a little tipsy when taking it all at one sitting.

Cliff Roberts from Goodin's crew went over to the Naval base one time and made a deal for some alcohol — or white lightning, or torpedo juice — made from corn meal mush or whatever else the Navy guys had available.

White lightning was the name the bootleggers back in West Virginia gave to the home brew that was sometimes made in bathtubs during the depression years to make some extra money, while torpedo juice was the name the Navy crews gave to the concoction they came up with, which usually consisted of alcohol (usually almost 100 proof) made from fermented corn meal and whatever else the makers could come up with to make it potent.

Cliff drank some of the torpedo juice and it was not long before he was as limp as a rag after he staggered around for a time. He went through the four stages of drunkenness pretty quickly, namely jocose (in which he was happy, joyful and silly), then bellicose (wanting to fight every one who tried to settle him down), then lachrymose (turning sad, feeling sorry for himself with fits of crying), and finally, comatose (passing out — and I do mean he was out.)

We laughed about it afterward because he went so much out of it that his muscles completely relaxed. We carried him to his tent, and while he was face up, his toes actually dug into the dirt as we drug him by holding him up under his arms. When he came to later, he threw up five times, and I believe, came as close to dying as a man could without quite making it. It took him two days to get over it, during which, fortunately for him, he did not have to fly any missions. I don't believe he touched another drop of alcohol after that experience for the rest of his time on the Canal.

Unfortunately, he was hit while flying at left waist gun while on a mission and was killed. The only good thing about it, I understand, was that it was quick and he didn't know what hit him. Cliff was replaced by Paul "Lefty" Leftowitz on Goodin's crew.

Those who smoked were also rationed to a small half-sized package of Old Golds, Lucky Strikes, Camels or Chesterfields — brands that were in vogue during the forties. Not many of us who flew smoked because of the danger around the gasoline used by the planes. Besides cigarettes were scarce and expensive. Some of us chewed gum when it was available. I never did smoke, so I saved a lot of money that would have gone up in smoke and ruined my health, too, as we found out much later when tests were made on its effects.

With regard to our own crew, after the two temporary guys made a few missions with us, and we went to New Zealand, they both went AWOL, the excuse being they didn't want to risk their lives flying with us. I think they were chicken, and just didn't have the guts for combat.

On our return from New Zealand, we picked up some replacements. As mentioned before, Hosfeth had decided to quit flying and was replaced by William "Bill" Humphrey. Griff was replaced by Victor "Vic" Meehan as assistant engineer. Norman "Johnnie" Johnson's sinuses finally caused him to be transferred to flying C-47's or DC-3's in the Air Transport Command. Johnnie was replaced by Donald "Don" Taylor.

So our flying was taking its toll of our crew, as well as the other crews in our squadron. A bad case of nerves was given names ranging from combat fatigue to neurasthenia, or a more severe psychoneurosis.

Some of the airmen just couldn't take the missions. Others took them, wanted to fight, to get even, or to forget the bad experience of receiving a "Dear John" letter, hoping to have a Jap bullet end it all for them.

But most of us did suffer some stage of combat fatigue, sometimes without being aware of the underlying causes.

Stories circulated constantly about those who could not take it anymore and wanted to go back home to the States. Of course, we all wanted the war to be over and to go home, with the exception of a few who, as I mentioned, saw a way out of a situation back home they would rather forget.

There was one story about an enlisted crewman who went in to see then Captain Norton R. Groth, the flight surgeon. He started acting like he was throwing something out of his hands on to the Captain's desk and on the floor, even though there was nothing there. The Captain, in his kindliest tone asked him, "What are you doing?"

The soldier replied, "I am throwing flowers on the desk and floor, Sir."

The Captain commanded, "Don't do that in here. Pick them up and take every one of them outside!" The guy, inadvertently had shown his good sense to give respect by having said "Sir." He had tipped his hand that he wasn't as bad off as he would have liked the Captain to think. Needless to say the crewman gave up on his "Section 8" and left. But sometimes it was no act and they did get to be moved back to the rear and eventually back home as unfit for combat duty.

Some crews bailed out and if fortunate enough, were picked up by ships, submarines or PBY's, or made their ways to the islands where coastwatchers hid them out until they could be picked up by our forces. Some were captured by the Japanese, but this did not happen often, for the Japs were not known for taking too many prisoners. Some made crash landings on island beaches — as Byrd's crew did — with all surviving due to the fine job by the pilot in the crash landing.

A normal tour was supposed to be twenty-five missions, but due to the lack of replacements and our losses, many of us were flying thirty, thirty-five and even as many as fifty missions before returning to the States.

August 29, A Respite at Buttons

We were to go on some other less active missions later further north after the successful raid on Kahili, but luckily, a new crew was on its way up from Buttons, so on the 29th of August, we finally made it back out of the combat area, or at least to a more secure location at Espiritu Santo on the New Hebrides Islands, known to us as Buttons.

We got a report on our last bomber raid at Kahili. I got credit for that Zero officially. Corny and Hutch got credit for another. One waist gunner on another bomber got creased on the head, but not too seriously. The P-40's and F4U's got 21 Japs and lost two planes. Not bad for our fighters.

The first thing we did when we got to Buttons was take a boat over to visit the Navy for a change, boarded the Battleship "U.S.S. Colorado" that was in the harbor there. It and its sister ship the "U.S.S. Maryland," were there together, along with some other ships. I did not realize how big they were, carrying almost 2,000 men. We went down into the ship and saw how the shells were loaded, too. The sailors really treated us nice — and they ate well, too.

CHAPTER 7

BATTLE OF QUEEN STREET

Rest And Relaxation

While at Carney and before flying back to Buttons and then on to New Zealand, we had not seen a woman (excluding the natives) for over four months. So, as I indicated, everyone was really looking forward to our rest leave in Auckland.

One of the busiest sections of Auckland, New Zealand was Queen Street, where the Red Cross Club and The Canteen were real jivey places to meet the girls. And there were plenty of them, too. We stayed at the Hotel Auckland a short distance away on Queen Street, and after being declared fit from our physical exams after arriving, we were ready to honor the service men who had preceeded us by "fighting the battle of Queen Street."

The closest we had even come to seeing a Caucasian female was perhaps one guy at Carney Field nicknamed "Broadway Billie" by some of the crew members who were flying on our B-24 Liberators. I would not say for sure that he was odd, queer, a fag, or to use the new expression, gay, but "Broadway Billie" had a problem.

His ways would now be popular in some areas of New York and San Francisco, both cities now noted for their large homosexual communities. I believe that was one of the reasons he was called "Broadway Billie." He came from Broadway in New York City and had acted in some plays there before entering the Army Air Corps.

"Broadway," as some called him, would not bathe in the river with the rest of us. We would go swimming in the nude sometimes (skinny dipping) and let it all hang out so to speak. We did not know if "Broadway" was bashful or not, but he would wait to go down to the river after the rest of us, including the natives, had left.

But the guy did fly and go into combat, so even though he was subject to some ridicule, lived a rough life of being avoided, a subject of speculation and suspicion, he was respected for being there with the rest of us rather than avoiding the draft or being a 4F for his "funny" ways, because at that time, those fellows were strictly kept out of our military.

One story about "Broadway Billie" that I must share with you concerned his solitary trips to the river. The path down to the river was through the dense jungle which had been cleared a few feet or so on each side. We always carried our carbine or pistol if away from the camp area. On this trip, "Broadway" had his carbine and on the way back to camp was unfortunate enough to meet a Japanese holdout.

Guadalcanal had been a very difficult campaign. The 1st and 2nd Marine Division had lost many men, as had other branches of soldiers, and the Japanese Imperial Marines. As a result of the Japs losses, many of the Japs fled into the jungles and hills, becoming holdouts who would not surrender. They lived by stealing whatever supplies they could find and sometimes ventured near our camps and compounds searching for food and weapons. The natives were friendly to us and would notify us when they located a holdout.

The holdouts had been known to kill some of our men from time to time when cornered. Some of them had been killed or captured by our men. That was why we carried our guns and the reason on this particular day "Broadway Billie" ran into a Japanese holdout coming down the path.

Both were surprised initially, and each turned and ran in opposite directions, with "Broadway Billie" dropping his gun in the excitement of the moment. The Jap also had a gun and let his drop to the ground, too, thinking only of escape from the armed American.

When "Broadway Billie" finally made it into camp, he reported the incident. Some of the guards, who were on duty around our camping area each day and night, went down to where the meeting had taken place. The guns were found just as they had been dropped.

It was then "Broadway Billie" found that he could have captured the Jap and been the hero of the day, because he had shells in his gun — the Jap did not. The Jap was carrying it only for the purpose it served, to scare the other guy into missing a shot or running away just as "Broadway Billie" had done.

I don't know if any of the rest of us would have done any differently, under the circumstances, but it sure didn't help his image with the rest of the crews in the camp. I don't know what happened to "Broadway Billie" after that because we were on our way to rest leave, and on my return "Broadway" was not around. He could have been shot down later or received a transfer back to the States.

Buttons had become almost civilized while we were up on the Canal. Goodin's crew came down on rest leave with us. Hansen's crew, Byrd's crew, and Ratti's crew were scheduled to get a break in New Zealand about that time, too.

On August 30th, we went down to the Navy to buy some things at the Post Exchange. Yes, they had one by now, or at least the Navy had a small PX where we could buy a few items. Corny and I bought a few things, but wanted to save our money for our New Zealand visit.

We saw the show that night, "Harrington's Kid." It was pretty good, if I recall. We went on a searchlight tracking, taking a Colonel who was in charge of defense of the island along with us. He flew back at the rear section of the plane, using the waist windows to survey the island from above. I guess he was checking security. He was a gentelman officer, a regular guy.

On August 31st I mailed some group pictures which were signed by the eight current members of our crew to my mom. I had a heck of a time getting it done, in fact it took all morning.

That night, we went to the show, "DuBarry Was a Lady." It was in technicolor which was a real treat as most of our shows were in black and white. It was in a theater used by the Seabees on the island. Corny and I had to catch a ride in a truck to get down there.

On September 1st, some of us went to shoot skeet. Boy, were we lousy. Hutch and I both only got three and four out of sixteen shots. I don't know what was wrong unless we had been using the turrets with a different sight too long.

On September 3rd we heard from the Canal. They had lost three bombers since we left Carney Field. The Japs lost 35 planes on the 30th of August. We lost one bomber and a tail gunner was shot in the back seriously, but that bomber had shot down seven Zeroes.

The Japs were dropping phosphorous bombs from the fighters. The phosphorous bombs, or some said they were magnesium, but whatever, would stick to the wings and burn a hole right through to the engines or gas tanks. They were like blobs of grease or jelly, and they smoked, leaving a white puffy-like trail behind them as they came down onto the bombers. It was hell to see them come down and not be able to take evasive action. We had some dropped above us on a few missions.

One was used to bring down a B-24 Liberator on September 3rd. We heard about it the next day, September 4th, when a guy brought Tommy's and my pay books down from the Canal. At least we got paid before going to New Zealand. The rest of the crew had already had their records brought down. We saw a show, "Priorities on Parade." I had seen it once before — somewhere.

The food at Buttons wasn't as good as on the Canal

because they didn't have a baker who was a miracle worker. On September 5th, 6th, 7th, and 8th, we didn't do much, just waited to get a ride down to Auckland. We went to gunnery school. They had improved on the training somewhat by using movies of planes coming in at different angles and directions which proved to be fun. Had it been the real thing, it would have been everything but fun, due to the effect of enemy planes flying right into our gun barrels if we failed to hit them.

I did some drawing on a pad I bought, using pen and pencil. I liked art and did occupy some of my time that way on Guadalcanal.

It rained quite a bit at the New Hebrides Islands, too. September 8th, we played some cards but didn't go to a show because of rain. We got word on the 9th of September we were going to Auckland tomorrow, the 10th, so we packed our bags.

We got the good news that Italy had unconditionally surrendered. We thought maybe we'd start getting some more replacements and help over in the Pacific now.

Well, we flew to Auckland in a C-47. It was a thirteen hour trip.

New Zealand was a beautiful sight from the air. The cliffs, the small colorful boats in the inlets and harbors and the brightly colored roofs of red, green, pink and blue, with the exteriors of the homes painted in pastel shades to blend with the contrasting roofs, gave us a warm feeling about the country even before we landed at the air field. We looked forward to the visit with great anticipation.

The farms were laid out in neat squares that were well cultivated, with gardens and pastures that provided grazing for large herds of cattle. In addition, the hills also had large groups of sheep along the slopes we passed as we lost altitude, which gave the impression New Zealand was a country rich in cleanliness and well kept by the farm owners. If money and health permitted, I would love to go back.

The first thing we did was go shopping in the PX. I

bought a watch, camera, ring, and an accordion to keep us company back on the Canal. I knew it wouldn't be too popular with the other crew members though, because I had to learn to play it. The only thing I could play at the time was the harmonica, which I had learned as a young boy.

Right away, we met some nice girls and of course, some nice bad girls, too. I made a notation in my journal all my girls have teeth and long hair, contrary to most. I'll just say, one problem the ladies had, as well as most other residents, was a lack of calcium or other correct minerals in the soil to protect their teeth from cavities. A wonderful place for a dentist to practice.

I eagerly got off the plane, as did the other crew members, then caught a bus that was waiting for us and headed toward downtown Auckland. The bus ran on the wrong side of the road for us, as in Great Britain, this being a small part of the British Empire. That was the first entirely different thing I noticed.

The second oddity was the English, or rather, the New Zealand accented English which the natives spoke.

The homes were quaint, beautiful, clean and well kept. The colorful houses, roofs, fences and pretty flowers completed the picture.

And girls! There were lots of girls, and very pretty too, in plain print dresses that fit well, to put it mildly.

I'm sure we were all impressed as we rode along the nice roads and streets leading to the downtown area. We were taken to a large office area, a three story building just off Queen Street, the main street of Auckland, and where the large Hotel Auckland was located.

We had to be processed in prior to beginning the ten day leave. This processing consisted of a physical and then an interview with a psychiatrist, who asked questions like, "Do you love your mother and father or hate them?" and "Do you feel someone is out to get you?" To this I replied, "Yes, the Japs."

He continued. "Do you masturbate or have you ever in

159

the past? Do you like girls or guys? Do you want to go home?" There wasn't any point in lying about those questions, or at least I didn't. "Do you sweat at night, have bad dreams or wet dreams?"

The doctor's exam included a "short arm", milking it down. I don't know what the doctor was expecting after we spent four months without seeing a decent woman. Oh yes, we even had to turn our head and cough as the doctor probed our testicles for hernias. It's true we could have ruptured ourselves lifting ammunition boxes or helping load bombs, but no one had that problem either.

The doctor, and the psychiatrist, gave us a thorough going-over before turning loose.

We were all pretty healthy, everyone passed the examinations and were pronounced fit to fight the battle of Queen Street, as it was called by those who had been down to Auckland previously. We had heard how nice it was and how wonderful the people were, and especially the ladies. We were to find it was all true.

What a battle it was, too, and we were more than ready. First, we went to the Hotel Auckland, the largest in town. The permanent party personnel had given us some recommended places to stay and to eat. We all had been paid prior to flying from Buttons on New Hebrides. Corny, Tommy, Hutch and I stayed at the Grand Vue Hotel, a small place, almost like a tourist home would be here in the States, but somewhat larger.

Some of the sights suggested were the race track, the museum in which the history of Maori people — original natives of the country — was presented, the beautiful beaches and harbors outside the city and other sites.

But for dancing and entertainment, including an opportunity to meet the ladies, the Canteen off of Queen Street and the Red Cross Club on Queen Street, were the meeting places of all the services and a real jivey place.

The local beauties, and there were lots of them, were very friendly and anxious to please us. I mentioned the problem with teeth and the fact about the girls wearing their hair short. In the States, the movie stars of the time wore their hair long most of the time, and that was what we were accustomed to back home. But the New Zealand girls liked to have their hair shorter for two reasons. It was less trouble to manage when swimming, dancing, and engaging in sports activities. Also, a curling iron provided enough curls not to have to worry about such things as permanents.

Many of the New Zealand men were in the service, flying or fighting up north in the Solomon Islands, or had been taken by the British Government to North Africa where they were helping Montgomery fight Rommel, the "Desert Fox" of the German Army. Many of the New Zealand men were lost in these battles. Others had been gone a long time and the women were as lonely as our men were from up in the Islands.

Everyone in New Zealand was expected to help in some way with the war effort. This included the women, too, and many served in the armed forces in the equivalent of our WAACS, WAAFS and WASPS in the United States.

We went to eat at the recommended restaurant at the Hotel Auckland. I asked some of the other guys there what would be good to order. They unanimously agreed that the steak and eggs were the best in town.

I listened to a New Zealand couple order after the waitress asked them what they wanted. They had the "Styke en aeigs," ordering in their best colloquial New Zealand accents. So when the waitress asked me, "What will you have Yank?," in her accent, I immediately replied, "I'll ave an order of styke en aeigs, plaese," using my best, just-acquired New Zealand colloquial accent, too.

She looked at me quizzically a few seconds, then said, "You mean an order of steak and eggs, don't you, bud?" It's a wonder she did not say, "Bloke," the word used to describe a smart aleck. She really put me in my place.

However, she laughed afterward and we later went to the theater together, which was also on Queen Street. I don't believe she had that happen before and it made a lasting impression on us both. I never used the native dialect again.

Needless to say, she was my favorite waitress during the rest of my leave in New Zealand.

When we attended the theater, the British national anthem, "God Save the King," was played prior to the beginning of any entertainment, requiring all to stand. They also had intermissions in the middle of every show which provided an opportunity to get popcorn, a drink of cola and make the welcome acquaintance of any females which may be alone and friendly.

After eating, we began the tour of the city. We visited Mount Eden and the Zoo. We rode the ferries to Bayswater and Devonport across the bay. We visited the Post Exchange, which was also downtown where the processing station was located.

The watch I bought was a Benrus, which I still have after these many years. A story about that watch will be related later. I bought a cheap camera with film since I had an interest in photography and had used the laboratory in our 307th Bomb Group on occasion, helping to develop the film which we had taken.

One of the lucky trinkets sold by the native Maori was their jade charm, a rendering of an unborn child, with large eyes and stomach. It was worn around the neck as a way to give good luck and ward off evil spirits. I bought a couple to give to my family when I went back to the States.

New Zealand, much like the original colonization of the United States, had been settled by those who had been classed as problems for Great Britain, due to nonpayment of taxes, being dissidents from the Church of England, causing political problems, and those accused of minor crimes against the state. Many, at their own option, just as those who came to America, chose to leave England for greener pastures and more freedom to worship and make a new life.

Because of these beginnings, they were very industrious, very religious, and good for their new country of New

Zealand. The citizens of Australia were of the same type of people. I believe that is why New Zealand and Australia are perhaps more closely allied with our own America in beliefs and progress.

I will have to say, too, the quaintness of this country of New Zealand was the way the people worked so hard to make it so clean and beautiful. They were probably twenty years behind the United States in modernization of such things as the telephone, automobiles, and other things we already had lots of, but their plain and clean manner of living was more like our rural life on the farms and small villages. A good clean life which impressed me greatly.

The people were friendly, and invited us to their homes to visit and eat with them. I did do that too, quite a number of times, because I felt at home, and I appreciated the fine job their sons were doing as fighter pilots up in the Solomons.

I liked the race track because it was very colorful. The horses were beautiful, the jockeys dressed very distinctively with bright yellows, reds and blues on their sashes and usually had matching horse blankets under the saddles with matching numbers and colors of their shirts, sashes and trousers (riding britches), making the races even more bright than our own horse races in the United States.

The grass was clean and green with white fences on both sides of the track. Betting was brisk and the viewing stands completely occupied. It was obvious that horse racing was one of their popular sports.

In recent years the New Zealanders have also proven themselves to be very competitive in boat racing. I can understand why, judging from all the boats in the harbors and in about every inlet and cove along the coast. You could see fishing and boating were other activities that added to the tourist possibilities of the country.

While the visit to the race track was spectacular, it was not a profitable visit for me, as I lost a few dollars. I don't believe the crew members had too much luck picking winning horses, at least no one bragged about their winnings.

We all went to the Red Cross Club on Queen Street, with dancing the main social event. The girls could jitterbug and had a lot of pep, and seemed to enjoy the company of our American boys. That's how we spent our first night. I didn't have much luck, but did meet some nice girls who held future promise, but most of them were dating some of the guys who were stationed there permanently. We sure envied them for getting that kind of duty. But I guess somebody had to do it.

The American marines, many who had fought on the islands in the Solomons, especially Guadalcanal, had been here before us, in 1942. I remember one story that was told about their activities involving the beauties of New Zealand. I don't say it caused us some problems, but it sure didn't help us when we came down on rest leave. And I don't blame the girls, either.

It seems some of the Marines overcame the objections and fears by the young ladies of becoming pregnant by telling them they could prevent it from happening. The Marines gave them Feenament and other chewing gum laxatives, with the accompanying story that the ensuing excess in bowel movements would rid them of the effects of their sexual indiscretions.

But, of course, it did not work and even though they had a very "moving" experience, in more ways than one as a result of what the Marines told them, in a couple of months, usually long after the men had left for the States or the islands again, the girls found themselves with child.

So they were not so trusting of the Army Air Corps crewmen, either abstaining altogether or insisting upon the use of prophylactic — a wise decision.

"Lew" Lewis of Goodin's crew, was fortunate to meet a nice looking girl at the Red Cross Club. He told me of his experience the next evening. They just danced and talked a great deal the first night they met, and made a date for the following evening at the Red Cross Club. She told him she was doing her required service in the civil defense guard at one of the bomb shelters provided throughout the city. After all, the Japs were not that far away should an aircraft carrier slip through and make a sneak attack like the one on Pearl Harbor.

Her father had been a pilot and was killed riding with another inexperienced pilot who became scared and froze on the controls, causing the plane to crash. Lew said she was very concerned about the men who were being sent back to the service hospital there in Auckland, the 39th General Hospital, and did volunteer work on the wards of the hospital in her off duty hours, helping them write letters, etc., when too wounded to write for themselves.

Lew said her name was Virginia, but she used the shorter version of Jenny. Her mom lived some distance from Auckland so she stayed at a local boarding house for young ladies, most of whom were in the service or worked right in the city. It was like a home, a tourist home.

On his second date, Lew said he was invited to visit her at her home, however the lady in charge put a limit on their visit to Jenny's quarters. She also shared them with another young girl who was in the civil defense forces.

Lew said he went into the room with her and the other girl was in bed on the opposite side of the room. One thing led to another and Lew said he finally was able to join Jenny in bed. But it was a very embarrassing situation because all was not quiet.

He said the girl in the other bed would giggle when she heard the bed making rhythmic noises. Lew said he felt like he should invite her in on the party, but felt Jenny would not appreciate the intrusion. Lew explained if he had not been up in the islands so long, the situation would have caused him to lose interest and dampen his eagerness. But it did not!

Meanwhile, the rest of the enlisted men of the Phantom Lady's crew took two adjoining rooms in the Hotel Auckland. The officers had taken up quarters in another location in the hotel, so I never did learn how they made out on their visit to Auckland.

But the enlisted crew had the very good luck at the Red Cross Club to meet a group of girls who joined them in their room for the next nine days — yes, that's right — the next nine days. Cliff Roberts, Pete Peterson, Joe Jamison and Andy Parker convinced the girls to come to visit them at their hotel suite. It must have been quite a party.

I cannot verify the facts, but Andy told me the girls stayed with them and did not leave the hotel. But I do know they did not go sight-seeing with us during our leave, except the first day. When our crew ate at the hotel restaurant, we saw Goodin's crew eating with the girls. Andy said they sent out for drinks and left the hotel only once, the last day, when they all went on a shopping spree for the girls.

The guys had some money left and I guess they felt obligated to treat the girls since they had contributed so much to the morale of the Phantom Lady's crew.

I understand there were some very revealing pictures taken and brought back to Carney Field on their return to Guadalcanal, but I was not privy to them. But I'm sure they would put the native women on the islands to shame, no matter how scarce their clothing.

They did enjoy talking about their leave when we got together in the evenings to reminisce about our Auckland trip. But every one of them were at the flight line when we got ready to go back up to the Solomons. All except the two guys I mentioned who went AWOL because they were afraid to fly with us when we returned to the Canal.

We rode all day on September 22, except for a stop to refuel at New Caledonia, then finally landed at Buttons on the New Hebrides Islands.

Before we left Auckland, we did a little more shopping. As a result, we bought a short wave radio. But we also decided to buy a small Sidney Silky Terrier dog. It was the cutest little pup you would ever want to see, with long, silver, silky looking hair. It was to bring us much joy and in the end, some sadness, too. Corny got the idea, then Hutch, Tommy and I decided to help pay for it. The total cost was one hundred dollars, a total which we divided into twenty five dollars each. The little terrier had registered papers, so it was a good breed.

That little dog, which we named "Ticki," after the New Zealand good luck charms depicting an unborn child, was to be our mascot. We learned to care for it very much. We had no problem bringing it up on the C-87 wrapped in a blanket.

It was the star of the camp whereever we went in the islands. Ticki was to get some darker hairs as he got a little older, but remained very small. The coloring of silver and black made it very pretty and cute.

Corny and Hutch did not come on up to Buttons until the next day, being bumped by some officers at New Caledonia.

When I left the Grand View Hotel in Auckland, I forgot and left my pocket book under my pillow. No money was in it because I had spent it all before leaving there. However, the manager of the hotel sent it up to me about a month later, to my surprise.

That just proved to me even more how wonderful the New Zealanders were to have such consideration, as well as honesty. While there was no money, I did have pictures and papers that were of some importance to me.

I might add, I passed my physical, as did Hutch, Tommy and Corny, so we were all ready for more combat. I had over thirty letters waiting to be answered when I got back to Buttons. I started to practice the accordion.

On September 23, I met a guy who could really play the accordion. We all sat around and listened to him. But I'll never be able to play like that, that is for sure. We went to the show, "The Youngest Profession," a comedy. I answered all those letters, too.

On September 24th through the 29th, we just did the routine things. We went to a couple of shows. "Holiday Inn" was one of them.

Under the palm trees is almost an ideal place to practice the accordion, it seems so peaceful. But the ships laying out in the harbor and the planes constantly droning overhead are reminders that there is no peace in this part of the world, or in most parts of the world in 1943, with war in Europe, North Africa and the Pacific.

I haven't flown much for almost a month now, as we are not yet transferred back to the Canal, and we lost some time while on rest and relaxation in New Zealand. Phillpot is not flying now on Byrd's crew, so they got a replacement. We still haven't gotten replacements for Griff and Hosfeth, but I'm sure we will when we go back up to the Canal. We just had some trouble because of our "devil may care" attitude.

But we have a prayer and a belief in God, too, to help us along during the next few months at Guadalcanal.

On October 1st, we saw a show, "Buckskin Frontier," read and listened to the radio. On October 2nd we didn't do much, either. I read a book called "Poems to Remember." I like poetry, especially this book by John Kieran. The show at the Seabees theater was "Stardust."

October 3rd, we saw "Frontier Bandit" and read some more poems and literature by Shakespeare, Milton and Bacon. I read many books to pass the time until we entered combat again. It rained quite a bit at Buttons. We saw a show, "Brother Rat" put on by the USO down at the Seabees theater.

Jelley had not come up to Buttons with us because he was being checked for night blindness, but he joined us on October 6th. We would all be flying together again. The rest of the officers got through their physicals, too. We saw a show, "Falcon's Brother."

October 8th, we were presented some medals and bid good-bye to some fellows going back to the States. We all wished we could go along, but it was not to be, for we were scheduled to go on a night mission or search mission the next day. We listened to "Tokyo Rose" on the short wave radio. We saw a show, "Savage Wild Women," but they were not as wild as it sounded.

On October 9th, we had an inspection of firearms, then

went on a search mission. We returned and went to the show, "Bataan."

First thing on October 10th, at 3 a.m., we went on search for eleven hours. We saw the show, "I Walked With a Zombie."

On October 11, we got the word — Johnnie would not be going to the Canal with us, due to his sinusitis. He went back to the States instead.

New Zealand Sights On R & R

(Clockwise, from left): Auckland, as seen from Mt. Eden; Ellerslie courts; Tamaki Waterfront Drive; Winter Gardens; Burn's Memorial and Memorial Museum.

CHAPTER 8

CLOSE CALLS & LOST FRIENDS

A Message of Hate From Toyko Rose

Some crew members of Frenisi and Shehasta on Guadalcanal in '43. Front, (l-r), Unidentified, Ira Jackson. Rear (l-r), Charles R. Thompson, Earl B. Cornelius, Henry E. Hutchings, and the author. Purple Heart's were prevelent. Out of 200 crew members who left Topeka, Kansas on 20 B-24's, only 27 returned, and most of them were Purple Heart recipients.

October 11th, we went to shoot skeet. I hit eleven out of sixteen, the highest anyone got, but poor by our usual performance.

Whitie Woytowich got his 1st Lieutenant bars today. That makes all the officers on our crew 1st Louies. Johnnie was a flight officer, but he is leaving us.

We listened to "Tokyo Rose" on her Zero Hour broadcast. She always gets us steamed up with her chatter about how well the Japs are supposed to be doing against our G.I. fighters. We played volleyball again with Byrd's crew with the same old results — they beat us. The enlisted men then played against the officers and we were beat again.

We were to go to the Canal in a couple of days. No flying today, though. We also received word two of our squadrons on the Canal lost a B-24 each, one going down in flames and the other just disappeared. It was obvious the war was still going on full blast at Kahili, Ballale and Buka on Bougainville.

We saw the show "Stormy Weather," with all black actors and actresses, starring Lena Horne.

On October 13th, we packed to go to Cactus. We saw a USO show with Little Jack Little and the dancer, Ray Bolger. He had starred in "Stage Door Canteen."

We didn't go to Cactus on the 14th as planned due to the discovery that our plane had a warped wing.

On the 15th, Corny and Hutch, and the rest of the crew went up to the Canal. But I didn't because Captain Groth, our flight surgeon, went in my place.

I joined my crew on October 16th, flying to Guadalcanal in a B-24. The rest of the guys pulled two strikes before I got up there with them. They said they missed the targets both times due to the weather. I'll start flying tomorrow.

I had 17 letters waiting for me to answer upon my arrival. We had started to garden some behind our tent with lettuce, carrots and tomatoes. All are coming on now, so we could eat the tomatoes. But just our luck, we changed tents, going back to our old one, since the crew that had occupied it was lost while we were down in Auckland on leave.

On the 17th I got a new heated suit. It hard to adjust the heat in the other one, I think it was shorting out sometimes. We were due to go out on a strike mission the 18th.

It seems while we were enjoying ourselves in New

Zealand, the top command was planning some work for us when we returned to Guadalcanal. We flew "The Rattler" on October 18th to Kara and Ballale, carrying eight one-thousand pounds bombs, and hit the target dead center.

Shehasta was back up at the Canal, but we didn't know if we would get her or Man-O-War again.

On October 19th, we were flying Shehasta. We wanted her back, and I guess it just worked out we got her back since she was our plane.

Our briefing was early in the morning, with take-off immediately after noon lunch. We were on another strike at Kahili on Bougainville. As I was to learn later, our mission was to neutralize the air fields on Bougainville and Ballale so we could take the airstrip on Munda, New Georgia and move to Munda for refueling and the longer trips to Rabaul on New Britain and Truk Island. So the missions from October 1943 and into 1944 were intensified. Our eventual goal was to retake the Philippines, and we needed fuel to do that task.

We were also getting some fighter escort from the P-38's and Marine F4U Corsairs. We hit the target of Kahili's runway all along the left side and all the way from one end to the other. Gene Bruce and the other bombardiers had spread them out pretty well. About 20 to 30 Zeroes attacked us after we left the target. We got one and our fighters got some, too.

Two of the P-38's collided, with one going down. I think the pilot got to the ground after bailing out without being strafed by the Japs. The other P-38 managed to fly back to New Georgia. The ack-ack was very intense and we got rocked around by it, a couple of pieces hit our wing but did not cripple us. A tail gunner from one of the other squadrons got hit with a 20 mm shell in the arm and shoulder, but not seriously.

We completed the afternoon mission with little trouble, except we encountered some phosphorous bombs which were set to explode above and in front of our B-24 Liberators. The streamers of burning phosphorous would stick where it hit like jelly or thick grease, burning right through the metal and into the wing tanks, causing the plane to explode. We were losing some of our bombers over Ballale and Kahili from those type of bombs. They just posed one more threat to us.

If it were not for war time, the white streamers would look like a part of a Fourth of July celebration, with exciting and beautiful fireworks.

We were also attacked by two fighters with Hutch and Tommy getting one of them as they passed over us for a probable. He came in at seven o'clock high, shooting as he came, pulling up right behind and above us. I did not get a shot at him as he peeled off to the left and high.

Bill Humphrey at the right waist was shooting. I could see the Zero as he came down from above, but out of my range, flaming as he went. He exploded before reaching the ocean and I did not see him bail out.

We had to pull some more night missions, too, which I really hated most of all. First, as I explained before, the master radar beam at Kahili was very accurate in picking us up on our bomb runs and at night, the beam blinded me in the lower ball turret. Then, when the flak ceased to explode all around us, we knew the Japanese fighters would attack.

When Jelley started evasive action by slowing down, cutting back on the power and dropping off to one side or the other, I never knew if we were hit or not, if we were going down or if we were being attacked by the fighters.

It was like a carnival ride which swings you up and down and around and around, the Octopus, I believe it is called. But here you are blinded by the light and heat of the beam.

I kept the turret rotating and also moving up and down, hoping to see anything if the radar beam should lose us and an attack was taking place by the Jap fighters. I sure didn't like the big flashes and black puffs of smoke when the flak exploded, but usually to see them and not feel them jar the plane was encouraging.

And, of course, the Japs were flying out there in the dark hoping the flak would cripple one of our planes. Just like a bunch of sharks, they were ready to complete the kill. We had no fighter cover at night or the strength of our combined firepower from the other planes on night missions.

Another Hap In My Sights

The next night mission over Kahili I got my fourth Jap plane, another Hap, making it two Zeroes and two Haps. He dived from two o'clock high some 600 yards out and came up directly under Shehasta. I followed him with my sight as he came up and after he completed his attack, he peeled off to the right.

I gave him six short bursts of about ten to twenty rounds each, judging from the tracers, starting my bursts from the time he got into range. Corny and Hutch had called him in, so I was really ready for him when he came down fast and started his climb toward us. He was out of Tommy or the waist gunner's range of fire, so it was up to me to get him.

He burst into flames immediately and never did complete his wing-over which would have placed him right side up again. When he exploded, I could see one wing fold back, so I must have hit his wing tank. Also, part of the stabilizer on the left side flew off. Black smoke immediately made a trail behind him. He had no chance to bail out.

The Japanese fighters carried plenty of guns and ammunition, but had hardly any armor plate, so when you hit one of their fighters, they were vulnerable to our machine guns and the firepower our bombers were capable of producing in a fight.

We were beginning to feel very uneasy when the Jap planes got too close, because it began to become more clear that they were more than willing to sacrifice their lives in a Kamikaze attack, and an attack could result in ramming a bomber if we didn't get them first. This was especially true if they were damaged and wanted to take us with them. Our losses were increasing in direct proportion to theirs.

While we could shoot down ten of theirs with one pilot each, a loss of one of our B-24 Liberator bombers also resulted in a loss of ten men that we did not want to lose, unless they were able to bail out or make a water landing to be rescued.

October 27

Our mission on October 27th was a memorable one. We were to hit Kara, but it was closed in and we hit Kahili instead. The flak was very intense. The Jap fighters were slow getting off the ground for some reason, perhaps because we had been pounding the air fields pretty hard with bombs, limiting the number that could take-off quickly. But the anti-aircraft guns were throwing the flak up like a blanket.

We were flying lead plane in Shehasta, in the first element while the Phantom Lady was in number two position. Andy Parker had signaled me by waving his guns up and down before the bomb run that everything was working all right and he was go for the bomb run. Frenisi was in number three position with Byrd's crew off to the right and riding in tight with us.

After the bomb run, which pasted the Kahili runway, we headed south hoping to elude the Jap Zeroes and Haps. We immediately began to close up for protection.

The New Zealand fighter escort of P-40's and Marine F4U's were already engaging the Jap fighters as we were getting further away from Kahili and Bougainville.

Feeling somewhat secure, I turned to signal Andy Parker in his lower ball turret that I was all right. I was horribly surprised to see his lower ball turret was missing. Flak had made a direct hit on his azimuth ring, or center support post, which supported the weight of the lower ball turret as well as the weight of the gunner flying in it.

It must have hit the turret directly, otherwise damage would have been done to those flying the waist guns, too. Andy had been salvoed right out of the Phantom Lady with the ball turret and had had no chance to get out or bail out. Perhaps he was killed instantly.

That's the way I'd want it, if I had no chance to bail out. I recalled his comments the other two times when his turret was hit and we had flown in different positions in the same element of the squadron. His fatalistic attitude proved to be well founded.

Immediately upon our return to Carney Field I checked with the crew of the Phantom Lady and no one else had been

Shehasta on Carney Field in '43. Note the number 324 is missing due to the accident at Buttons. This day, I was cleaning the guns in the lowered ball turret. Also note the bombs with the fins removed in the foreground.

hit by the flak. That's fate for you. The ground crew went right to work putting another turret in from one salvaged from a B-24 that had been wrecked. He had collapsed a nose wheel, leaving the rear part of the plane in relatively good shape for parts.

In explaining the fate of Andy Parker, I failed to mention our own problems, for we lost two engines on one side over Kahili, numbers 3 and 4, but managed to make it back without too much trouble. Lt. Francis and his crew gave us protection on our way back. Shehasta did it again. It usually would have been fatal to lose two engines over enemy territory and still get out without getting shot down by enemy aircraft. Luck was with us again.

But after something like this happening, not only to Goodin's crew on Phantom Lady, but our own problems with Shehasta, it was easy to begin thinking time was running out. We all had the urge to quit, but we wanted to finish our missions, so we stayed to win the fight, stayed with our crews, had enough desire for revenge, pure hate and a desire to beat the Japanese and to stay the course.

Some would call it patriotism, but there was more than that to it. The real truth was we did not want to let our buddies down, to turn chicken, to break up the team or to appear cowardly.

After sharing the good times of Tucson, Clovis, Topeka, and Alamogordo, of El Paso and Juarez; of beautiful girls; of tequila, and the pink drink that would make you see pink elephants, or better yet, drink it with the worm for the good luck we needed right then; it would not be right to bow out of the bad times in helping to sink the Japanese rising sun.

We were slowly accomplishing our goal. We were moving north, securing more islands in our march toward retaking the Philippines and positioning for an attack on Japan proper.

The United States Navy was moving forward, too, shelling islands held by the Japs, establishing repair and refueling bases in the harbors at New Georgia, the Russells, and moving north toward Empress Augusta Bay at Bougainville. Submarines, PT boats, destroyers and cruisers were operating out of these advance bases to intercept the Japanese supply and troop ships.

Corny and Hutch took a PT boat over to the Florida Islands to visit Tulagi. Hutch wanted to see the grave of his brother who had been in the Navy and was lost a year earlier when his PT boat sank in a fight with the Japs. I didn't know at the time, of course, but I was to go to a joint funeral later at Eatonton, Georgia, along with Ira Jackson of Byrd's crew, when they brought Hutch and his brother back to the States for burial.

I was also to learn later that Major Gregory "Pappy" Boyington was among those Marine F4U Corsairs that helped to provide us with fighter cover on the missions over Ballale, Kahili, Buka, and later on over Rabaul. He was shot down at Rabaul after our own fatal mission and Jelley's crew had already gone back to Auckland, New Zealand.

With the securing of Munda, "Pappy" moved up from the Russells. Later he went to Vella Lavella with his Black Sheep Squadron. We were in good company with the likes of John Kennedy in his PT 109 and Pappy with his Black Sheep.

October 29

The next mission that stands out in my mind was a strike on Buka Passage on October 29th, 1943 — and it's a mission I won't forget.

Our crews were to observe a sight that hardened many of us and fueled our hatred of the Japanese almost beyond reason. As mentioned previously, I cannot understand restitution in any form for displaced Japanese in the United States when our men not only left their homes, their families and loved ones, but they lost their lives, too.

We needed to neutralize those ships and planes in the Passage because it was a staging area for support of the ships and air fields at Kahili, Ballale, Kara and Munda. So we made a long mission to Buka to knock out the shipping as well as fighters and bombers stationed at the two airfields on each side of the strait known as Buka Passage. We had no friendly fighter cover and flew north of the coast of Bougainville hoping to take the Japs by surprise. But this was not to be, for they were up in the air and waiting for us.

We had three squadrons with a strength of approximately twenty-seven B-24 Liberators, all carrying one hundred pound bombs. I know Ratti's crew, Byrd's crew, Hansen's crew, Goodin's crew and quite a few others I cannot recall were on the mission. We were met by fighters that were probably notified by Jap ships plying the waters off the coast of Bougainville.

There were Jap Tonys, Zekes, Haps and even some Betty Bombers in the air. Lt. Ratti's crew shot down one Betty Bomber that day. I had observed an in-line engine version of a Tony before that looked like a German ME 109, and it seemed more narrow than the radial engine types we had encountered previously at Kahili and Ballale.

There were many enemy fighters in the air. I do not recall the flak being too severe, but one of our bombers was hit by fighters or flak, and part of the crew bailed out.

I counted four chutes. The Jap fighters dove down toward the chutes, strafing the airmen in their chutes. Then they dove down close to them, going over them at a fast rate of speed. This caused the parachutes to collapse, rolling them up or getting them entangled with the shrouds. It was a revolting sight and being in the ball turret, I got a first hand view of it. I tried to reach some of the fighters with bursts from my guns, although they were too far below to shoot at them effectively.

We did get some Jap fighters in spite of their inhuman actions. I got a Tony and I know Byrd's crew got two on that mission. Ratti's crew got one Betty, but then one Betty got away. Goodin's crew got two. Tommy Thompson, our tail gunner, got one Zero coming in from the rear, though I didn't see it. All in all, our bombers did well and got their share of Jap planes, but it did not make up for seeing what the Japs did to our men, shooting them in their parachutes.

It is one thing to have guns to fight back with, but another to shoot defenseless men. From then on, I can't vouch for the others, but our crew became as mean and vicious as the Jap bastards we were fighting. But I had already made my mind up on missions long before this one to give them hot lead any time and any way I could.

A report was given by Tokyo Rose that we had been up the Slot and tried to bomb Buka Passage, without success. Her statement that two of our bombers had been shot down and that *"the American flyers were dealt with in a manner they deserved"* made us mad as hell. We were ready to go up as soon as possible to meet the yellow bastards. It only embittered us more for the next missions.

We did get down on their level, I will have to admit, and showed no mercy on our future missions. We pulled more missions, but none like the Buka strike.

Many of the crews were working now with replacements for those lost. They were pickups from other crews that had suffered losses, or where part of a crew that didn't make the mission when a plane was lost.

Victor J. Meehan and William "Bill" Humphrey were in that category as replacements on our crew as was our co-pilot Don Taylor. Jack "Dave" Davison was the new ball turret gunner on Goodin's crew of Phantom Lady.

As a result of the loss of Andy Parker when he was salvoed out of the ball turret of Phantom Lady, one of the squadrons had two ball turret gunners quit. But those men who had been on that mission, had seen our bombers explode, had seen Jap suicide kamikaze pilots ram our bombers, and had seen our men being shot in their chutes stayed on, fighting and fighting some more, never giving in to their fears and other emotions.

October 30

We made the October 30th raid on Kahili, but not without problems. The Japs must have brought in more antiaircraft guns because the flak was heavier than I remembered on prior missions. The Japs had more than fifty fighters in the air and we had no fighter cover with us.

Byrd's crew, Ratti's crew and Hansen's crew were right up front with us in the first element, and Goodin's crew was back in the second element. We were flying number one in the first element with Gene Bruce as our lead bombardier. Due to the flak we started to spread out some after the bomb run.

There was one straggler that had been hit by flak. The Jap fighters began to close in for the kill. We all cut back on our air speed to stay with the damaged bomber, to provide some firepower as support.

I couldn't tell from looking back what was wrong, as there was no smoke or fire and all engines were still running, but maybe not at maximum power. There may have been a problem in the cockpit, but at least they were able to stay on the straight and level, just not as fast as the rest of us.

We had left the target and had headed back out to sea when the Jap fighters hit us. I don't believe I had seen as many enemy fighters before, and we had a damaged plane to protect, too, which meant we could not increase our speed too much. The damaged B-24 Liberator still had full fire-power for protection, but was falling back slowly.

The Japs seemed extremely aggressive, sensing our problem with the one bomber. But we were getting further away from land and we knew they would not follow us too far out into the ocean before turning back. We had dropped down from 19,000 feet to 12,000 feet so we could go off oxygen.

The Jap fighters finally began to break off to return to Bougainville. The damaged Liberator kept losing altitude and finally made a ditched landing in the water just off of Choisel Island, where I'm sure at least some of the crew made it to shore — and help from the coastwatchers. I never learned their fate, but I'm sure it was better than if they had gone down near Bougainville, or bailing out as floating targets for the Japanese fighters, as we had witnessed on the prior missions to Buka.

Byrd's crew got two Jap planes and two probables on the mission. Ratti's crew, Goodin's crew and Hansen's crew got one each. On our crew, Corny got one and Tommy and Hutch shared one. I got another one in a very similar manner to the last one.

There had been plenty of Jap planes coming in at Shehasta from the forward area. There were Zekes, Haps and the new Tony in-line engine fighter.

My hit came up under Shehasta after a dive from about seven o'clock high from some distance out, with his guns blazing as he came up in a loop at two o'clock low, exposing his belly as he peeled off to the right. Tommy said he had tried to reach him from way out as he came down but didn't know if his shots were effective.

But I raked his under belly until he started to belch smoke that was black immediately on sight. I saw a part of his elevator break away, too, so I knew I had scored a hit on the engine as well as on his tail assembly. The resulting spin did not cease as he spiraled down to the ocean waiting below to swallow him up forever.

More Routine

After that mission, we cleaned guns and went to the show, "Swing Shift Mazie." We had made stencils to put our names on Shehasta in the various positions which we flew, and we were able to finish finally. I had made my own and placed my name near the lower ball turret. Hutch, Tommy, Corny, Gene, Jelley, Taylor, Meehan, Humphrey, and Woytowich all had their names in various locations, too. It was quite impressive, and something few planes had done yet.

I helped develop some pictures. Corny, Hutch, Tommy and I went over to the 5th Bomb Group where the B-17's were leaving for the States or New Guinea, due to their incompatibility with the faster and longer range B-24's.

On October 31st, we took off at 6 a.m. for Kara. We hit the runway with our bombs. There was little ack-ack and we returned with no interception by the Japs. It was a milk run compared to the October 27th mission.

We made another night mission to Kahili with Ballale as the alternate target the first part of November, 1943. Kahili was closed in, which made me happy because Ballale had much less flak and their searchlights were not nearly so accurate as those on Bougainville's Kahili runway.

A positive sign though, was the report our troops had landed on Bougainville on November 1st, 1943, at Empress Augusta Bay area, with many supporting ships of our fleet engaging the Japanese navy in a major battle. We were ready to consider longer missions soon.

November 3rd, we saw "Arsenic and Old Lace" at the show. Later we went to a briefing for a raid on Buka in the morning.

For the first time, we hit Buka going right down the runway with little ack-ack and no fighter incidents. They did not try to intercept us. I didn't understand why, unless the last mission was too much for them. But we knew better than that, and figured supplies were not getting down from Rabaul to Bougainville as quickly as before.

We had heard the planes of the U.S. Aircraft Carriers "Saratoga" and "Princeton" had bombed Jap ships in Simpson Harbor at Rabaul, trying to cut off troops and ships going south to Bougainville and west to New Guinea. The Japs had almost 100,000 troops with five airfields ringing Rabaul, and many naval vessels in Simpson Harbor. Some of the B-17's from the 5th Air Force on New Guinea had hit Rabaul before, but they did not have the distance to travel we would have, and they had fighter cover to accompany them, while we had none, due to the distances involved. But, that was to change.

I mentioned Gregory "Pappy" Boyington had been in the fighter cover that helped us on our raids on Ballale, Kahili and Kara on Bougainville. His Black Sheep squadron had left

Russells and moved to Munda after our forces had taken that field. This extended their range so they could go all the way up to Buka, too. By then, Pappy had made a name for himself and his renegade crew.

Pappy had flown in General Claire Chennault's group of "Flying Tigers," helping the leader of China, General Chiang Kai Shek, fight the Japs with the Flying Tigers establishing his reputation and shooting down six Jap planes while there.

He went back to the States, then got back into the Marines and came down to New Hebrides, came on up to Guadalcanal, then to Russell Islands, then moved with his men to Munda. They moved on to Vella Lavella, and after the troops landed at Empress Augusta Bay on Bougainville, and an air strip was secured there, his Black Sheep moved up there, placing them closer to Rabaul.

In China, Pappy had flown P-40 Warhawks, but his squadron flew the F4U Corsairs in the Solomons. He was an Ace, a "Flying Ace," shooting down 22 more Jap planes in the Solomons for a total of 28 enemy aircraft, a record for which he earned the Congressional Medal of Honor.

Pappy took off from the marsden runways which the Seabees had placed on the coral runways at Torokina, on the coast of Empress Augusta Bay, Bougainville, and started to fly up to Rabaul. His fatal mission came just one month and twenty-five days after our own over Rabaul, but he was not so fortunate.

Pappy was shot down on January 3, 1944 over Rabaul at Simpson Harbor. He was taken from the water after bail out and became a prisoner of war of the Japanese for a year and a half before being released, or rather rescued when we won the war with Japan.

I should say, his exploits, and those of his men, made him famous, and his book just added to his legend of drinking, fighting and bravery, but most of all to his good example of leadership against great odds. But at that time, we were all challenged to do our best.

The New Zealanders, flying their P-40 Warhawks, were doing their best, too, as were the P-38's, P-39's and F6F's, flown by their respective units of Army Air Corps, Navy and Marines. All were up in the Islands flying from small airstrips under hazardous and less than ideal living conditions. Other Navy and Marine pilots were flying from our carriers.

When the landing of our troops at Empress Augusta Bay on Bougainville took place, there were many Navy vessels involved. Admiral "Bull" Halsey was in charge of the big Navy operations in that area of the Pacific. But the Battles of Empress Augusta Bay and Battles of Cape St. George also had a Captain Arleigh "31 Knot" Burke (who later retired with the rank of Admiral) in charge of the task force known as "The Little Beavers, Desron 23" and consisted of three Cruisers known as "Desron 12" — the U.S.S. DENVER, U.S.S. MONTPELIER, and the U.S.S. CLEVELAND. Admiral Merrill commanded these cruisers.

The accompanying destroyers for "Desron 23" were U.S.S. AUSBURNE, DD 570; U.S.S. SPENCE, DD 512; U.S.S. CONVERSE, DD 509; U.S.S. DYSON, DD 572; U.S.S. STANLEY, DD 478; U.S.S. FOOTE, DD 511; U.S.S. THATCHER, DD 514; and most important to me personally, the U.S.S. CLAXTON, DD 571, with Captain Herald F. Stout commanding.

"Clicking" With The U. S. Navy's Little Beavers

Symbols like these revealed the pride and determination of our naval forces. Clockwise, from upper left: The Desron 23 destroyer squadron adopted the comic book character "Little Beaver" as its mascot, and hand-painted a likeness of it (right) on its ships. The symbol of the U.S.S. Claxton (left), a destroyer, carried this slogan: "Click With The Claxton."

These cruisers were protecting our troops in their landing at Bougainville. Two big battles they engaged in against the Japanese Navy were on November 2nd and November 25th, 1943, when they took on the Japanese ships ONAMI, MAKINAMI, AMORGIRI, YUGIRI and UGUKI. They sunk the YUGIRI and damaged the ONANRI and MAKINAMI. They gave an excellent accounting in the battle with the Japanese Navy, and went on to distinguish themselves in other battles of the Pacific in World War II. And Commander Stout retired with the rank of Rear Admiral.

On November 4th, we made another raid on Buka without any intercept from the Jap fighters, but the mission was seven hours long. The ack-ack was not too heavy either. We returned to the Canal, cleaned guns and then went to the show, "Mr. Big," about a bunch of jitterbug kids. Not bad.

On November 5th, we worked at the flight line most of the day, cleaning guns and checking turrets. The show was no good that night. November 6th we didn't fly due to bad weather, so I helped develop some pictures we had taken of the different crews and of some of the nose art on the planes.

On November 7th, we headed up to Buka again but canceled it out due to more bad weather. We went to the show that evening, "The Sky's the Limit."

November 8th, we went to code class, then Captain Groth taught us in a first aid class. That was to come in handy later on during the Rabaul mission.

Our next mission was to Kahili, but it was closed in so we hit Ballale. The fighters were up and the tracers were lacing the sky immediately, even before we made our bomb run. Since it was a night mission, we went over in intervals spaced about eight minutes apart and the Japs had plenty of time to work us over before the next B-24 Liberator came in for a bomb run. They were extremely aggressive in their attacks. I could sense they were feeling the pressure to get us out of the war as soon as possible because supplies were not getting down to them like they had in the past. We were getting concerned that they would start the Kamikaze attacks from desperation.

Corny called in a Zero at ten o'clock high, flying right over us. He got in some shots and Hutch finished him off as he passed over. He broke into flames and exploded just as he left us behind going north at four o'clock high.

Another came in from a dive and passed right under Shehasta. I caught him head-on and must have hit his propeller and engine, because he almost blew up right in my face, just barely missing our plane. He put some bullets into the tail section of Shehasta, but failed to hit a vital part of the plane or damage the rudders sufficiently to cause us any trouble.

I heard and felt a bullet hit my turret and jar it, but did not feel anything other than that, so figured no damage was done. When we got back to Guadalcanal, I found two bullets had hit near the turret's azimuth ring. It was a real close call and I began to feel like Andy Parker did before he was hit and salvoed out of the Phantom Lady, turret and all.

That was the last Jap fighter I would get. But there was still one more probable to be shared by our crew.

And the price would cost us three men.

Our crew: (l-r, front row) Bill Humphrey, Lt. Taylor, Jim Jelley, Ralph Bruce, Julius Woytowich. Back Row (l-r), Charles Thompson, Henry Hutchings, the author, Victor Meehan, Earl Cornelius. All received the purple heart. Three were fated to receive their medals posthumously.

Chapter Nine

Rabaul Raiders

Fatal Missions

Of course, this is the way we wanted all the Japs to look in the Solomon Islands in 1942-44. War breeds a hatred all its own.

When we were briefed for our next mission, it was for a strike on Rabaul on New Britain. We were to go up to Munda, land, refuel, take on a bomb load and head to Rabaul on November 11, 1943. Shipping in the harbor was the target.

I had seen the show, "My Heart Belongs to Daddy," the night before we left the Canal. I believed after the mission to Rabaul on November 11th, Armistice Day, that my heart would belong to the Lord, for I did a lot of praying that night, as did many of the other crew members.

This was to be a tough mission, almost the maximum range of our B-24's, with no fighter escort. We would be the first B-24 Liberators to hit the Rabaul area. Some B-17's and B-25's, flying from New Guinea as well as some Navy Dive Bombers had hit Rabaul, the harbor and some of the five airfields nearby. But they also had fighter cover. We would not have any to accompany us on the mission. The alternate target would be Rapapo Airfield.

General of the Army Douglas MacArthur. From a U.S. Signal Corps photo.

General Douglas MacArthur had issued the order, "All men and planes are expendable until Rabaul is neutralized." Quite frankly, we cussed him out for putting an order to us in such harsh terminology. Little did we know the reason for such an order, but we were to learn later why he was so concerned about Rabaul.

The mission was possible because we had secured Munda as a refueling stop and could load bombs closer to our target. The 424th Squadron was to lead the way on the mission, to be accompanied by all the other squadrons, the 370th, 371st, and the 372nd — a total of 36 planes. It was an all-out strike at the heart of the enemy's stronghold in the South Pacific.

We made an early 6 a.m. take-off on November 10th from Carney to Munda. On arrival, we were assigned quarters for the night. Tommy and I went souvenir hunting, and there were some to find as a result of the fight for possession of the airstrip.

It was apparent the great damage our ships and planes had done to secure New Georgia. The Seabees had pushed the wrecked planes and dead Japs off to the side of the runway, and we could see the arms and legs of the Japs sticking out of the piles of coral and wreckage. The stench of death was still in the air from their rotting bodies, and the smell of death hung in the air near the runway. Expended shells lay everywhere and large bomb craters had not been filled in along the hillsides. But the matting to extend the runway was laid down on a bed of coral dozed out by the Seabees parallel with the ocean shoreline.

The morning of November 11th, we were glad to get back into Shehasta at 6 a.m. for the trip north. We were loaded with 500 pound bombs, a full load for such a long trip.

The skies were clear and we were flying at a low altitude for much of the trip, and passing over some of our own naval vessels about thirty miles out from the coast of Bougainville. As we approached Rabaul, we started to gain altitude. We put on oxygen masks in our turrets and charged our guns, test fired a few rounds and then waited for the target to come into view.

Eighteen planes, or two squadrons of nine planes each were in our formation. Others were to follow us later.

I don't know if all the crews that were listed on the mission sheets for the November 11, 1943, Armistice Day trip to Rabaul made it or not, but the following were listed, by pilot and plane: Alexandre in Plane #819; Worban in #215; Jelley in #324; Hansen in #221; Goodin in #310; Friend in #141; Bisbee in #966; Ratti in #266; Marshall in #858; Francis in #107; Byrd in #925; Pueppke in #260; and Scott in #137.

As a result of mechanical problems or the loss of a plane, some changes were made in the plane number that a crew would fly, but usually we flew in the same one as much as possible. We were in Shehasta #324 on our missions now, and Man-O-War #966 had gone back to its old crew. I'm sure most of them did make the trip to Rabaul, since it was the first and all were in the 424th Bombardment Squadron (H), 307th Bombardment Group (H), 13th Air Force, USAFISPA.

Our attack altitude would be at 19,500 feet, all in tight formation. We came in over the city but went out into the harbor area where the ships were taking evasive action, circling, zig-zagging, leaving wakes that would have been interesting to observe had we not had our minds on the enemy aircraft that was climbing fast up to our altitude.

I don't know how the bombardiers picked the targets because there was so much to choose from down below, including big troop ships as well as many smaller vessels.

We began to experience some flak as it was evident the ships as well as ground antiaircraft fire from shore was throwing up all they could. We were already starting on our bomb run out over the ships in the harbor.

We did not see any fighters in close until Gene Bruce had dropped his bombs in trail, targeting the ships. As we were leaving the target area, I could see some of the bombs hit the water, but others were hitting right on or alongside some of the ships. One ship appeared to be a large troop or cargo vessel and some of the bombs hit close enough to penetrate the side of it, but not right on top of it.

The fact we hit some of them was a good feeling. The mission is successful if the target is hit, for as Gene Bruce, our bombardier said, "That's what the whole mission is about, the delivery of the bombs and hitting the target."

He would kid and say, "That's what makes the bombardier so important, they should name the crews after him." He had a very good point, too. We knew the Japs would be paying a price for any losses we would have on this mission.

There were hardly any fighters in the sky that I could see

as we left the harbor. We must have caught them by surprise. But I could see some coming up from far below. Also, high above and some distance away, some P-38 Lockheed "Lightening" fighters were getting ready to engage some Jap fighters. They must have come from New Guinea, but did not come near us. No P-40's or F4U's were in sight.

Where ever they were from, they were too far below us to distinguish from the Jap fighters.

We were already turning south, heading for home when we spotted some other Jap fighters off to our right at two o'clock high, climbing up above us. Some of them were met and engaged by the P-38's as we began to lose altitude.

Suddenly, I heard Corny and Hutch on the intercom call out, "A Zero at two o'clock high closing fast on our squadron." There was only one reported, which was unusual since they usually came in pairs, one the leader and the other his wing man, or one after the other at short intervals.

I heard Corny yell, "HE'S COMING IN!" Corny, Hutch, and Bill were all blazing away. I don't know if the waist gunners were getting in any shots or not, at least the one on the right waist, Bill, sounded like he was shooting. But the Jap had singled us out, coming in and down past our plane. I don't know why he picked us out of all our B-24's.

He came back up out on the right side at about three o'clock, and it was obvious he was suicide bent because there was no way he could escape the fire that was coming from our guns. I had been shooting as he went below and came back up, as had all the other gunners who could get some shots in at him. He went out of sight above the plane.

Then I realized he had hit our plane on his dive back down, because I could feel Shehasta shaking and I could hear and the sound of shells ripping into her side in rapid succession. He had shot four or five 20mm shells into Shehasta, and all the 7.7's he could get off at us. It sounded like a hammer hitting the metal sides of our plane.

But I had been too intent on the Jap Zero to notice our own problems. Just as suddenly as he had hit us, I saw his plane coming down on its back — with no pilot in its cockpit. Just a second or two later, I saw the Jap pilot floating down by our plane, not more than one-hundred fifty feet away.

He had on a heavy brown leather flight suit which was shiny looking in the sun, as though it was brand new. He had his helmet on, also brown leather, with the white band and red sun of the kamikaze, either painted on the helmet or a cloth band tied around his head, I could not tell which, but it was enough to make up my mind what to do about him.

All of this happened in a few seconds.

As he floated down in his parachute, I sighted in on him and put rounds into him, watching the tracers tear into him, jerking his body around. Other gunners from the waist and ball turrets of our formation joined in, too.

As he drifted down out of range, he looked like a little doll, hanging in his parachute.

I was feeling pleased with myself because I had never seen a Jap bail out before, but I had seen how the Japs had shot our guys in their chutes at Buka, and this was just pay-back time. I yelled into the intercom, "BALL GUNNER TO PILOT — WE GOT HIM!"

Jelley came back, "GOT HIM HELL — HE GOT US. GET OUT OF THAT TURRET. WE'RE GOING DOWN!"

I pushed forward on my control sticks, pointing the guns down and putting my back up against the exit door. I then began to feel my cheek and head burn, and realized I had been hit — but with only minor wounds.

I did notice after Jelley called me on the intercom that I didn't see any other fighters at our level, which was unusual, because the Japs liked to pick on crippled planes that were vulnerable to their guns. But our B-24's in the 424th Bomb Squadron began to tighten up around us, giving us protection. We appeared to be the only plane hit on this first mission to Rabaul. And on November 11th, too, Armistice Day, a day to celebrate peace. But peace was a long way off, as far as we were concerned. I heard later Marshall's crew was hit, too.

I learned later a waist gunner on another plane did get hit in the arm on that attack, the only wounds suffered other than our plane.

Upon opening my turret door to climb up into Shehasta's belly, a sight hit my eyes I'll never forget. I went up looking for a chute, as I had none on. I was not even wearing a harness for a snap-on pack. I spotted, and grabbed, a seat pack from behind the armor plate at the right waist gun.

I saw Vic Meehan laying on the floor of the fuselage, below the left waist gun. Bill Humphrey was sitting on an ammunition box with a dazed look on his face, blood running down from his shoulder. Vic had blood coming from his lower stomach. The shell had hit low, near his crotch, and came out his back, leaving a large wound.

Charlie Thompson was coming from the tail section, having left his tail turret, and his right arm was bleeding. All of us in the back of the plane had been hit.

Some of the Jap's seven point sevens, or twenty milli-meter shells, had also hit the small cardboard-like bomb-shaped markers nearby in a rack in the wall of the fuselage which contained gold-colored powder. They were used by the navigator to gain a fix on location, to measure wind drift, etc.

The incoming wind had blown the powder all over the rear of the plane. Meehan, Humphrey, as well as myself, were covered with it — our faces as well as our clothes. It gave an eerie cast to everything as it was sucked out the waist windows.

I looked out the waist window and saw the number four engine was feathered and we were losing altitude. The instru-ments were out, too. Some shrapnel glanced off my turret, gone through number one engine and cut an oil line. Jelley had feathered it, too, so both outboard engines were out.

Jelley called on the intercom, "We're going to try to make it back. Throw everything out that's loose or will come loose."

Corny came to the rear from up in the front of the

plane. He said things were bad up there, too. Hutch and Bruce came back to join us. Hutch checked for damage to the cables and other controls. Whitie came behind them, all trying to help as best they could to lighten the plane by throwing out ammunition boxes, guns and anything else that would go out the waist window or camera hatch.

Everyone had some injuries. I asked Corny to get a first aid kit for Vic and Tommy. I tried to stop the blood flow from Vic, but with no success. I wadded up a jacket and laid him down on it after placing gauze from the first aid kit over the wound. But the blood just did not stop.

Gene got out the morphine kit and put the little needle into Vic's arm to help reduce any pain he may have, but he seemed to be only semi-conscious at best. He muttered something which Gene and I thought was "letter," but as he repeated it we knew he said "water." I started to give him a drink, but Gene said no, not with internal injuries.

I told Gene, "It won't make any difference, now."

"Go ahead," Gene said, as he realized the extent of Vic's injuries, and I gave him a small drink.

In the meantime, Hutch was trying to inflate Vic's life vest, in case we went down for a water landing, but the vest would not inflate. After checking the containers on each side, we found both were missing. Hutch took one out of his life vest and I took one out of mine, and we put them in Vic's vest and inflated it. Had we thought of it, we could have inflated it by blowing through the tube provided to inflate by mouth, but under the stress of the situation, neither one of us thought of it. Hutch then went back to the cockpit to help Jelly and Taylor.

Gene borrowed my knife and cut the small hook-shaped shrapnel from Bill Humphrey's neck. Bill then went up front to use the radio to call the other B-24's and to ask for help from the Navy PBY's in case we went into the water.

Gene and I agreed Vic needed another shot of morphine, to keep him out of as much pain as we could.

Gene had been a coach in high school and had experience in first aid, so he was in a position to know more about it than the rest of us.

But it wasn't long after that, as I cushioned Vic's head, and held his hand, that he stopped breathing.

Just about that time, we sighted some United States Navy ships. We were about forty miles off the coast of Empress Augusta Bay at Bougainville.

We had not reached the ships, consisting of three light cruisers and eight destroyers, when Jelley came over the intercom to tell us to bail out over our Navy ships if possible.

Those ships were a welcome sight, for I could feel Shehasta vibrating from the damage done to her. The number two engine was starting to smoke and Jelley had to cut the throttle and feather the prop on it, too. I don't know what kept the plane from exploding.

Jelley had asked us first if we wanted to stay with the plane and we had all indicated we did, but when we lost the number two engine, he gave the order, "BAIL OUT!"

Only Jelley, Taylor, Hutch, and Meehan were to stay with Shehasta in an attempt to make it to Vella Lavella. But she was losing altitude — fast.

Gene and I had opened up the camera hatch, as it was good to throw things out of and also for bailing out. Tommy, who had been relaying messages to us from Jelley from his seat on an ammunition box at the waist window, was pretty dazed from his arm injury. He said his arm was all right, but I could see he could not use it, although the blood had stopped running down his arm.

I had put my seat pack on but did not take time to tighten up the leg straps which was a mistake. We were still some distance from the Russell Islands or Vella Lavella, but our altitude was down to seven thousand feet.

For once I really thought that the saying, "Rank has its Privileges" should apply, and the officers should jump first. I said to Gene and Whitie, "Go ahead." Gene said, "No, you go first. We'll follow you!"

I walked back to the camera hatch and without looking back, said, "So long," and jumped. I didn't even bother to think about it. If I had, I wouldn't have had the nerve to do it.

We were then at about 1,800 to 2,000 feet up, and still some distance from the Navy ships, but from the air, they looked closer.

I pulled the rip cord immediately after my feet left the floor of Shehasta. There was no time to waste. I didn't hold on to the rip cord, either. Going out the escape/camera hatch, we didn't worry about catching the drag chute, or the parachute catching on the tail section due to pulling the rip cord too soon. So when my chute opened, I was head down and the straps were too loose.

I was jerked around into an upright position, and the buckle across my chest came up and hit me under the chin, stunning me temporarily. Before I knew it, I was seeing the waves coming up to meet me.

I still had on my heated suit, a blue color that was to blend in with the ocean water. But the Mae West was yellowish orange and more visible. Around my waist I had a cartridge belt with my pistol on my left side and a canteen of water on the right side.

I did not inflate my Mae West until I felt my feet touch the water. I remembered my days of instruction on bailing out and the warning not to inflate it or the impact might make it burst. Also, not to free myself from the chute too soon, thinking I was close to the water, when I may still be some feet up.

I did remember to unhook the leg straps and to unfasten the buckle in front that crossed my chest, but to keep my arms down so I would not drop out of the harness.

As a result of not inflating my jacket until after hitting the water, the weight of the equipment caused me to go very deep into the water before I was able to come back up and surface again. My first breath of air was partly salt water.

Only one side of my Mae West had inflated, because I had given the one capsule to Vic. I thought when I threw my hands up, the chute would leave me. But one strap caught on my canteen and was pulled down into the ocean with me. The loss of air on one side of the vest didn't help.

Hutch and I were up for consideration later, or so I was told, for the Soldier's Medal, because we had endangered our own chances of survival when we used the CO_2 capsules to inflate Vic's Mae West. But I guess since Vic didn't survive to need the Mae West later, and Hutch didn't either, the top brass decided we didn't deserve it, or it was just lost in the paper shuffle, as were many recommendations for our men.

Medical records also seemed to get lost or be misplaced after months and years of island hopping and losses of men as well as equipment. Perhaps some Unit Histories or records of flight surgeons' daily notations could provide some evidence to support injuries, treatment and citations of special acts which warranted recognition and consideration later in the life of a serviceman.

Anyway, with only one side inflated of the Mae West, I was not able to stay above the water, due to the weight of my heated suit, the pistol and the canteen.

I took the canteen out of the canvas cover, unsnapped my belt, and let the pistol and belt go. I retained the canteen of water by holding it over my middle finger by the chain attached to the cap and top. I thought the water would come in handy later on if I was to be left out there in the ocean for a long period of time, not located or picked up. I swam as best I could under the circumstances, to stay afloat.

The next problem was not only to stay above the water, but to keep the waves from washing over me, preventing me from taking a breath of air without getting a mouthful of salt water. I found the best way, since the waves were so high, five to ten feet (perhaps higher), was to swim into the coming wave. Facing the waves I found the water raised me up as the cap of the wave went over me, so it was only a few seconds my head was covered by water before the wave lowered me, prior to the next oncoming one.

I was a relatively good swimmer, but had never had any

occasion to swim in an ocean with such huge swells. The best I had ever done was to swim from plant number two of the Glen L. Martin Plant at the junction of the Middle and Back Rivers, which were at the mouth of the Chesapeake Bay near Baltimore over to Dundalk, Maryland. It was a distance of about three miles, but I had two buddies who escorted me across the bay in a row boat, just in case I had trouble getting across.

But this was quite different. The ocean water was not cold, but the waters in the areas around the Solomon Islands are some of the deepest in the world and very rough. I was far from any shore, and virtually alone.

My next worry was sharks. The depth of the water really did not concern me, as people have drowned in a bathtub — but sharks, that's a different story.

I had blood on me. They could attack at any time and I had nothing for protection. I found out later I was not attacked because of the distance we were from the shores of Bougainville, almost 30 miles, while the sharks usually stay within ten miles of the shores and the activities there. An exception is when they follow ships for the garbage or other things sharks find edible that are dumped or dropped overboard.

Since I was the first to bail out, I was some distance from the three small cruisers and eight destroyers we had sighted. I learned later everyone else was picked up a very short time after bail out. I was in the ocean about one and one half hours before finally being sighted by the destroyer, the U.S.S. Claxton, number DD 571.

As I found out later, our tail gunner and assistant radio operator, "Tommy" Thompson had bailed out right after me, but his parachute did not open. I don't know if it was due to shrapnel which had pierced his chute, or if it was due to his own weakness from the wound to his arm. In any event, his falling almost contributed to my own loss of life.

The Captain, later Rear Admiral, Herald F. Stout, informed me they debated whether one or two men had

Rescue At Sea

"Thank God for the U.S. Navy and for the U.S.S. Claxton!" (Left), Rear Admiral (Ret.) Herald Franklin Stout. (Below) The author's drawing of his dramatic bail out from Shehasta. The Claxton searched for 1 1/2 hours before rescuing him.

jumped some distance ahead of them. They had made twelve circular passes looking for me, and had just about given up searching for me for two reasons.

First, the others had all been picked up, and the crew disagreed on whether or not one chute opened or if the airman in the unopened chute was Tommy, who was already lost, or me. Second, the U.S.S. Claxton had left the main body of the task force, losing the protection of the other destroyers and cruisers, exposing the Claxton to possible attack from enemy planes or submarines without any supporting firepower.

Commander Stout decided on one more circular pass before giving up. Thanks to his perseverance, and the risk taken by the crew of the Claxton, I was spotted on the thirteenth pass. I was not to hear about this until years later, from his own lips.

Even more amazing was the numbers of the Claxton, 571, also added up to thirteen. It would seem the number thirteen is an important one in my life, being in the Thirteenth Air Force, too, and a very lucky number for me.

The U.S.S. Claxton had been the first United States Destroyer to reach the South Pacific at Noumea in April 1943. The first "Claxton" was named for Midshipman Thomas Claxton, killed on the U.S.S. Lawrence at the Battle of Lake Erie, 10 September, 1813.

The second "Claxton," DD 571, was launched 1 April 1942 by Consolidated Steel Corporation, Orange, Texas; sponsored by Mrs. A.D. Bernhard, and commissioned 8 December 1942, with Commander Herald F. Stout in command. Commander Stout was in command when I was picked up from the ocean on 11th November 1943.

The Claxton was turned over to the German Navy after World War II, bearing a new number, 0178, serving as Z-4 since December 15, 1959 — loaned under the Military Assistance Program with the Federal Republic of Germany.

It is hard to imagine, waiting for the rescue, but on seeing the destroyer approach, sighting it on rising in the water on a high ocean wave, I worried they would overrun me or still not see me. As it approached, it looked larger than a big building, which it was, and I had a fear of being run over.

But shortly afterward, I saw a whale boat (rescue boat) approaching with three sailors in it. The boat had a motor, and all three men wore life jackets. My first words to them were, "Thank God for the Navy."

One of the men, with a black beard, said, "Where are you from?" I said, "West Virginia."

"I'm from Fairmont," he said.

I said, "I'm from Weston." Weston is about fifty miles south of Fairmont. His name was Hank, or Henry, or something like that. In the excitement, I was too shook up to pay attention or remember. What a coincidence, the first man I talked to out in the large Pacific Ocean was a man from my own area back home. We met only once more on board ship, which was most unfortunate, because he seemed to be a very nice person.

Years later, after he was deceased, I learned his name

Two
Views
of
The
——————————— U. S. S. Claxton ———————————

(Left) After an overhaul in New York shipyards, the Claxton was placed on reserve at Charleston, South Carolina on April 18, 1946. She was to sail again, after she was loaned under the Military Assistance Program to the Federal Republic of Germany on 15 December 1959. Though she was given a new number, her old number, DD571, continues to stand tall in the memories of those who served aboard the ship during World War II. (Right) A scanned image of the Claxton plying South Pacific waters, circa 1942.

was Encil Hawkins. I mentioned the man with the black beard to one of his shipmates who said his nickname on the Claxton was in fact "Blackbeard," and he told me his name.

The second fellow, whom I learned later was named James "Jim" Quinlan, was a very jovial fellow who reminded me of "Popeye," and was a real sailor in every respect. I met him again years later, along with Rear Admiral Herald F. Stout, at a ship's reunion in Anaheim, California. I never learned the third man's name.

My rescue boat returned quickly to the Claxton, where I was hurriedly hoisted to meet the crew and to receive treatment. They wanted to get moving again as fast as possible, just in case the enemy was out there somewhere. As I mentioned, we were pretty far from the other ships.

I was taken immediately to the ship's dispensary, where I was treated for shock, exposure and shrapnel wounds. My back was sprained from the jerk of the parachute, an injury which gave me more trouble later, but for which was denied an application for service related injuries by the Veteran's Administration, a point of much contention — which I still find very disturbing.

The ship's doctor was Walter H. Brown, Lt (JG). He gave me a small dose of hospital brandy and proceeded to examine the extent of my injuries. I was so happy to be rescued that I didn't even know what all he did do at the time. Maybe his medical records would reflect the results.

Shortly after my examination by the doctor, I was informed Whitey Woytowich, our navigator, had been picked up by the Claxton some time earlier and was up on the bridge with Commander Stout.

Someone gave me Navy issue sweat jersey and trousers, with socks and slippers. My clothes and shoes, which had miraculously stayed on my feet through the bail out, were sent to the laundry room to be washed and dried out.

I gave my heated suit to a fellow who was assisting me. His name was Beuford Helms. He had the suit for some time, then sent it to the laundry for cleaning, but it came all apart in the wash, exposing the wires and almost messing up the washer. It obviously was not made for laundering.

Years later, when at the Anaheim Reunion, I laughed to learn what had happened, but I asked Beuford not to comment on how badly that suit needed washing — as scared as I was bailing out, then worrying about sharks, then wondering if I would be abandoned to the deep Pacific Ocean.

I found out later, too, what happened to the rest of the crew. Ralph "Gene" Bruce and Earl B. "Corny" Cornelius were picked up by the U.S.S. Stanley. William "Bill" Humphrey was picked up by a destroyer, too, but I don't know which one.

James "Jim" Jelley, Donald "Don" Taylor, Henry "Hutch" Hutchings and Vic Meehan were in Shehasta when she did a belly-landing in the ocean about twenty miles from Vella LaVella Island, just north of the New Georgia Island Group.

The plane broke in half with Vic going down with her, having expired even before I had left the plane. The top turret came loose and struck Hutch on the head, causing a brain concussion.

Shortly thereafter, Jim, Don and Hutch were picked up by a PBY and returned to Munda on New Georgia, then moved on down to Guadalcanal, and the 42nd Station Hospital there. I visited Hutch in the hospital when I finally got back to the Canal, but he died in the hospital on the 20th of November, 1943.

I had had enough of combat and was looking forward to my return to Guadalcanal with no more action. But the Claxton was attacked the next evening, along with the other ships, by two Japanese torpedo planes. One torpedo went alongside the Claxton, as the plane came from ahead of the bow, just missing us. Another Jap torpedo plane dropped his torpedo so close it went deep enough to pass under our bow, but went on over and hit the Cruiser U.S.S. Denver, killing or wounding twenty of her men.

The Denver was damaged and had to go back to the Russell Islands for temporary repairs. I heard it went back to Hawaii for extensive repair work later.

Commander Stout said to me, "Looks like you jumped from the frying pan into the fire, Son." I agreed. He was very nice, as was the rest of the crew. He spent most of his time on the bridge, sleeping in a bed provided there. He told Whitie and me to use his quarters on the deck.

Commander Stout looked a great deal like Jerry Colona, a fine comedian of that era who worked extensively with Bob Hope in his USO tours during the war. His large mustachioed and large eyed face, with a smile that would melt the heart of any lass, worked well with his comedy routine. I'm sure Commander Stout was also aware of the resemblance, as were his men.

I would be remiss if I did not mention the feeling of pride, and relief, at the sight of the Flag of the United States of America flying from a staff about midway of the ship. Just the sight of it as I approached the Claxton in the rescue boat brought mixed feelings.

First, a feeling of safety — to know I was in the hands of my own countrymen, then, of strength — to know I was fighting on the side of the greatest military might in the whole world, a country I knew would eventually win this struggle, and last, a feeling of pride — a pride in what our country stands for most of all, FREEDOM FOR ALL, more freedom than any other country offers to its people.

Yes, I had placed God first. I had prayed for His forgiveness, even making some commitments that were not so easy to keep later, and which did eventually lead to my acceptance of Him publicly, surrender to Him and Baptism.

I admit I have not kept the faith as strictly as I should, but have no doubt, I will never forget what my God and my Country have done for me. I know that others who were walking along with me through the ordeal of combat at the time felt as I did, for they confirmed it without any reluctance.

I believe that is what makes our people and our nation so strong — our belief in our God and our Country. That is why an atheist who does not believe in a Supreme Being and a coward who does not believe in his flag or country are total failures as human beings and of no worth to their fellowman.

Commander Stout invited Whitie and me up to the bridge to observe, from that vantage point, the movements of the other ships and any activity as we moved along north toward Empress Augusta Bay area of Bougainville.

But when the Jap torpedo planes dropped their torpedoes, they also strafed the deck of the Claxton. I was in the cabin with the ship's doctor, Lt. JG Walter H. Brown, but could hear the machine guns going, as well as the ship's big guns, 3-inch, 40mm, 30mm, plus depth charges and two banks of torpedo tubes on each side of the ship, which would have been used in a surface attack from other ships or submarines. The entire ship vibrated.

Lt. Brown and I started to go out on deck to observe the battle, but he went back into the dispensary, indicating I should follow him. I stayed long enough to see the torpedo planes and their torpedoes that went alongside and under the ship. They did shoot down one of the planes as he pulled away after dropping his torpedo. The other pulled away and headed back toward Bougainville. We were very fortunate that day.

The next day, Commander Stout told us why they were up into the Solomon Islands that far, just off the coast of Central Bougainville. There were forty thousand troops headed up the slot to make a landing at Empress Augusta Bay, establish a beachhead and move inland. This was why Admiral "31 Knot" Burke and his forces were clearing the water up above Bougainville of any movement south by the Japanese navy from New Britain, New Ireland, New Guinea or other northern bases.

In fact, before we were picked up and brought back to the Russell Islands, Burke's task force had been up the slot and engaged the Japanese Navy in the battle of Empress Augusta Bay and another in the battle of Cape St. George. They were awarded the Presidential Unit Citation for their performance.

I then understood why General Douglas MacArthur had issued the order to "neutralize the air fields and harbors at Rabaul with all men and planes expendable until the mission was accomplished." While a harsh order, what were two- to four-hundred men and their planes when it was necessary to protect forty-thousand troops. After that, I never was much to question a decision of my President, our Commander in Chief, or any lesser Command Officers, because I realized they always know what is best for the whole, having a more thorough knowledge of the mission to be accomplished.

It does not pay to criticize those in the know, when we have limited knowledge. The same is true in other areas of life, I have found, for it is easy to be an "arm chair quarter-back" — of a football game or any other game in life. It is quite different when you *are* the quarterback.

Whitie and I were let off the Claxton after stopping at Rendova, then proceeding to the northern side of the Russells, where a P.T. Boat carried us ashore. We walked across the island, which was difficult and painful for both of us, along a small jungle trail that had been cleared for jeeps.

We caught another P.T. Boat to Tulagi where the P.T. Base was located.

We were in the same area that future President John F. Kennedy had his experience in P.T. 109. That part of the Pacific was an area of activity for many well known airmen, soldiers and sailors who later rose to fame and fortune.

We then caught a ride on a Patrol Boat to Guadalcanal. Five days had passed since Shehasta had left for Rabaul on the 11th of November, 1943.

My mother had been notified first by a telegram delivered by the Red Cross Lady in our town, Mrs. Zobrist, that I was "Missing in Action." It was another five days before she received a telegram indicating I was alive and wounded in action, though the nature of the wounds was not specified.

So she worried until she received a letter from me telling her I was not seriously wounded — no loss of limbs, eyesight, or any of the other things a mother, or a loved one, can imagine. Even then, I'm sure she was not real sure I was all right until she saw me personally, much later, upon my return from overseas.

Guess who met Whitie and me at the Patrol Boat Base on Guadalcanal? Yes — Jim Jelley and Don Taylor.

Jim had his arm in a sling and his leg bandaged, but he was driving the jeep. We jumped right in it and headed back to the 307th Bombardment Group at Carney Field. We were taken to the 42nd Station Hospital for a checkup, treatment as needed, and released.

The next day, Corny, Humphrey and I went over to see Henry Hutchings. He could not hear due to either the concussion or some other problem, nor could he talk, but he knew us and squeezed our hands to let us know he knew us. He died November 20th. The losses of our crew were very severe as a result of our strike on Rabaul.

We were grounded pending evacuation to the 39th General Hospital at Auckland, New Zealand. Other crews on subsequent strikes who had been shot up, or partially lost (as ours was) were there with us, and were also airlifted to New

Zealand. Some of the men I knew or met were Red McCarthy, Daniels and McGee. Helmuth Schultz and Salvadore Fatigato were also along on the flight.

A few of the men stayed with us for a month and were eventually returned to the States on a troop ship, the U.S.S. Seabarb. Others were sent back to Guadalcanal and took part in further strikes on Rabaul and Truk Island. These crews usually were short on the number of missions.

During one mission briefing I attended while waiting for further evacuation, one crew member who was sitting on a railing in the operations room, suddenly fainted and fell off the railing onto the floor when the first strike on Truk Island was announced. The thought of the distance, and no fighter cover, was too much for him. I don't believe he made the mission.

Part of Goodin's crew had also been evacuated to the 39th General Hospital. They had been shot up a few days after our Rabaul mission in a strike on Buka Island and Buka Passage. Ben Pudder, Mike Reeder, Pete Peterson and Joe Jamison had been lost, either prior to or during a water landing in the ocean just a short distance from the Shortland Islands. The others were picked up by a PBY. They were lucky to be picked up, because the area was still held by the Japs.

It is interesting to note, again, how we seemed to ignore or refused to accept the loss of our crew members and other buddies. In my diary, as I read it many years later, it was amazing how a loss was accepted so matter of factly, without further comment, almost as if it didn't happen.

Blocking it out of the mind was a defense set up to help cope with our losses. Any memory of the incident or the loss would result in anger with the enemy, and a sworn purpose to get even. To reflect on it any further could have developed an incapacitating fear, rendering our effectiveness as a member of a combat crew useless.

CHAPTER 10

FAREWELL TO THE LIBERATORS

Goodbye To Good Buddies

The author, Savadore Fatigato from Ratti's crew, "Red" McCarthy from Hansen's crew and Earl B. Cornelius, all at the 39th General Hospital in Auckland following action in the Solomon's and Rabaul. Ratti's crew had made a second run on Rabaul Harbor with us due to bombs hanging up in their plane, or perhaps a good target on the run. Ratti's crew followed us after we were hit and provided protection for us on our return. Hansen's crew was on the Rabaul mission, too, on November 11, 1943.

Before we left Guadalcanal, some interesting things occurred I will tell you about because they show just how things are in combat situations.

One guy that was good at metal work had developed a small hobby into a money making venture. He was making watch bands out of the aluminum taken from the Jap planes (or perhaps our own) that were shot down, or damaged beyond repair, over Guadalcanal. To make them sound more interesting, he always told the metal was from enemy planes.

Prior to my last mission, I had given him my watch to make a band to fit my wrist. He had measured for it. Also, he was to replace a scratched crystal with plexiglass from one of the planes. But upon my return to the 307th, when I went to pick up my watch, he had sold it because he was told I had been lost and would not be returning. He had to go to the guy who bought it and buy it back for me. This was no problem because he had been in that position before and no one wanted to keep something that was not actually available to buy. I have it to this day, having bought it in Auckland, New Zealand on rest leave.

Also, all my clothes and personal effects had been gathered up in a duffel bag, locked and prepared for shipment back to my family in West Virginia, as were the other missing crew members' effects. I had to leave the accordion that I was learning to play and sold it for twenty dollars, about one fourth its value. Many of the photographs I had taken and developed in the 307th Photo Lab were lost or fell into other hands before I got back to Carney Field. These I did not recover, although some were saved — the ones that were personal and packed for shipment.

I had a chance to tell Ira Jackson, of Byrd's crew, and some of our other buddies good-bye. Byrd's crew was one of the fortunate ones that came through a tour in relatively good shape. Ratti's crew also survived, the last I heard.

I was told later, and have little reason to doubt it, that of the original twenty B-24 Liberators leaving Topeka, Kansas, a total of two hundred men, only twenty seven of the original crews survived, excluding replacements coming later. It may have been better, but it was hard to be sure because many Liberators were lost. New replacement crews, as well as survivors from broken crews continued to fly to their destiny — survival or death.

As the new replacement crews kept coming in, perhaps five of the replacement planes and crews were lost before one of our older crews met a similar fate. Some portions of crews were injured or killed and replaced, too. Three of our own crew were replaced prior to our raid on Rabaul, when Meehan, Thompson and Hutchings were lost, and Griff Griffith was lost on a night raid.

I do know, out of the twenty that came down to Guadalcanal over a short period of time to the 424th Bomb Squadron, we were the seventeenth plane and crew to be lost. Ratti's crew, Byrd's crew, and I believe Hansen's crew, or parts of these crews, were still there when we were shot down.

Joe Binder and his crew had just joined us, as I recall, and made raids up into 1944 on Rabaul, Truk and other northern targets in the South Pacific on the way to the liberation of the Philippines. He had brought the plane — "Little Mick" — down about that time from the States, but turned it over to another crew, flying the break-in runs with some of the old timers already there.

Joe later had an incendiary bomb explode in his bomb bay over Rabaul, and lost one of his crew who bailed out. He was reportedly a Jap prisoner in the camp with Pappy Boyington, but it was never confirmed when Binder talked to Boyington at Oshkosh, Wisconsin. Pappy did not remember the crewman.

Much of survival was due to training and experience, if you survived long enough to get experience. But another important factor was luck, being in the right place or in a wrong place at a particular time. I do not know what part a belief in God and prayers to Him made, but I'm sure my own belief made a difference as far as I was concerned. He was called upon many times by us all, in our own way, some very openly, some privately, but always when we faced near or certain death. Very few were too proud to admit a need for help from the Almighty God, to trust in His Judgement and ask for His forgiveness of unkept promises.

We said good-bye to all our good buddies, perhaps never to see them again, except for the lucky ones we did get to see years later at reunions.

Once again, we were given complete physical and mental examinations, testing for the extent of injuries. After a traumatic experience such as our crew had been subjected to, it was not at all unusual to be processed for return to the United States. Besides, we had many more than the expected missions to qualify for return.

We looked forward to the trip south to Auckland again, and did not know if we would be coming back to Guadalcanal, or perhaps to Munda on New Georgia, which was rumored to be our next move north.

Our visits to Auckland while in the 39th General Hospital did not result in the same kind of successful pleasures as the July rest leave. We were limited to short passes, but were able to go into Auckland on a few visits. We went swimming at a well-used beach called Milford Beach, a popular picnic and swimming area. But we were too excited about the prospect of returning home and very happy to have survived our combat tour.

Most of us were bothered by the question of why some were lucky and came through the ordeal while many others did not, but we didn't dwell on that question too long. Only later, as with delayed stress syndrome (a modern term for frayed nerves as a result of combat), did the question come back to haunt us, and perhaps contribute to many sleepless nights, as well as some unstable actions and decisions, with detrimental results to many who served their country in vicious combat against the enemy.

After a month of rest, relaxation and examinations, we were all placed on the "return to States" list, except Jim Jelley who insisted on a return to Guadalcanal. I do not know the wisdom of that decision, but I do know he made some additional missions after the rest of us returned to the United States.

Later, I learned he returned to the States and flew C-54 transport planes for the Military Air Transport Service (MATS), served through Korea and went to Viet Nam, too! I can say he was a very exceptional, patriotic and brave pilot with expert background obtained from actual experience. No other pilot could have done a better or more courageous job of bringing us back from the Rabaul mission, or the other close calls we had over the period of time our crew flew with him in training and combat.

I would just as soon forget our return to the States on the U.S.S. Seabarb, one of the so called "Liberty Ships", or troop ships. It was seventeen days of bad food and poor treatment.

The ship was overcrowded. For some reason there was hardly any food — except hard boiled eggs every day. I don't believe there was a cook on board, or so it seemed. We would go up in the morning from the hold where we slept, crowded together like sardines, to get some fresh air and a cleaner place to sleep on deck.

The highlight of the whole trip was the crossing of the Equator and International Date Line. One of the men dressed-up like King Neptune. He was crowned and an initiation was performed as we crossed the Equator. It did create some fun on an otherwise uneventful trip which left much to be desired.

There was some gambling and fighting, as a result of cheating at cards in the quarters below deck, seasickness, and homesickness, too.

I got into a gambling game of Put-N-Take with some New Zealand Airmen going to Canada for advanced flight training on British Bombers and Fighters. They had a small top that had four sides numbered one to four, which was spun around and around on the deck. When the top slowed down to a stop and fell, those who bet on the number which was on the top side won. Of course, if four played, three of the players had to lose. Others also bet on the side as observers.

I lost forty dollars before I realized I couldn't win against the odds if the other three players were together and splitting the winnings. They had me outnumbered three to one. At

Medals

(Top) Members of the 307th Bombardment Group (HV) receive medals for heroic action against the Japanese in 1943 at Carney Field, Guadalcanal. (Above Left) The Author receiving the Distinguished Flying Cross from General Oliver at MacDill Air Force Base, Tampa, Florida in 1944. (Above Right) Colonel D.B. Faust, Commanding Officer of Battey General Hospital, Rome, Georgia presents medals to crew members from 307th Bomb Group. (L-R) Col. Faust, the author, Michael A. Venezia, Earl B. Cornelius and William F. Humphrey. The author, Humphrey and Cornelius recieved Purple Hearts. Venezia received the Air Medal with Oak Leaf, as did the author.

that time, forty dollars was a large amount of money — a month's pay if you were not on flying status.

Many passengers became seasick, especially in the choppy waters close to shore at New Zealand, and again when we approached the coast of the United States. I didn't get seasick, perhaps due to being accustomed to flying, but the action at sea is somewhat different — a rolling motion rather than the gravitational ups and downs of an aircraft. But I will admit to being somewhat queasy at times.

The greatest sight was the Golden Gate Bridge coming into view out of the fog, or haze, which blanketed the coast line as we approached San Francisco and the Bay. When we finally debarked, many of the men cried and kissed the cement dock, not even waiting to get to the soil and grass. That was a sight to see, too.

We were immediately boarded on buses and taken to Letterman General Hospital in San Francisco. Within a week we were sent to Battey General Hospital at Rome, Georgia. In the transfer were members of the B-24 Liberators Shehasta and Phantom Lady. They included Cornelius, Humphrey and me, as well as Mike Venesia, Lew Lewis, Lefty Leftowitz, Phil Tabor and Dave Davison.

Corny, Humphrey, Venesia and I received Purple Heart Medals from Colonel D.B. Faust, Commander of the Hospital. Three of us received Air Medals, too. Paperwork for Goodin's crew had not arrived. The orders on my Distinguished Flying Cross did not catch up with me until I had been transferred to MacDill Field, Tampa, Florida.

One of our men met a beautiful young lady while on pass to Rome, Georgia, and their relationship developed very quickly into talk of marriage. With no waiting period for blood tests in the next county, we went with them one evening and they were married by a justice of the peace.

I don't know what the result of that union was, but at the time, both swore they were in love, and who were we to put a stop to romance? It was probably the fastest marriage I had ever taken part in witnessing. Based on some long term romances, it had an equal chance of survival, I found out later.

All of the surviving enlisted members of Phantom Lady and Shehasta were given rest leaves at Miami Beach, Florida. That city was also a redistribution station.

I am reminded, while there, Corny, Humphrey and I were in the President Madison Hotel. All of the hotels were very plush, with not only the beach behind the hotels, but fresh water pools were also within the area owned and operated by each hotel. We enjoyed ourselves very much.

We were short on money, though, and had a difficult time getting extra money for the essential items such as soap, towels, etc., because our records hadn't arrived from Battey General Hospital yet.

We went to the Red Cross and found we had to itemize every little thing we needed just to get ten dollars to carry us over until our pay records arrived. That incident soured me, and the others, for any future contributions to that agency, even until now.

However, we went down the street to the Salvation Army (which was noted even then for coming through in a pinch) and received a donation without any problems whatsoever. Of course, even overseas, the Red Cross went first class — officers uniforms, vehicles and all, but still taking up collections when they served a cup of coffee.

While the Red Cross was taking credit for the task of notifying next of kin at home of wounded and killed, or prisoners of war and missing in action, all of which was channeled out of Washington and the War Department, we were receiving free coffee and donuts, as well as personal items we needed, from the Salvation Army. They also met the troop trains and troop ships along the way into battle. So you know how I feel about that, as do many other Airmen, Soldiers, Sailors and Marines.

Corny and I went to Miami while on rest leave at Miami Beach. The first trip proved interesting and the second trip even more so when we wound up in the park. We met two girls and asked if they would like to go to the show with us. Both agreed and we went to the Hippodrome Theatre to see a live show consisting of magic, dance and patriotic themes.

We had seats very close to the front of the theatre, about the third row. As a part of the show, the master of ceremonies told some jokes and asked for a volunteer lady from the audience to assist him with some of the tricks and patriotic parts of the show. Guess what? The girl with me was selected and after some urging, did go up on the stage and helped with the program. She was very attractive and the showman complimented her — and me on my wise choice of companionship as she came back to her seat.

We had dinner later and parted company, heading back to the President Madison at Miami Beach. That was the last we saw of the ladies, sorry to say, but we did have a good time at the show.

The next evening, Corny and I went to the USO in downtown Miami, where we met two new and charming ladies.

I wish now to compliment the United Service Organization (USO) for their fine job throughout World War II, Korea and Viet Nam, especially for their shows with name stars such as Bob Hope, and for the companionship provided at their canteens along the way.

The young ladies we met had a mission to help entertain the servicemen and to help them forget the battles they had left overseas. We were very pleased to have their company, until one of them suggested it would be nice to go to the fine, patriotic show advertised at the local Hippodrome Theatre. How were we to tell them we had already seen it the night before, without perhaps losing the benefit of their cheerful and very promising company, especially since we had gone with two other girls? So, we went along with their suggestion, and desires.

When we entered the theatre, Corny managed to guide his friend into a row of seats perhaps ten rows back from the stage. However, my young lady friend was very enthusiastic about getting up close to the stage. Being very attractive, she was getting me deeper into a bad situation.

Guess what? That's right! The showman looked down at the front rows and said, "I need a beautiful volunteer for this part of the program. Sergeant," pointing his finger at me, "how about that beautiful lady with you?"

Being complimented, she quickly jumped up and headed for the steps at the side of the stage, dressed in her bobby socks and pretty red, white and blue skirt and blouse that showed off her voluptuous form, just ideal for the situation. She performed her part well. After the windup of the last part of the show, the showman thanked her and looked down at me and said, "I thank you, too, Sergeant. By the way, she doesn't look like the girl you had with you last night... Oh, my lands, I'm sorry!"

Everyone laughed, thinking he was just joking. But as the laughter died down, I could hear someone behind me, loudly, hysterically and uncontrollably laughing, completely broken up by what had happened. I knew who it was, and I knew his lady friend must have wondered what was going on with him. I had turned very red in the face, completely embarrassed, perhaps more than at any other time before or after that incident.

Corny continued to laugh loudly and finally got up with his friend and went out into the lobby to wait for us. When we joined them, he was still laughing, and by then I was getting pretty hot about his behavior. I don't know if he told his friend why he broke up with laughter, but I do know when we went to a fast food restaurant to eat after the show, the girls went to the wash room. We waited for them for some time, but when they had stayed much longer than the ex-pected time, we guessed it. They had slipped out a side door and left us "sitting," another form of "stood up." I couldn't blame them, considering Corny's actions. But being the good buddy he was, I never doubted he had not shared his secret with his date, but concluded the girls had guessed the awful truth of the situation — the showman was **not** joking!

The next evening we went to the Frolic Danceland, home of renown bands, where Ina Ray Hutton and her all lady dance band performed. Corny and I had our pictures taken and autographed by Miss Hutton.

Miami Beach served as a redistribution station as I mentioned previously, as well as a recreation and processing point for overseas Army Air Corps returnees, so we were pretty up tight about our next duty assignment. But as luck would have it, most of the enlisted crew who were survivors of the combat duty were sent to MacDill Field, Tampa, Florida.

Corny was sent to the Pas de Grill Hotel near St. Petersburg, Florida, which was not too far from Tampa, for further rest and relaxation. I visited him once. I have never seen or heard from him since. Neither have I heard from Julius T. Woytowich or William "Bill" Humphrey. I have tried to locate them to no avail. Some members of the Phantom Lady came to MacDill Field, too.

MacDill Field was a phase training base for B-17 Flying Fortresses headed for Europe. I had heard much about the bombers from accounts of their missions in Europe, but had not had an occasion to fly on them.

Immediately upon assignment to a Squadron, I was placed back on flying status as an aerial gunnery instructor on the B-17's. My experience and record as a ball turret gunner with the 307th Bombardment Group on Guadalcanal contributed to receiving that assignment in March 1944.

I liked being back on flying status and life began to return to normal, the same as before we left the States to go to the South Pacific.

So I left the old buddies who had been on my crew flying on Shehasta, and began a new adventure on B-17's, flying with many inexperienced pilots and crews, just going through the initial training that was required before being sent to European assignments. It was a new beginning I looked forward to with pleasure. But I was to find it represented a new time for excitement.

Just before starting the new assignment, I was given a

ten day leave to see my family at Weston, West Virginia. Everyone welcomed me with open arms, and I saw some girls and school buddies who were still home for some reason or another. But everyone was all patriotism, and since my combat record had been in the local papers, I even had an opportunity to speak to some service groups.

Perhaps the happiest person was my mother, who seemed to doubt I had all my limbs and eyes, and was in good physical and mental shape after receiving the telegrams I was missing in action, then later , just wounded, with minor injuries. My father took it all pretty well, too. I had an opportunity to visit a town to the north of Weston where I saw a young lady who had been of great interest to me before leaving for the service, and to whom I was engaged and eventually married. But that is another story, long after my missions in Shehasta.

I did forgive the American Red Cross long enough to speak on their behalf to the local glass plants and service organizations, such as the Lions, Rotary and Kiwanis, to tell the need for buying War Bonds and helping the Red Cross, too. I did this because the lady who represented the Red Cross was so nice to my family when taking them the telegrams. But it was difficult to forget the incident in Miami Beach.

It was on that visit I almost had a fight with Bill Nolan when he stood in the local drug store and bragged about not going to service because he had obtained a deferment to do farm work.

That wasn't so bad, but when he made fun of other guys going to do their duty and said, "I'd rather be a live coward than a dead hero," I lost my temper and would have worked him over right there, if it were not for some intervention by the owner of the store and some other men who were there. But he wasn't too well thought of after that incident, even by others who stayed home for legitimate reasons.

I could not help thinking about my friends on my crew who had lost their lives, and others lost in combat. It is still sickening to think some persons have so little regard for their country and their flag, who would give in to an enemy, or trample our flag, or even burn it. They are traitors — to their country, to their families, and to themselves! THANK GOD FOR PATRIOTS!!

A Time To Remember

(Above) They were the only two children of Fannie and Francis Hutchings. Norman Hutchings 1/C Water Tender in the U.S. Navy, killed on November 30, 1942, and his brother, Henry E. Hutchings, who died on Nov. 20, 1943 from wounds received on our Nov. 11 raid on Rabaul. Their bodies were returned for burial at their home in Eatonton, Georgia in 1948. It was an emotional time for all of us. (Left) The funeral was the first time I had seen Ira Jackson since our days on Guadalcanal.

About God, Country, Democracy and Patriots

"Proclaim liberty throughout all the land unto all the inhabitants thereof." Inscription on the Liberty Bell

"Do your duty in all things. You cannot do more. You should never wish to do less." Robert E. Lee

"Worth, courage, honor — these indeed your sustenance and birthright are." E.C. Stedman

"We have room for but one loyalty, loyalty to the United States." Theodore Roosevelt

"When we assumed the soldier, we did not lay aside the citizen." George Washington

"Independence now and independence forever." Daniel Webster

"Even God lends a hand to honest boldness." Menander

"The right is more precious than peace." Woodrow Wilson

"Resistance to tyrants is obedience to God." Thomas Jefferson

"Patriotism is a lively sense of collective responsibility." Richard Aldinton

Americanism consists of utterly believing in the principles of America." Woodrow Wilson

"Loyalty is the holiest good in the human heart." Seneca

"There is no record in the history of a nation that ever gained anything valuable by being unable to defend itself." H. L. Meneken

"We have room in this country for but one flag, the Stars and Stripes." Theodore Roosevelt

"He who would save liberty must put his trust in democracy." Norman Thomas

"He serves me most, who serves his country best." Homer

"He who loves not his country, can love not." Byron

"The nation's honor is dearer than the nation's comfort." Wilson

"Don't spread patriotism too thin." Theodore Roosevelt

"He loves his country best who strives to make it best." R. G. Ingersoll

"A courage mightier than the sun—you rose and fought and, fighting won!" Angela Morgan

"The chief bond of the soldier is his oath of allegiance and his love for the flag." Seneca

"Freedom exists only where the people take care of the government." Woodrow Wilson

"O America! Because you build for mankind, I build for you!" Walt Whitman

"Fate only picks on the cowards and quitters; So give em both barrels—and aim for the eyes." Grantland Rice

"One man with courage make a majority." Andrew Jackson

CHAPTER 11

SEPARATE WAYS

New Beginnings & Endings

The author (left) and Corny in the "Frolic Danceland Club" in Miami, Florida. We were on rest leave at the Redistribution Station. April, 1944.

While moving about the base I saw two old buddies, Paul "Lefty" Leftowitz and Dave Davison occasionally. Lefty was working in engineering on engine maintenance and Dave was assigned to turret maintenance, as well as some armament on bomb racks, etc. Neither was flying anymore. And from their comments, I believe they were happy to leave it that way.

We discussed some of the fun things going on from time to time at MacDill and in Tampa. We rode the ferry boat across to Davis Island and went across the bridge to downtown Tampa together to look things over. As a result, we shared a few experiences.

Training of the gunners on B-17's was quite interesting, as well as hazardous. We flew over the Gulf of Mexico to practice air to water gunnery. We had cameras mounted on the guns which took pictures of the floating targets which the gunners were hitting — or missing — when they pulled the triggers to fire their guns.

After we had been out on the firing range, shooting from turrets and waist guns from about four hundred feet up, depending on the pilot or copilot at the controls, we would have a class in which we viewed the pictures. In this way we could discuss how to improve their accuracy.

Part of my job was to check turrets, guns, ammunition and cameras prior to each gunnery mission. The target area was outlined by large floating signs stating the area was restricted to boats of any type, with large lettering which read, "WARNING, RESTRICTED AREA, GUNNERY RANGE."

A very disturbing incident occurred shortly after I started as an instructor. A very immature young pilot, who had little regard for himself or the safety of his crew, began to show his lack of responsibility shortly after take-off.

I had flown with good pilots, and I knew the difference between proficient and reckless flying. This guy was definitely reckless.

But I was assigned as the gunnery instructor, so I proceeded to go through the training steps with the gunners, preparing them for when we would approach the floating targets in the restricted area of the range.

While flying to and from the range, the pilot was in command, and of course, even on the range his authority was superior, but I had the right to challenge the actions of any of the crew when it threatened the safety of others and of myself, regardless of the rank, and especially where operation of the turrets and guns were concerned.

When we made the runs over the targets, it was up to

the pilot to maintain a safe altitude, usually between four and eight hundred feet above the water. This still provided a safe distance from the target, yet was closer than any crew member would want to see an enemy aircraft approach their plane.

We would usually make a somewhat flat banking turn to give the top turret gunner an opportunity to take some shots at the targets, too, but his targets were usually some distance away in relation to those of the nose, tail, ball and waist gunners.

On one pass over the targets, a ball turret gunner had a link hang up, jammed his gun and was unable to free it. Sometimes the inexperienced gunner would break the link, but this was easy to correct. However, if it jammed, the cover plate was difficult to raise, and the bolt hard to pull back with the charging handle.

This gunner put the guns in a downward vertical position, opened the exit door and climbed out so I could enter and try to clear the link. I climbed into the turret, fastened the safety belt, but left the exit door open, so the student gunner could see what I was doing.

I finally got it freed and placed the belt of 50 caliber bullets back into the gun. Then I closed the door, raised the guns to a more horizontal position to test fire the guns on the next pass over the targets.

The turret was fixed on the azimuth ring permanently and did not raise up into the fuselage as with the B-24, which had a hydraulic lift lever to bring it up high enough to permit a landing without scraping the surface of the runway. The B-17 was high enough to clear the runway with the ball turret down in a fixed position.

As I came around to aim at the target, I heard the pilot say, "Pilot to ball gunner, see if you can read the small print on that sign down there."

He was approaching much too low, and I could see one wing was low. Just as the spray from the gulf waters began to come over the ball turret, I realized we were so low we could clobber in if the wing tip touched the water. I yelled, using my throat mike, "Get this plane up, you're too low! This is the gunnery instructor! I'm in the ball!"

By that time, we were climbing again. I said, "Head for MacDill!"

He had brought the plane up just in time, but not before some of the spray from the props had come back over the turret. I WAS SCARED!

I called the gunners out of their positions at the turrets and guns at the waist, and we headed home.

When we got back I made a report to the Major in charge of training. The next day, I was asked to report formally on the incident, which I did, but the brass continued to let the Second Lieutenant fly with his crew. The copilot chose not to take issue with what the pilot had done on the gunnery mission.

I was ordered to report to the flight surgeon for evaluation of my flying status. As it turned out, the flight surgeon had returned from the 307th Bomb Group on Guadalcanal just a short time before, and he had been on the Canal when our crew was shot down.

He was aware of my having bailed out, and the circumstances of our Rabaul raid. He said in view of my rough time in the ocean, and having had the experience of bailing out, perhaps I needed a few days off from flying, and grounded me for a couple of weeks.

He had served in one of the other Squadrons when Captain Groth was my flight surgeon, in the 424th, knew we had lost part of our crew, and in consideration of that fact, I could well understand his decision. But it was a fatal one.

Just two weeks later — to the day — that same pilot and his crew were lost while flying on a training flight along the Gulf Coast southward from MacDill. They were off the coast again, flying too low over the ocean, when the pilot dipped one wing, touched the water, and cartwheeled, breaking up and resulting in the loss of the ten men on the crew and the B-17 Flying Fortress.

This time, there were other B-17's on the flight close enough to observe what had happened. Needless to say, I was placed back on flying status the next day by the flight surgeon, with his apologetic statement that he should have listened to me and grounded the pilot instead, who turned out to be a hot -rodding sky jockey who had no business with the responsibility that had been entrusted with him.

That was one of the problems in flying with new pilots and crews. Their inexperience increased the risks, just as phase training was costly at Alamogordo, Clovis and Tucson, when our own crews were in training. Our losses of B-24's in Alamogordo, for example, were sometimes compared to combat losses.

Another incident I had during my time as an aerial gunnery instructor involved a ball turret gunner who was also too smart to listen to good advice, but the results were not so devastating.

After getting close to the target area, I gave him instructions for getting into the turret, which began by manually lowering the guns to gain access to the turret. Then, open the exit hatch door, climb in, fasten the safety belt, which went behind his back and which I observed him doing prior to his reaching up on each side of the door and fastening it. The handles were painted red, and operated from both sides of the door, inside and out, so I could observe whether or not he did latch it properly.

He was not wearing a chest pack but did have on a harness which could accommodate a parachute, with rings to snap the chute onto, if needed.

To wear a parachute or not, was usually optional with the turret operator in the ball turret because of the small space of the turret. A big man just could not ride the ball turret, and even I, at 119 pounds, did not choose to wear one. At most times, the harness was not very comfortable.

The choice also depended on how one felt down there swinging around, with the possibility of the hydraulic or electrical systems going out. It was more critical in combat.

Further, the gunner's feelings about the plane, the pilot and purpose of the mission had a lot to do with making the decision.

The turret usually attracted the guys who wanted to see it all, from the water or ground up, and it was like having your own little roller coaster down there, ups and downs, and around and around. You could ask anyone who flew one, or other crew members who chose not to fly in one, and they could still tell you their feelings about it now.

With the guns straight down, they were also clear of the gun wells, which were to the rear of the plane, and allowed the turret guns to be stowed up close to the fuselage on landings and take-offs. You never stayed in the turret during that time, so you had to know how to exit quickly in event an emergency developed on the plane.

Or if you had your chute on, you could turn the guns forward and vertical, which provided enough clearance for you to unhook your safety belt, unlatch the door and push yourself out into space. But I never did cherish the thought of doing that, and never did consider that option.

After getting into the turret and unlocking the safety latches, you could then turn on the master switches to all electricity and open the hydraulic lines (on the B-24), then connect your oxygen hose and throat mike for talking (which left your hands free), plug in your heated suit and test your guns with a short burst after pulling back the charging handle on each gun.

All this kept you pretty busy for a time immediately after entering the turret. Set your rheostat to the correct lighting on your sight and you were ready for the range and/or combat.

On this particular training mission, the student gunner pulled the door shut and suddenly I heard the power come on and the gunner bring up the guns to the front position. I called him on the intercom, but he ignored my call or he had failed to plug in his earphones.

I believe he did put on the earphones and throat mike

because that was the one thing I emphasized to all students entering a turret, and therefore he had ignored my call to come back up into the plane.

He had failed to make sure his hatch door was locked properly before turning on his switches. Instead, he had swung the turret around with the door to the rear, creating a certain amount of suction on the door, sufficient to cause it to open and fall downward. That caught his attention!

He still didn't hear my frantic call to him, "Instructor to ball turret. Come up, come up. Lock your door, lock your door!"

Feeling the air at his back, daylight coming in, he panicked. He pushed forward on the controls, bringing his turret up and snapping off the door when it hit the azimuth ring. It broke loose and fell away. When he got up far enough he started to get out. I pushed him back down into the turret, reached down and locked it in place. Had that not been done, the turret could have swung back down, decapitating him, or at best, injuring his back.

He didn't take time to turn off the power switch, but of course, when he let loose of the control handles the dead man switches in the controls shut off all electric power to the turret. He tried to get out with his safety belt still fastened. He was white as a sheet. I helped him and he wasted no time getting out, after I unfastened his safety belt.

On return to base, I did not have to recommend he be grounded — he couldn't quit flying soon enough.

That experience gave me a good story to tell new turret jockeys who felt they didn't need to study or listen to the instructions prior to using the turret in the air. They did have a mock-up to practice on prior to actually flying the turret in the air, but for some reason, things always happen differently in actual situations. The suction of the air, for example, would not come into play at all in a turret used for training purposes on the ground.

Even other hazards presented the first time in the air have greater meaning to a new crew member. Training to develop team spirit and cooperation can only be developed under simulated combat conditions. The constant search for enemy planes, aircraft identification, reporting of sightings by the crew using the clock system, could only be developed in the air and with real experience.

I enjoyed the experience and the assignment, but not the risks of inexperienced crews. To complicate matters, weather and mechanical problems added to the hazards.

Those who were more proficient were already over in Europe or in the South Pacific keeping the planes flying.

After ten months of instructing, I finally put in for engineering or radio training, thinking of the advantages of a profession outside the military. Aerial gunners were not in demand in civilian life, nor were armorers. Guns and bombs would not be the thing after the war.

I was transferred to Wichita Falls, Texas, for reassignment to Scott Field, Belleville, Illinois.

But before leaving MacDill Field, Lefty and Dave filled me in on some of their experiences. They were almost as interesting as my own.

Dave had an assignment every two weeks on the flight line at the supply room where the parachutes, Mae West Life Vests, watches and other flight equipment was checked out to the crews. These were issued to crew members as needed before a flight and then returned after a mission. This duty was sometimes on night shift, from midnight until eight in the morning.

One evening, Dave got sleepy and dozed off while laying on the counter in front of the supply room, which made it impossible for anyone to get past him to the supplies. But sleeping on duty was still a court martial offense if you were caught and reported. The door to the supply room could not be opened without lifting a part of the counter top, so I guess Dave felt safe.

A very pretty little Corporal WAC (Women's Army Corps) came into supply to check and see if one of her friends had turned in his supplies from an overnight flight.

But finding Dave sacked out, she punched her finger into his ribs to wake him. Dave, a Staff Sergeant reacted violently by swinging his fist outward, catching the Corporal right in the eye, and knocking her down.

She hit up against the back wall of the supply room first and sunk to the floor. Dave jumped off the counter and started to help her up as she struggled in a dazed condition. As soon as she regained her composure, she became very angry and indignant, threatening to report Dave for sleeping on duty.

Dave apologized and asked her not to report him. Seeing his ribbons, and realizing he was just back from combat overseas, she must have thought it over and decided to become more civil to Dave. She said she shouldn't have punched him in the ribs, either.

Dave liked her looks and asked her if he could buy her a piece of pie and coffee later when he got off duty. She agreed.

Her eye did get black, and she had a hard time explaining it, but he said, she seemed proud of it when the others kidded her, saying they ought to see the other guy.

Dave implied all went well. They found their way later up on the walkway above the planes in one of the hangars that was being worked on in the daylight hours. Dave said the walkway was pretty hard, but her soft body melting close to his made it all worthwhile.

She was shipped out on another assignment not long after that, and Dave was still trying to get over that experience.

Lefty also had a situation develop that he fell into quite innocently. He developed a friendship with a very cute little lady who worked in the Base Commissary. She had an apartment across the bay at Davis Island. There was convenient transportation on the ferry that many of the servicemen rode, as well as the workers at the Field. Lefty met her while crossing the bay on the ferry.

She lived with another girl who worked at the Base

Hospital. I had a couple of dates with her roommate, so I knew the girl Lefty was talking about, and the location of the apartment. But Lefty became very involved with Melody Markley.

Melody and Lefty became close, and even shared the apartment when possible. They lounged about on the shore of the bay, a common practice in the evenings by lovers. The next thing I knew they were talking of engagement and even of marriage.

However, when I received orders to ship out, it turned out Lefty received his, too. We traveled together to Wichita Falls, Texas.

But when Lefty went into the apartment to tell Melody of his transfer, he got the shock of his life — even more traumatic to him than his combat experiences, or just as bad. She told him she had something very important to tell him. No, she wasn't pregnant, though that was the first thing that came into his mind. He was prepared for that, and would have married her.

To Lefty it was worse, but better that she wasn't pregnant, too. Melody was already married. Her husband only had a year to complete his training as a doctor of chiropractic. He was in the navy stationed overseas at Tripoli, North Africa.

She told Lefty she wanted to go with him, would divorce her husband and follow him to Wichita Falls. Lefty was too stunned to answer, but he said he would never let that happen. She had not been fair to him, or even honest with her husband. Over the months they had been so close and shared so much, it was a real blow to Lefty. He was thankful she was not pregnant, and was relieved that the farce of an engagement had not become a fact of marriage.

Lefty told her to forget him, play fair with her husband and left immediately for Texas, never to see or hear from her again. Lefty had a pretty tough time getting back into any female relationships again. His distrust was to last for some time, until he got settled in at Scott Field.

Lefty expected to enter training for maintenance on B-29's. Instead, he was assigned to Scott Field, Belleville, Illinois, just as I was, and we both served the balance of our time before the end of the war and demobilization as Military Policemen, working on the field and in downtown Belleville and East St. Louis. I have not covered the MP Duty.

There he met a very nice girl who had one child and who had recently lost her husband. He had been a fighter pilot, a first lieutenant, who crashed on a training mission off the coast of Virginia. Lefty needed someone like her who was suffering a loss, too. They were good for each other.

Since I had a few more points, I was discharged before Lefty. But when I left, Sheri and Lefty were talking marriage. Lefty had intended to stay there at Belleville, Illinois.

The war with Japan drew to a close after we dropped the Atomic bombs on Nagasaki and Hiroshima from the newest bomber, the B-29. The order was given by President Harry Truman, a wise decision which saved thousands of lives of American soldiers, sailors and marines. It eliminated the need for an invasion of Japan by our forces.

Demobilization and the point system resulted in my leaving Scott Field for an honorable discharge at Camp Atterberry, Indiana. After receiving my discharge on September 6, 1945, I caught a ride into town, taking my duffle bag along, went out to the edge of town and started hitchhiking back to the wild and wonderful hills of West Virginia.

Two days later I was sitting in the living room of my family's home quite early, September 8, 1945, due to my decorations, points and overseas time. Just seven days later, on September 15, 1945 I was enrolled in West Virginia University.

While many veterans began looking for jobs or filed for the 52-20 benefits ($20 per week for 52 weeks), I immediately entered the University as the fall term was just beginning. Without giving it much thought, I entered pre-medical courses. After two terms, I transferred to West Virginia Business College where I obtained a degree in Advanced Accounting and Business Administration.

Working in a bank proved boring, and after three years, I reenlisted in the U.S. Air Force, rose to the rank of Master Sergeant, and went overseas twice more, once to Guam during the Korean War and again to Japan. I will not cover those years, as that is another story. So is my civilian life, which I may cover at another time, in another story.

But a few years ago, I had a reminder of my days in the South Pacific. While reading my Veterans of Foreign Wars Magazine, I noticed under Navy reunions, the U.S.S. Claxton crew had one scheduled for September 4th, a Labor Day weekend at Anaheim, California. The secretary's name and address were listed.

I wrote a letter to Bill Daddario, including the facts of that fateful day, November 11, 1943, and that I was rescued by the Claxton. Bill called me and asked if I could attend the reunion as their guest, stating he remembered the events of that day well. He especially recalled my description of Commander Herald F. Stout as being accurate, and our attack by torpedo planes the next evening. I agreed to be there.

My wife and I attended, stayed at the Jolly Roger Inn, where the reunion was held. Rear Admiral Stout and his wife were also there.

As I had explained previously, it was a great reunion, "where a great time was had by all," as they say. I was made an honorary member of the U.S.S. Claxton by her crew, and was given great treatment by those in attendance.

When I arrived at the Inn, Bill Daddario met me at the door. He had been waiting to let me know I was to be a surprise guest. Bill advised me to say I had heard about the great reunions the crew held, was a friend of his and was attending as his guest. I had told two fellows why I was there, so I looked them up and asked them to keep my identity quiet. They were agreeable and thought it would be great fun.

That evening, I had the first opportunity to meet Jim Quinlan, one of those in the whale boat who came out to get me after I was spotted in the ocean. He was enjoying the reunion already and he let me know in no uncertain terms he had no respect for a 4-f'er who stayed home and worked in a defense plant to get a deferment and not go to fight.

He didn't like it much when I asked to have my picture taken with him in front of a large picture of the U.S.S. Claxton that was in the lobby of the hotel. We had all changed greatly in the passing years, and since my time on the ship was somewhat limited, it was even more difficult to recognize someone who had dropped out of the sky to visit with them a few days back in November, 1943.

The reunion was beginning to look like a successful surprise as far as my visit with them was concerned.

While eating at the cafeteria, I was seated with Rear Admiral Herald F. Stout and his wife, Zoe, with my wife Ardith, across from her. Bill Daddario's wife asked Admiral Stout if he had ever picked up any airmen in the Pacific Ocean.

He said, "Yes, I remember one skinny fellow who looked like a drowned rat we picked up out of the drink on Armistice Day of '43." (I knew he was talking about me.)

"We almost didn't get him. We had gotten too far away from the main body of our other destroyers and cruisers, which could have created a risk to our crew. We had made twelve passes looking for him, and some of the men said only one person had fallen from the plane, and only one chute opened. Others said two bodies had come from the plane up front. Other men had bailed out after passing over the Claxton.

"Safety had become a factor for the crew, so I decided to make one more pass across the area. It was the thirteenth, and last one. Our man up in the crows nest spotted something orange bobbing up and down on the waves, so we sent a boat out to check it out and sure enough, they came back with this fellow. He was yelling and almost jumping up and down in the boat. He couldn't get on the ship fast enough."

I must have let my emotions show, for I was hearing for the first time just how close a call I really had. Mrs. Stout

Admiral Arleigh A. "31 Knot" Burke graduated from the U. S. Naval Academy in 1923. His first duty was aboard the U.S.S. Arizona, then the U.S.S. Procyon. He then obtained an M.S. degree in engineering in 1931, and had other assignments in Naval Ordinance. In 1943, he was made Captain and took over as commander of "Destroyer Squadron 23," known as the "Little Beavers" after Fred Harman's comic strip, Red Ryder. The U.S.S. Claxton was a part of the Little Beavers. The squadron's swift attacks on the Japanese in the Solomon Islands earned him his nickname. Later, President Eisenhower nominated Admiral Burke for the post of Chief of Naval Operations, where he served three terms. In 1991 an AEGIS Destroyer, U.S.S. Arleigh Burke, DD51, was commissioned in his honor. It's first commander is John G. Morgan, Jr. U.S. Navy photo.

---

looked at me and said, "Are you the one?" She was speaking in a very low voice, and I nodded my head up and down.

Admiral Stout then grinned his wide and friendly smile, which was emphasized by the Jerry Colona style moustache which he still maintained, and his large friendly eyes. He had let me know how close my rescue was to failing. Only by his persistence, and risk taking by the entire crew, was I finally sighted and picked up. It was a stirring bit of information. He agreed to keep our secret a little while longer.

When it was time for me to speak, I started by paying tribute to the fine crew of the Claxton, but still did not say why I was there with them. Then I delivered the line I had yelled when I was picked up many years before out in the Pacific. "Thank God for the Navy." But I continued, "Thank God for Jim Quinlan. Thank God for Rear Admiral Herald F. Stout. For you are the ones that helped save me on November 11, 1943." Jim Quinlan was visibly moved. Now he knew why I wanted a picture with him. He and I, and our wives, talked a lot after the dinner.

I told the crew of giving my heated suit to one of them, and Beuford Helms yelled, "That was me." The laundryman said he remembered washing the suit which came apart. It was then I made him promise not to tell how badly that suit needed cleaning after my experience over Rabaul, the bail out and the fear of not being rescued. I'm sure all the washing he had to do to it is why it came all apart in the wash.

Since Admiral Stout's home state was Ohio, he joked about my being a West Virginian when he introduced me. He told about the West Virginia boy that got one of the attractive Ohio girls in a family way.

When the young man and his girl friend went to her father to tell him, and to ask for permission to marry, being an honorable and dependable man of character (as you know we West Virginians are), the father said, "Hell, no! I would rather have a bastard in the family than a West Virginian!"

Of course, even though he was from Ohio and was joking, he got a big laugh, especially since some of the crewmen were from his neighboring state of West Virginia, including Encil Hawkins from Fairmont, West Virginia, who was in the whale boat with Jim Quinlan when I was picked up. I regret he was not alive to make that special reunion.

That reunion was so great, I attended another a few years later in Philadelphia. I will always honor that membership of the U.S.S. Claxton which was made at the September 4th, 1978 meeting in Anaheim, California. I could not have served in the Navy with a better crew, even for that short time. I hope to attend another in a couple of years, too.

In much the same way, I found a reunion for the 307th Bombardment Group listed under those for the Army Air Force in the Disabled American Veterans Magazine. As a result, my wife and I have attended two more reunions, one in Milwaukee, Wisconsin and another in Nashville, Tennessee.

After forty-five years, I was happy to see another surviving member of my crew on Shehasta. That was Dr. Ralph E. "Gene" Bruce, our bombardier, and his wife, Margaret. Gene was one of the best bombardiers in the 307th Bomb Group.

I later met the pilot of our B-24, James D. "Jim" Jelley, and his wife, Winnie. Jim retired from the Air Force as a Colonel after having served his country well in World War II, Korean Conflict, and Viet Nam.

It is interesting to note we had all become "traveling men" — Rear Admiral Herald F. Stout, Dr. Ralph E. "Gene" Bruce, Colonel James D. "Jim" Jelley, and myself, even though over the years we had gone our separate ways, and did not see each other for over forty years, had no way of knowing we shared common interests in life. William Daddario and Rear Admiral (Retired) Arleigh "31 Knot" Burke must be included, although I did not know of them until recently. And we must not forget General Douglas MacArthur, President Franklin D. Roosevelt and Harry S. Truman.

I would say it is more than a mere coincidence, a statement, perhaps, of the kind of men who would fight and even die for their country, to protect America, their God, and their friends, and men who practice the motto, "Love Your Fellowman, Lend Him a Helping Hand."

I have also met some other crews' members at the reunions who were on that ill fated first mission over Rabaul — Helmuth Schultz from Ratti's crew, Ira Jackson and his pilot Byrd, and pilot Edwin M. McConnell, who provided copies of mission sheets during that time frame. And I met Joe Binder, who joined our group just about the time we were leaving Guadalcanal, also flew over Rabaul and had the experience of an incendiary bomb exploding in the bomb bay of his B-24. He lost one man who bailed out over Rabaul, and later some others on Francis' crew at Truk.

Many of the crews stayed with the 307th Bomb Group, moved up north and eventually helped in the liberation of the Philippines. They have their own stories to tell covering the period 1944 through 1945.

Top Left: Ira Jackson, a good buddy from Byrd's crew. Right: Helmuth "Bud" Schultz kept good records of the missions. Middle Left: Edwin M. McConnell was a great help in providing mission sheets and other information. Right: USAF Lt. Col. (Ret.) James D. "Jim" Jelley had a long and distinguished career, even after World War II. He served at various posts in the Air Force, Viet Nam. Bottom Right: Joseph C. Binder, pilot of "Little Mick" with the author in his well-decorated A-2 jacket. Below: The author and Gene Bruce, bombardier on Shehasta. Gene left us with pleasant memories of him on October 12, 1989. Great guys, every one.

The Nashville Reunion in 1988

I have enjoyed writing of my adventures in the best, bravest and most patriotic military force in the whole world then and now. I am proud of it. I am hopeful you will enjoy this book, or portions of it, and as a result will visit your old buddies and friends at every opportunity in the future. There will never be another time like it.

While I have enjoyed remembering, and writing it, but at times there has been great sadness, too, especially for those who have already made that last long flight. May God be with them, and with all those who are the survivors these many years.

You can slip off your parachute now, after you unbuckle your harness straps, and enjoy the balance of the good life we all fought for, so many long years ago.

It is difficult to report as this book is finally completed that two of the principal patriots in this book who I have had the good fortune to enjoy a renewed fellowship with at recent reunions of the 307th Bombardment Group and the U.S.S. Claxton, have made their last voyage to that Celestial Home above, that House not made with hands, eternal in the Heavens: Doctor Ralph E. "Gene" Bruce, bombardier on Shehasta, and Rear Admiral (Retired) Herald Franklin Stout, U. S. Navy, Commander of the Claxton.

Postscript

It is ironic that as this book goes to print after many years of writing, typing, researching and soul searching on my part, that this postscript is added on Pearl Harbor Day, December 7, 1991. Just 50 years after the sneak attack by the Japanese, our President George Bush has expressed regrets for our internment of those Japanese-Americans after the attack. But no apology from the leaders of the Japanese government for their "Day of Infamy."

After spending nine months in Japan in 1955, I can have respect for the Japanese people (many not born at that time) and I have since met Japanese students I liked where I taught, but I cannot find it in my heart to completely forgive, and I'm sure I will never forget what the Japanese government did in 1941, and their subsequent actions of inhuman treatment to our servicemen as prisoners of war.

It is more obvious as time goes by that we won the war (no one really wins) but we have lost the peace. I have 15 grandchildren and it is a concern for the future of my children and those grandchildren that we do not forget the lessons of the past, but that our nation remains strong, not only militarily, but financially and morally strong, as well.

While they buy our land, buildings, businesses and educational institutions, we are not allowed to own and/or control anything in Japan. Let's wake up, America! We do not need a new world order— we need the old belief in accepting the responsibility for America's future FIRST. We need to provide for those who have borne the battle in defense of this Great Country, FIRST. I am not an isolationist, but I believe in fairness in trading with foreign countries, and with an open market for our products to their country, creating jobs here, FIRST.

Thank God For Patriots!

Acknowledgments

I thank the following sources for help in completion of this book including pictures, biographical information, and historical background: U. S. Army Air Force; U. S. Navy and Marine Corps; U. S. Army Signal Corps; National Archives; 307th Bombardment Group (H) Reunion Association; U.S.S. Claxton DD571 Reunion Association; Mrs. Margaret Bruce; Mrs. Zoe A. Stout; Lt. Col. James D. Jelley; Edwin H. McConnell; Ira Jackson; Helmuth Schultz; Joseph Binder; Smithsonian Institute; 13th Army Air Force; 5th Army Air Force; Maxwell Air Force Base Historical Research Center, Montgomery, Alabama; the Fairmont Library, Fairmont State College Library, Benedum and Morgantown Public Library, in Fairmont, Bridgeport and Morgantown, WV, respectively—as well as my daughter, Connie Gail Lucas for her help, and my wife, Ardith, for her patience with me over the period this book was in progress.

RECOMMENDED READING

"Ba Ba Black Sheep," by Colonel Gregory "Pappy" Boyington, USMC Retired. Publisher: G.P. Putnam's Sons, NY, NY

"Lonely Vigil (Coastwatchers of the Solomons)," by Walter Lord
Publisher: Viking Press, 625 Madison Ave., NY, NY 10022

"Up The Slot," by Samuel L. Walker
Publisher: Walker Publishing, 5721 NW 48th, Oklahoma City, OK 73122

"Charlie, Memoirs of a 13th Air Force Flight Engineer in the Southwest Pacific, 1944-1945," by Charles B. Dowdy, Jr.
Publisher: McDowell Publications, 11129 Ridge Rd, Utica, KY 42376

"PT 109: John F. Kennedy World War II," by Robert J. Donovan
Publisher: McGraw-Hill Book Company, Inc., 330 W 42nd St., NY, NY 10036

"Destroyers," by Antony Preston,
Publisher: Bison Books, Limited, London, England, U.S. Edition by Printice-Hall, Inc., 1977, Englewood Cliffs, N.J.

"Diary of the 307th Bomb Group (HV)" by Sam S. Britt, Jr., 1921 Lake Hill Parkway, Baton Rouge, LA 70808

EPILOGUE

"AROUND A FAR CORNER"
(Adopted From the Old Poem)

AROUND A FAR CORNER I HAVE A FRIEND
IN THIS LARGE WORLD THAT HAS NO END.
YET DAYS GO BY AND WEEKS RUSH ON,
AND BEFORE I KNOW IT, YEARS HAVE GONE.
AND I NEVER SEE MY OLD FRIEND'S FACE,
FOR LIFE IS A SWIFT AND PRESSING RACE.
YET HE KNOWS I THINK OF HIM JUST AS OFTEN AS IN THE
DAYS
WHEN I GAVE HIM A CALL, AND HE RETURNED IT IN KIND.
WE TALKED OF THINGS PAST THAT CAME TO MIND,
OF A SHARING OF ADVENTURES WAY BACK IN TIME.
WE WERE YOUNGER THEN, COMBAT AND FLYING FRIENDS.
BUT NOW WE ARE SO BUSY AND JUST TIRED MEN.
TIRED WITH PLAYING A FOOLISH GAME,
TIRED WITH TRYING TO MAKE A NAME,
OR APPEAR IN A PARADE, OR THE RACE TO SAY, "I'VE GOT
IT MADE."
TOMORROW, YES, TOMORROW, I WILL SAY, "I'LL CALL HIM,"
JUST TO SHOW THAT I'M THINKING OF HIM.
BUT TOMORROW COMES AND TOMORROW GOES,
AND THE DISTANCE BETWEEN US GROWS AND GROWS.
THEN FROM AROUND THAT FAR CORNER, MILES AWAY,
"HERE'S A TELEGRAM, SIR, YOUR FRIEND DIED TODAY!"
AND THAT'S WHAT WE GET AND DESERVE IN THE END,
AROUND THAT FAR CORNER, A VANISHED FRIEND.

Lyman Austin "Ace" Clark, Jr.,
for his friends around a far corner.

An Airman's Scrapbook

Memories of Men Who Gave Their All...

Corny and Red McCarthy

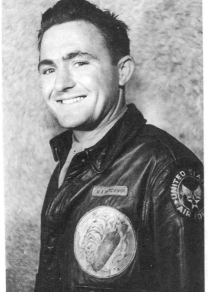

Hutch

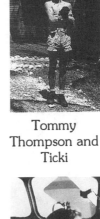

Tommy Thompson and Ticki

Jim Jelley

(Left) Julius T. Wytowich and Ralph E. Bruce

The Big Chapel on Guadalcanal

...And Of The Beliefs That Brought Them Together

Bill Humphrey

(L-R) Humphrey, Clark, Cornelius

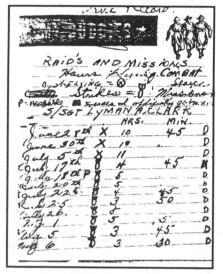

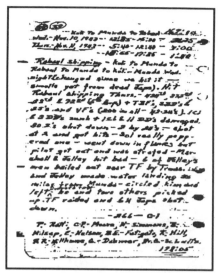

A sample from the author's diary.

Memories of Shehasta's fatal mission as recorded in the diary of Helmut "Bud" Schultz.

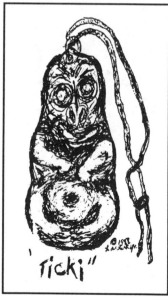

"Ticki"

We bought our mascot, Ticki, a registered Sidney Silky Terrier, in New Zealand and named him after the good luck charm of the New Zealand Maori natives, which they called ticki. The charm represented an unborn child of their ancestors and was carved from jade, wood or stone. They wore the charm around their necks. Ticki was a source of great pleasure to us, a friend who never let us down.

(Above) We enjoyed having Ticki around, and he would meet us when we returned from a mission. (L-R) The author, Corny and Hutch. Tommy took the picture. Unfortunately, neither Hutch nor Tommy made it back. Ticki also met with a bad end. He followed the cook into the freezer, as a result his life was lost after we left Guadalcanal. (Below) A typical village in the jungles of Guadalcanal.

Living On The Edge...

Although the native villages were primitive by American standards, our accommodations in the camp were not that much better. (Top Left) A sturdy, open air hut in one village. (Top Right) A not so sturdy tent that we called home. (Above) Two native children pose for the camera in 1943. Perhaps you can observe the diseases on their arms and legs. 13th AAF photo. (Left) Sitting in the tent, June, 1943— Carney Field, Guadalcanal.

Living It Up!

While most servicemen stationed in the South Pacific slogged through jungles and put up with Spam, mosquitoes, heat and endless rain, most also got a taste of the good life on their way to or returning from their assignment by a stopover in Hawaii and a visit to the Royal Hawaiian Hotel, as shown here in January of '43.

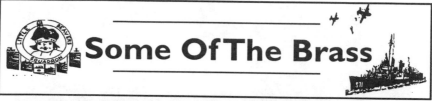

Some Of The Brass

(Above) The Captains of Destroyer Squadron 23 at Purvis Bay HQ, Solomon Islands, 26 May 1944. (L-R) Commander H.A. Gano, U.S.S. Dyson; Commander L.K. Reynolds, U.S.S. Charles Ausburne; Captain Arleigh A. Burke, Commander Desron 23; Commander B.L. Austin, Commander Desron Division 46; Commander D.C Hamberger, U.S.S. Converse; Commander Herald Franklin Stout, U.S.S. Claxton; and Commander H.J. Armstrong, U.S.S. Spence. Photo courtesy Zoe E. Anderson Stout (Below) Not an armchair general, Brigadier General William "Bill" Matheny, Commander of the 13th Bomber Command, 13th AAF, led many missions up the slot.

A Tribute

Rear Admiral Herald Franklin Stout,
United States Navy
**THE Commander of U.S.S.
Claxton, DD571**
1942-1944
b. 15 June 1903 d. 23 March 1987

This author found it very difficult to touch on all of the accomplishments of the man, a child of God with a deep Christian Faith, a patriot, a brother who had traveled east as well as west, a Sojourner of the 33°, a loving husband, father and grandfather, but to this author, he was a man who risked his men to rescue one lonely airman when reason and the odds were not with him. For this I am truly thankful. But he was much more. I have talked to the sailors who served under him, and they say he was firm but fair, kind and thoughtful, had a sense of humor, but most of all a leader who cared for his men.

Admiral Stout served his country from 1926 to 1956 as a commissioned Naval Officer, with most of his service on destroyers with the Pacific Fleet. He graduated from the Naval Academy in 1926. He was in command of the U.S.S. Breeze, anchored at Pearl Harbor on December 7, 1941.

He moved out to sea with his crew to do battle.

He was put in command of the U.S.S. Claxton when it was commissioned and took it to the South Pacific and participated in the last surface battle of World War II, the battle of Cape St. George, put the Japanese Navy to route and earned the only squadron citation ever given for conspicuous gallantry and extraordinary heroism. For this and other action in the Pacific he twice received the Navy Cross, a Silver Star, and a gold star in lieu of a second Silver Star. He was awarded the Distinguished Service Medal for action in Korea where he was in command of Mine Squadron 9 and the Western Pacific Mine Sweeping Force of 30 ships. In 1956 he was Commandant of the 11th Naval District when he retired as Rear Admiral.

As a civilian, he was a member of the design engineers with Convair, which produced Atlas Missiles.

He was a avid student of history and as a skilled printer, photographer, typographer and genealogist. He wrote his storied of his family covering nine generations of English ancestry.

After ten years as a widower, he married Zoe E. Anderson on July 25, 1976. His first marriage was to Louise Frederica Finley on the day he graduated from the Naval Academy. They had three sons, all military men, and eight grandchildren as of 1988.

This eulogy lovingly composed by Zoe E. Anderson Stout is very appropriate: HOME IS THE SAILOR... Safe, Safe at Last... The Harbor Past... Safe in His Fathers Home.

In honor of Rear Admiral Herald Franklin Stout, the Aegis Guided Missile Destroyer DDG-55 is to be named U.S.S. Herald F. Stout, under construction at Pascagoula, MI with the christening October 1992 and commissioning in early 1994.

(Courtesy of Zoe E. Stout)

Admiral Halsey graduated from the U.S. Naval Academy in 1904, first serving on the U.S.S. Missouri. He received the Navy Cross in World War I, and later commanded destroyers and the aircraft carrier Saratoga. He graduated from Naval War College in 1933, and Army War College in 1934, and became a naval aviator. He was a vice admiral on the U.S.S. Enterprise delivering planes to Wake Island when the Japanese hit Pearl Harbor on December 7, 1941. In 1942, he led attacks on the Japanese on the Gilberts, Marshals and Wake Islands and received the Distinguished Service Medal. He was then given command of the South Pacific area Naval Forces, including "Desron 23." U.S. Navy photo and bio.

Fleet Admiral William Frederick "Bull" Halsey, Jr.   b. 1883 d. 1959

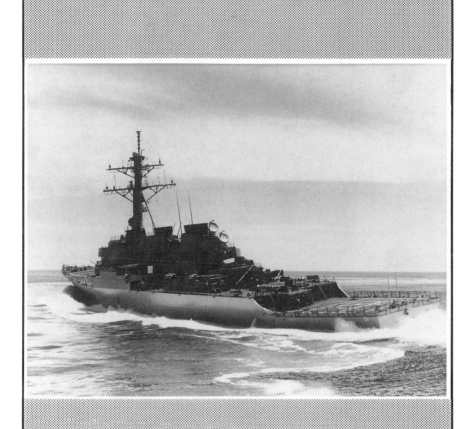

A Burke Class Aegis Guided Missile Destroyer like the one shown above (U.S.S. Arleigh Burke, DDG-51) will be commissioned DDG-55 in 1994 in honor of Rear Admiral Stout.

Buddies

(Top) Gene Bruce in flight training at Carlswell Air Force Base. (Bottom) He gets a check on his "GI Haircut" from some friends. (Right) James D. "Jim" Jelley in 1946.

(Above) We shot down three zeros the day this was taken. Front Row (L-R): William F. Humphrey, Lt. Taylor, James D. Jelley, Ralph E. Bruce, Julius T. Woytowich. Back Row (L-R): Charles R. Thompson, Henry E. Hutchings, the author, Victor Meehan, Earl B. Cornelius. (Right) USAF Lt. Col. (Ret.) James D. Jelley rode herd on his crew in the Solomon's, and rode down main street in a 1974 Ft. Worth, Texas parade as part of the Sheriff's Possee. (Below) The author, Corny (holding Ticki) and Hutch in front of the photo lab in camp.

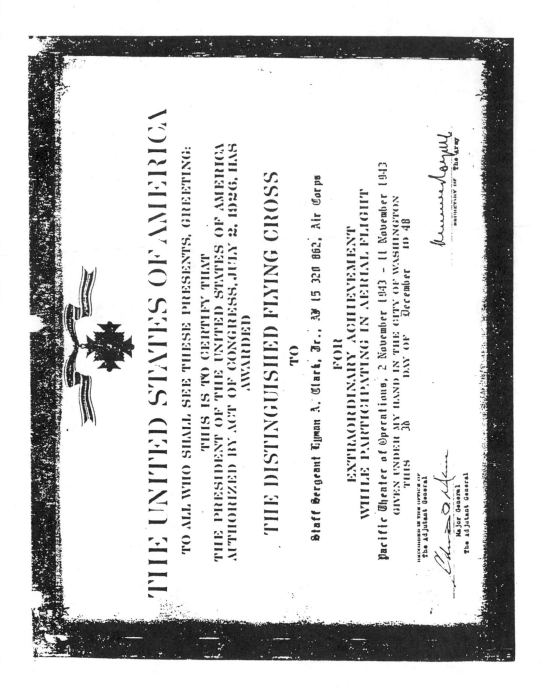

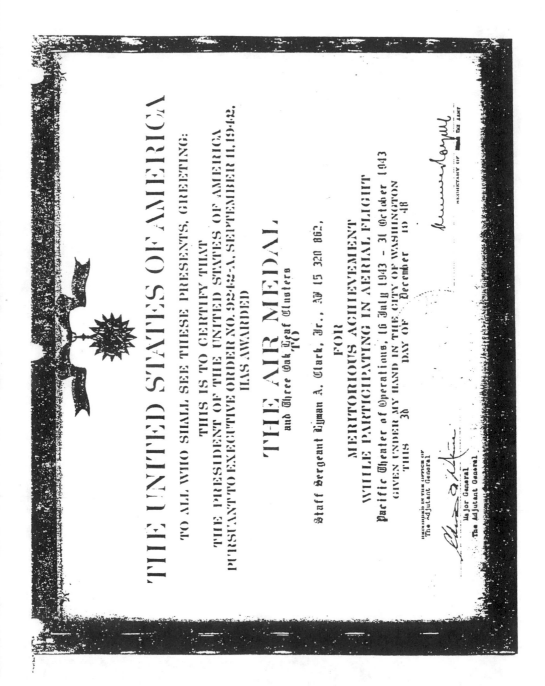

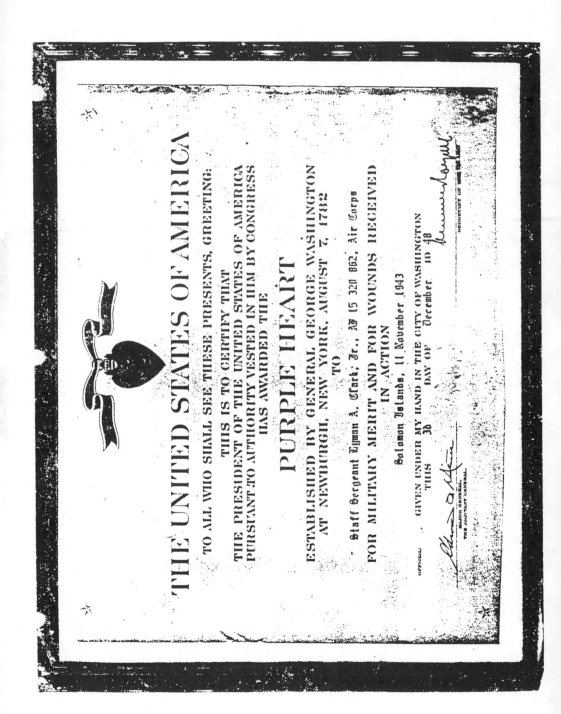

13th AAF Photo

Appendix A

A Sampling of
MISSION SHEETS
424th Bomb Squadron
The Office of the Operations Officer
307th Bomb Group (H)
13TH AIR FORCE

Courtesy of Edwin H. McConnell

424TH BOMBARDMENT SQUADRON (H), AAF
OFFICE OF THE OPERATIONS OFFICER

APO # 709
JULY 10, 1943.

FLIGHT SCHEDULE

PILOT	SHIP #	CALL LTRS	T/OFF	ROUTE ALT	ATTACK ALTITUDE	TARGET	ATTACK TIME
PRICE	040	11V27	1800	9,000'	10,000-14,000'	KAHILI	2045
ALEXANDER	002	12V27	1810	9,500'	10,000-14,000'	KAHILI	2050
MCNEESE	170	13V27	1820	10,000'	10,000-14,000'	KAHILI	2100
HANSEN	323	14V27	1830	9,000'	10,000-14,000'	KAHILI	2115
HOLMES	533	15V27	1840	9,500'	10,000-14,000'	KAHILI	2125
MCCLOSKEY	606	16V27	1850	10,000'	10,000-14,000'	KAHILI	2135
WARD	025	17V27	1900	10,500'	10,000-14,000'	KAHILI	2145
BOMBAR	212	10V27	1910	11,000'	10,000-14,000'	KAHILI	2150

SPARE SHIP 877

ROUTE OUT: NORTHERN CIRCUITOUS   ROUTE BACK: DOWN THE GROOVE

ALTERNATE TARGETS: BALLALE & VILA.

BOMB LOAD:

REMARKS: START ENGINES 20 MINUTES PRIOR TO TAKE-OFF, OBSERVE RADIO SILENCE ON TAKE-OFF AND MAKE ONLY ONE CONTACT WITH TOWER FOR LANDING INSTRUCTIONS.

GROUND STATION CALL LETTERS - MGX (INITIAL CALL TO THIS STATION ONLY) 2V3 OR TWO WAY ANSWER IN CASE OF MGX'S SILENCE.

RADIO RANGE 338 KCS - CALL LETTERS DX

CARNEY FIELD HOMING BEACON 370 KCS; 3D SECOND DASH FOLLOWED BY 2 CALL LETTERS DK.

GUADALCANAL RADAR BEACON IN OPERATIONS SIGNAL RC

FREQUENCIES: 6970 PRIMARY 7000 SECONDARY   LIAISON: 4435 PRIMARY 3825 SECONDARY

HENRY L. MILLEDGE,
CAPTAIN, AIR CORPS
OPERATIONS OFFICER.

THESE MISSION SHEETS CONTRIBUTED
BY EDWIN N. MCCONNEL

424th BOMBARDMENT SQUADRON (H), AAF
Office of the Operations Officer.

APO # 709
16 October 1943

FLIGHT SCHEDULE

PILOT	SHIP #	T/O'S	CALL LETTERS	TARGET	ATTACK ALT.	ATTACK TIME
Alexandre	137	0630	1V27	Kara Airdrome	18,000'	0930
Warbon	215	0631	2V27	"	"	"
Jelley	925	0632	3V27	"	"	"
Hansen	221	0633	4V27	Kara Airdrome	18,000'	0930
Darr	212	0634	5V27	"	"	"
Byrd	877	0635	6V27	"	"	"
Ratti	092	0636	7V27	Kara Airdrome	18,000'	0930
Bisbee	145	0637	8V27	"	"	"
Francis	107	0638	9V27	"	"	"
(Spare ship #658)						

REMARKS: Start engines 20 minutes prior to take-off. Landing by new squadron procedure.

SQUADRON ASSEMBLY: Overfield at 2,000'. Squadron leader will make 1 circle over field and start climbing toward Savo Island. Rendezvous over Savo at 10,000' between 0735 and 0745. Meet fighters over Visu Visu at 18,000' between 0840 and 0850.

ROUTE OUT : Savo, Visu Visu, to SouthSide of Shortland, to Moila Point to target.

ROUTE FORMATION : V of Squadrons, Javelin down within Squadron. 72nd Squadron will lead, 424th in # 2 position and 370th in # 3 position.

PLAN OF ATTACK : Right turn across Shortland, slight left turn from Moila point Point to heading of 330°. Right turn away from target across North Side of Tonelei Harbor North of Kolombangara. South Side of channel and home. 424th Bombardier sight for range.

ATTACK FORMATION : Javelin Down

TARGET : Kara Airdrome, South Side of dispersal area. Alternate:

BOMB INTERVALS : 40 Stations 125 feet   20 Stations 250 feet

STANDARD NAVY RESCUE CRAFT

AREA	CONTROL	BOAT CALL	FREQ.
Segi			6050
Munda-Rendova	Quartz	Joe	6050
Barakoma	Diamond	Pluto	6050
Russells	Sirius	Dick	6050
Dumbo at Munda	Y-59	30V28	6050

BOMB LOAD: MAXIMUM 100# GP Inst. Nose Fuse .025 Tail Fuse

FREQUENCIES: Stand by on 5620 KC & 6050 KC until beyond Russells and 6050 KC & 4500 from there on. Reverse on return.

LIAISON: 4575 KC Continous Secondary
3550 KC 1700-0800 Primary
7890 KC 0800-1700 Primary

XII BOMBER COMMAND GROUND STATION OOV21 GUARD AT ALL TIMES
(Unless in case of emergency)
(IFF WILL BE TURNED ON IN ALL SHIPS)

412th BOMBARDMENT SQUADRON (H) (J) AAF
Office of the Operations Officer

19 October 1943.

FLIGHT SCHEDULE

PILOT	SHIP #	T/O	CALL LETTERS	TARGET	ATTACK ALTITUDE	ATTACK TIME
Alexandre	137	0830	14V27	Kara	19,500'	1130
Harpster	566	0831	15V27	Kara	19,500'	1130
Jolley	324	0831	16V27	Kara	19,500'	1130
Werben	218	0833	17V27	Kara	19,500'	1130
Darr & Friend	225	0835	18V27	Kara	19,500'	1130
Byrd	146	0834	19V27	Kara	19,500'	1130
Hansen	866	0836	20V27	Kara	19,500'	1130
Scott	212	0838	21V27	Kara	19,500'	1130
Francis	107	0837	22V27	Kara	19,500'	1130

REMARKS: Start engines 20 minutes prior to take-off. Leading by wave Squadron Procedure.

SQUADRON ASSEMBLY: Over-field at 8,000'. Squadron Leader will make one circle over field and start climbing toward Kara Island. Rendezvous over Kara Island at 8,000' between 0910 - 0930. Meet fighters over Slabe at 17,000' between 1040 - 1050.

ROUTE OUT: Kara, Slabe, across West side of Shortland, West of Wells Point, on run approx. 330°.

ROUTE FORMATION: V of Squadrons, Javelin down in Squadrons. 370th will lead, 424th in #2 postion, 72nd in #3.

PLAN OF ATTACK: V of Squadrons descend from 20,000' before run. On break away mate right turn descending at 700' per minute across Lake Tahale, Across Faure, North of Telle LaVella to Base.

ATTACK FORMATION: Javelin down.

TARGET: Kara Runway, Alternate Ballale or Kahili.

STANDARD NAVY RESCUE CRAFT

AREA	COVERAGE	BOAT CALL	FREQ.
Sagi	Juaria	Joe	4050
Munda-Bandoma	Diamond	Pluto	8040
Baratoma	Sirius	Dick	4050
Russelle	L-59	--	6060
Dumbo at Munda	MOVES	MOVES	6660

FREQUENCIES: Stand by on 4680 KC & 6060 KC until beyond Russelle and 6060 KC & 4580 from there on.
Reverse on return.
LIAISON: 4575 KC Continuous Boundary
6650 KC 1°00 - 0600 Primary
7060 KC 0600 - 1700 Primary

XIII BOMBER COMMAND, COMMAND STATION 6060, Guadalcanal
AT ALL TIMES (BUTTON 6 IN CASE OF EMERGENCY)
(IFF WILL BE TURNED ON IN ALL SHIPS)

Maximum 100% CP Inst. Nose .025 Tail.
40 Station Ships 100', 27 Station Ships 200'.

424TH BOMBARDMENT SQUADRON (H), AAF
Office of the Operations Officer.

APO #709
24 October 1943

FLIGHT SCHEDULE

PILOT	SHIP #	T/o	CALL LETTERS	TARGET	ATTACK ALT.	ATTACK TIME
Alexandre	137	0600	1V27	Kahili	13,500'	0900
Werban	215	0602	2V27	Kahili	13,500'	0900
Jolley	324	0601	3V27	Kahili	13,500'	0900
Hansen	321	0603	4V27	Kahili	13,500'	0900
Darr	928	0605	5V27	Kahili	13,500'	0900
Byrd	104	0604	6V27	Kahili	13,500'	0900
Ratti	211	0603	7V27	Kahili	13,500'	0900
Blabe	966	0608	8V27	Kahili	12,500'	0900
Francis	107	0607	9V27	Kahili	13,500'	0900

REMARKS: Start engines 20 minutes prior to take-off. Landing new squadron procedure.

SQUADRON ASSEMBLY: Over field at 2000 ft, squadron leader will make one circle over field and start climbing toward Buraku Island, Rendezvous over Buraku Island at 12,000 ft. by 0715. West fighters over Simbo at 19,000 ft at 0815.

ROUTE OUT : Base, Buraku Island, Simbo, North side of Faure, north of Lake Lahale, left turn into target, left turn away from target.

ROUTE FORMATION : V of Squadrons, javelin down within each Squadron. 424th #3 position, 500 ft. below lead squadron.

PLAN OF ATTACK : Left turn into target on run of approximately 130 degrees Mag. V of Squadrons. Left turn away from target. Descending 1000 ft per minute and 180 to 190 m.p.h.

TARGET : Kahili, primary - Kara, secondary.

BOMB INTERVAL : 300 feet.

BOMB LOAD : 8 - 1000 GP - .1 second nose and .1 second tail.

STANDARD NAVY RESCUE CRAFT

AREA	CONTROL	BOAT CALL	FREQ.
Sogi	Quarts	Joe	6050
Munda-Rendova	Diamond	Pluto	6050
Barakima	Sirius	Dick	6050
Russells	Y-69		6060
Dembo at Munda		NOV28	6060

FREQUENCIES: Stand by on 5620 KC & 6050 KC until beyond Russells and 6050 KC & 4500 from there on. Reverse on return.

LIAISON : 4575 KC Continuous Secondary
3550 KC 1700 - 0900 Primary
7890 KC 0800 - 1700 Primary

XIII BOMBER COMMAND, COMMAND STATION 00V21, GUARD AT ALL TIMES (UNLESS IN CASE OF EMERGENCY)

IFF WILL BE ON AT ALL TIMES IN ALL SHIPS

423RD BOMBARDMENT SQUADRON (H), A.AF
Office of the Operations Officer.

AFO ? 709
27 October 1943

FIELD OR CLUE

PILOT	SHIP #	T/O	Call Letters	TARGET	AT ACK ALT.	ATTACK TIME
Alexndro	137	0730	11V27	Kara	13,000' Ind.	1030
Carpucor	146	0732	12V27	"	"	"
Jello	324	0731	13V27	"	"	"
Harbon	215	0735	14V27	Kara	13,000' Ind.	1030
Marshall	350	0736	16V27	"	"	"
Barr	066	0734	10V27	"	"	"
Hanson	221	0736	17V27	Aara	13,000' Ind.	1030
Batti	211	0738	18V27	"	"	"
Francis	107	.0737	19V27	"	"	"
Scott	212	0739	80V27	"	"	"

REMARKS: Start engines 20 minutes prior to take-off. Landing new Squadron Procedure. Squadron leader will make one circle over field and start climbing over field at 2000'. Squadron leader will make one circle over field and start climbing toward Cape Esperance. Assemble with 372nd over Cape Esperance as at 8000' between 0820-0830. Proceed on course at 0830 Southern Circuitous route. No fighters.

FLYIN BAGS: Southern Circuitous.
ROUTE OUT: Southern Circuitous.
A. IS ASSEMBLY: Javelin Down in Squadron, 8 500' below 372nd on their left wing.
METH OF ATTACK: Right turn into target approx. 30 seconds after 372nd. Right turn away from target, north, of Treasury.

COLOR: Primary Kara dummy - Secondary Sahill - third Selelo
BOMB INTERVAL: 300 feet. Aim 100 yds down runway.
BOMB LOAD: 8-1000# GP .1 sec nose .1 sec tall

AIR SIGNALS	COLOURS	SMOKE CALL	BOMB
Aim	Quartz	Joe	6050
Squadron leader	Diamond	Pluto	6050
Javelin	Sirius	Dick	6050
Element	Y-59		6050
Chng at Start		30.23	6050

FLYING: Stand by on 6020 KC & 6050 until beyond friendly coils and 6050 KC - 4600 from there on. Reverse on return.
LIAISON: 4075 KC continuous Secondary
3560 KC 1700 - 0800 Primary
7030 KC 0800 - 1700 Primary
XIII BOMBER COMMAND, CARILO STATION WILL DO ALL IN THEIR
(UNLESS IN CAPS OF EMGENCY)

424TH BOMBARDMENT SQUADRON (H), JAP
Office of the Operations Officer.

APO # 709
29 October 1943

FLIGHT SCHEDULE

PILOT	SHIP #	T/O	CALL LETTERS	TARGET	ATTACK ALT.	ATTACK TIME
Alexandre	137	0600	1V27	Buka	19,000'	0800
Urban	215	0600	2V27	"	"	"
Jelley	324	0601	3V27	"	"	"
Hansen	221	0604	4V27	Buka	19,000'	0802
Marshall	308	0608	5V27	"	"	"
Friend	925	0605	6V27	"	"	"
Byrd	115	0607	7V27	Buka	19,000'	0803
Babos	906	0608	8V27	"	"	"
Francis	107	0609	9V27	"	"	"
Patti	811	0610	10V27	"	"	"

REMARKS: Start engines 10 minutes prior to take-off. Landing new Squadron Procedure.

SQUADRON ASSEMBLY: Over field at 5,000'. Formation leader will then start climbing toward Cape Esperance. Will leave Cape Esperance at 0705 at 9,000'. Proceed en course at 0705 Souther Circuitous

ROUTE OUT: Souther Circuitous
ROUTE BACK:
ROUTE FORMATION: V of Squadrons. 424th in No. 1 position, 372nd in No. 2 position, Navy in No. 3. 372nd
Squadron will be 500' above lead Squadron. Navy will be 500' below lead Squadron.
RUN OF ATTACK: Left turn into target approx. 20 seconds after Navy. 372nd will follow 424th by approx.
30 seconds. Navy will make slow right turn after bombs away. 424th will make a somewhat
sharper turn and will resume lead of formation. 372nd will make a right turn and rejoin
the formation.

TARGET: Buka Runway.
BOMB INTERVAL: 300 Feet. Aim 300 yds down the runway.   BOMB LOAD: 8-1000# Gr. 1 sec Nose 1 sec Tail

EMERGENCY: Stand by on 5420 KC & 6060 KC until beyond
Russells and 6060 KC & 4830 KC from there
on. Reverse on return.
LIAISON: 4875 KC Continuous Secondary
3650 KC 1700 -0800 Primary
7980 KC 0800 - 1700 Primary
IFF SQUELCH CHANNEL CHANNEL 0V21 GUARD AT ALL
TIMES (CHANGE IN CASE OF EMERGENCY)
IFF WILL BE ON IN ALL SHIPS

STANDARD NAVY RESCUE CRAFT

AREA	FLEET	CONTROL	BCST CALL	FREQ.
		Quartz	Joe	6060
Munda-Rendova	Diamond	Plate	Plate	6060
Barakoma	Sirius	Dick	Dick	6888
Russells	Y-59			
Dumbo at Munda			10V28	6060

Cclcf - Silver 1
Fighter-View 96

424TH BOMBARDMENT SQUADRON (H), AAF
OFFICE OF THE OPERATIONS OFFICER

A.P.O. # 709
31 OCTOBER 1943

PILOT	SHIP #	T/O'S	CALL LETTERS	TARGET	ATTACK ALT.	ATTACK TIME
ALEXANDRE	137	0610	11V27	Kara	17,500' Ind.	0856
HARISTER	858	0612	12V27	Kara	17,500' Ind.	0856
JELLEY	524	0611	13V27	Kara	17,500' Ind.	0856
WORBON	215	0613	14V27	Kara	17,500' Ind.	0856
FRIEND	819	0615	15V27	Kara	17,500' Ind.	0856
BYRD	146	0614	16V27	Kara	17,500' Ind.	0856
RATTI	925	0616	17V27	Kara	17,500' Ind.	0856
BISBEE	986	0618	18V27	Kara	17,500' Ind.	0856
FRANCIS	107	0617	19V27	Kara	17,500' Ind.	0856
HANSEN	221	0619	20V27	Kara	17,500' Ind.	0858
SCOTT	212	0620	21V27	Kara	17,500' Ind.	0858
SPARE SHIP	211					

REMARKS: Start engines 20 minutes prior to take-off. Landing new Squadron procedure.
SQUADRON ASSEMBLY: Over field at 2,000'. Rendezvous with 372nd on their right wing at 7,000' over Savo. Leave Savo on course at 0705.

ROUTE OUT: Direct to Lulual Point.
ROUTE BACK: South of Shortland & then direct to Base.
ROUTE FORMATION: V of Squadrons javelin down within Sqdn. 372nd leading. 424th 500' higher on their right wing.

PLAN OF ATTACK: Left turn around Lulual point, left turn on to target, approximately heading 160°. 424th attack 30 seconds behind 372nd.

TARGET: Kara Runway. Secondary: Kahili Runway. Tertiary: Ballale Runway.
BOMB INTERVAL: 500'
BOMB LOAD: 8-1000' GP., 1/10 Second Nose & 1/10 Second Tail.

STANDARD NAVY RESCUE CRAFT

AREA	CONTROL	BOAT CALL	FREQ.
Segi	Quarta	Joe	6060
Munda-Rendova	Diamona	Plute	8060
Barakona	Sirius	Dlok	6060
Russells	Y-59		6060
Dumbo at Munda		30V28	6060

FREQUENCIES: Stand by on 5620 KC & 6050 KC until beyond Russells and 6060KC & 4500 from there on. Reverse on return.

LIAISON: 4676 KC Continous Secondary
3550 KC 1700- 0800 Primary
7890 KC 0800-1700 Primary

XIII BOMBER COMMAND, COMMAND STATION OOV21 GUARD AT ALL TIMES.

424th BOMBARDMENT SQUADRON (M), AAF
Office of the Operations Officer.

APO # 709
2 November 1945

FLIGHT SCHEDULE

PILOT	SHIP #	T/O'S	CALL LETTERS	TARGET	ATTACK ALT.	ATTACK TIME
Alexandre	187	0710	1V27	Kahili	19,800'	1000
Warben	215	0712	2V27	"	"	"
Jolley	324	0711	3V27	"	"	"
Hansen	925	0715	4V27	Kahili	19,800'	1000
Darr	819	0715	5V27	"	"	"
Taylor	966	0714	6V27	"	"	"
Ratti	211	0716	7V27	Kahili	19,800'	1000
Marshall	868	0718	8V27	"	"	"
Francis	107	0715	9V27	"	"	"
Byrd	146	0719	10V27	"	"	"

REMARKS: Start engines 20 minutes prior to take-off.; Landing new Squadron Procedure.
SQUADRON ASSEMBLY: Over field at 2,000'. Assemble with 372nd over 'Save at 8,000'. Leave on course at 0810.
ROUTE OUT: Save thru Manning Straits, along North coast of Choiseul, to Lolual Point & left turn.
ROUTE BACK: South of Treasury & direct to base.
ROUTE FORMATION: Echelon of Sqdns. Javelin down within Sqdn. 424th Leading 372nd #2 position 500' higher.
PLAN OF ATTACK: Left turn around Lolual point, left turn on to target. 372nd will attack 30 seconds after 424th.

TARGET: North West end of Kahili Runway. Secondary Ballale.
BOMB INTERVAL: 300'

BOMB LOAD 8-1000# GP .1 Second Nose .1 Second Tail

FREQUENCIES: Stand by on 5620 KC & 3050 KC until beyond
Russells and 6050 KC & 4650 KC from there on.
Reverse on return.

LIAISON: 4574 KC Continous Secondary
3050 KC 1700 - 0800 Primary
7090 KC 0800 - 1700 Primary

XIII BOMBER COMMAND, COMMAND STATION, OOV21 GUARD AT ALL
TIMES (EXCEPT IN CASE OF EMERGENCY)
IFF WILL BE ON IN ALL SHIPS

STANDARD NAVY RESCUE CRAFT

AREA	CONTROL	BOAT CALL	FREQ.
Segi	Quartz	Joe	6050
Munda-Rendova	Diamond	Pluto	6050
Barakoma	Sirius	Dick	6050
Russells	Y-69		6050
Dumbe at Bunda		30V2a	6060

442th Bombardment Squadron (?) ???
OFFICER OF OPERATIONS OFFICER

A.P.O. # 709
4 November 1945

PILOT	SHIP#	T/O's	CALL LTRS.	ATTACK TIME	TARGET	ATTACK ALT.
ALEXANDER	619	0825	13VRY	1200	Buka Runway	18,500'
HARPSTER	157	0827	14VRY	1200	Buka Runway	18,500'
JELLEY	396	0826	15VRY	1200	Buka Runway	18,500'
Werber	215	0828	16VRY	1200	Buka Runway	18,500'
FRIEND	141	0830	17VRY	1200	Buka Runway	18,500'
EIGME	906	0829	18VRY	1200	Buka Runway	18,500'
HANSKI	925	0831	19VRY	1200	Buka Runway	18,500'
MARSHALL	497	0833	20VRY	1200	Buka Runway	18,500'
FRANCIS	107	0832	21VRY	1200	Buka Runway	18,500'
RATTI	211	0834	22VRY	1200	Buka Runway	18,500'
BYRD	145	0836	23VRY	1200	Buka Runway	18,500'
SCOTT	213	0835	24VRY	1200	Buka Runway	18,500'

REMARKS: Start engines 20 minutes prior to take-off. Landing new Squadron procedure.
SQUADRON ASSEMBLY: Over Field at 2,000'. Assemble with the 372nd over Save at 7,000'. Leave on Course 081T.
ROUTE OUT: Save to Baga Island. Meet 16 Fighters at Baga at 11,000' between 1035 - 1045. Leave on Course 104T.
to 156° 36'E., 6° 16'S then to 154° 50'E., 5° 14' S.

ROUTE BACK: South of Empress Augusta Bay, South of Treasury and home.
ROUTE FORMATION: Echelon of Sqdns. Javelin down within Sqdns., 372nd Leading. 424th 500' higher on their right
wing.

PLAN OF ATTACK: Left turn to run of approximately 228°. Right turn away from target and left turn on course.
TARGET: Buka Runway SECONDARY: Benis Plantation. THIRD: FOURTH: Poporang Seaplane base.
BOMB INTERVAL: 800' BOMB LOAD: 8-1000# OF 1/10 Sec. Nose & 1/10 Sec. Tail.
STANDARD NAVY RESCUE CRAFT

AREA	CONTROL		BOAT CALL	FREQ.
BUKA	QUARTZ	JOE		6050
MUNDA-RENDOVA	DIAMOND	PLUTO	6050	
BARAKOMA	SIRIUS	DICK	6050	
RUSSELLS	Y-69		6050	
DUMBO AT MUNDA		30TR8		

IFF WILL BE ON AT ALL TIMES.

XIII BOMBER COMMAND, COMMAND STATION COT51 ON
GUARD AT ALL TIMES (UNLESS IN CASE OF EMERGENCY)
FREQUENCIES: STAND BY ON 5820 KC AND 6050 KC UNTIL BEYOND
RUSSELLS AND 6060 KC AND 4500 KC FROM THERE ON
REVERSE ON RETURN.
LIAISON: 4175 KC Continuous Secondary
3050 KC 1700 - 0800 Primary
1785 KC 0800 - 1700 Primary
ALTERNATE FREQ: 5550 KC 1700 - 0800
7890 KC 0800 - 1700 Primary

270

[illegible] [illegible] 1005
Leave on [illegible] 1025

424th BOMBARDMENT SQUADRON (H), AAF
Office of the Operations Officer.

APO # 709
7 November 1943

FLIGHT SCHEDULE

PILOT	SHIP #	T/O'S	CALL LETTERS	TARGET	ATTACK TIME	ATTACK ALT.
✓Alexandre	157	0810	1V27	N.W. Dispersal Area at Buka Runway	1150	20,000'
Warben — A-1	216	0812	2V27		1150	"
➤✗Jelley	324	0811	3V27	"	"	"
Hanson	926	0813	4V27	"	"	"
Darr	141	0815	5V27	"	"	"
Taylor	910	0814	6V27	"	"	"
Ratti	819	0816	7V27	"	"	"
Marshall	858	0818	8V27	"	"	"
Francis	107	0817	9V27	"	"	"
Byrd	145	0819	10V27	"	"	"
Pueppke	260	0821	11V27	"	"	"
Scott	212	0820	12V27	"	"	"

REMARKS: Start engines 20 minutes prior to take-off. Landing new squadron procedure.
SQUADRON ASSEMBLY: Over field at 2,000'. Assemble with 372nd over Save at 7,000'. Leave on course at 0910 for Pilelia Island.
ROUTE OUT: Save to Bikella - Approximately 20 miles off coast of Bougainville til turn in toward Buka.
ROUTE FORMATION: Echelon of Sqdns. Javelin down within Sqdn. 424th leading. 372nd 500' below on left wing.
PLAN OF ATTACK: Turn left to run of approximately 225°. "B" Flight will move out to left, "C" Flight will move out to the right. "D" Flight will follow "A" Flight. Right turn away from target. Left turn and return by Northern Circuitous route.
TARGET: Northwest Dispersal area at Buka. Secondary: Dispersal area at Bonis. Third: Kahili Dispersal area.
BOMB INTERVAL: Buka Dispersal Area - 40 Stations 125'
20 Stations 250'
Kahili Dispersal Area 40 Stations 125'
20 Stations 250'
Bonis Dispersal Area - 40 Stations 50'
20 Stations 100'

STANDARD NAVY RESCUE CRAFT

AREA	CONTROL	BUOY CALL	FREQ.
Segi	Quarts	Joe	6050
Munda-Rendova	Diamond	Plato	6050
Barakoma	Sirius	Dink	6050
Russells	Y-59		6050
[illegible] at Munda		80V28	6050

FREQUENCIES: Standby on 6620 KC and 6050 KC until beyond Russells and 6050 KC & 4530KC from there on. Reverse on return.
LIAISON: 4675 KC continuous Secondary
5050 KC 1700 - 0800 Primary
7768 KC 0800 - 1700 Primary
ALTERNATE FREQ: 3860 KC 1700-0800 .. 7360 KC 0800-1700

424th BOMBARDMENT SQUADRON (H), AAF
Office of the Operations Officer

APO # 709
9 November 1943

FLIGHT SCHEDULE

	PILOT	AIRPLANE #	T/O's	CALL LETTER	TARGET	ATTACK ALT.	ATTACK TIME
A	Alexandre	137	1045	13V37	Bonis	18,500'	1100
A	Marpster	366	1047	14V37	"	"	"
A	Jolley	324	1046	15V37	"	"	"
B	Werban	316	1048	16V37	"	"	"
B	Friend	141	1050	17V37	"	"	"
B	Blakee	966	1049	18V37	"	"	"
C	Hanson	381	1051	19V37	"	"	"
C	Byrd	926	1053	20V37	"	"	"
C	Francis	107	1052	21V37	"	"	"
D	Ratti	319	1054	22V37	"	"	"
D	Puephe	360	1056	23V37	"	"	"
D	Scott	868	1055	24V37	"	"	"

REMARKS: Start engines 20 minutes prior to take-off. Land new squadron procedure.

SQUADRON ASSEMBLY: 372nd will circle field twice while climbing to 2500'. 424th will circle once while climbing to 2000'. Op assembly over Have at 7,000'. Leave on course at 1140. (Alternate Op assembly over Bingina Island)

Route OUT: Northern circuitous from Have to point where left turn is made in toward target.

ROUTE FORMATIONS: Echelon of Squadrons. Javelin down within sqdn. 372nd loading. 424th 500ft below on right wing.

PLAN OF ATTACK: Left turn into target. 424th will fall back and make individual sq run. Each flight leader will make a PDI run (Lead bombardier in each flight sight for range and deflection) B,C &D flights will have to fall back enough to permit flight leader to make PDI run. Run will be made at 165MPH.
Left turn away from target over Tadel Island. Return Southern, circuitous route.

TARGET: (1) Bonis (2) Buka (3) Kahili (4) Kara (5) Ballale
BOMB INTERVAL: 200' (Aim 1/4 way down runway)

STANDARD NAVY RESCUE CRAFT

AREA	CONTROL	BOAT CALL	FREQ:
Bogt	Quarts	Joe	6050
Munda-Rendova	Diamond	Plute	6060
Barakoma	Sirius	Dick	6060
Russelle	Y-59		6060
Dumbo at Munda	JOVRD		6060

BOMB LOAD: Maximum 500# of 1/10 Nose 1/10 Tail

FREQUENCIES: Standby ch 5620 KC and 6050 KC until beyond Russells and 5050 KC & 4500KC from there on. Reverse on return.

LIAISON: 4878 KC Continuous Secondary
5050 KC 1700 - 0600 Primary
7765 KC 0600 - 1700 Primary

ALTERNATE FREQUENCY: XXXX N880 KC 1700-0600 P, 7890 KC 0600-1700
TIMES: (GROUND COMMAND, COMMAND STATION 00V21, GUARD AT ALL TIMES IN EMERGENCY)

IFF WILL BE ON IN ALL SHIPS

SHASTA'S FATAL MISSION

MISSION SHEETS CONTRIBUTED
BY EDWIN M. McCONNELL   414th BOMBARDMENT SQUADRON (H), AAF
Office of the Operations Officer.

APO # 709
10 November 1943 &
11 November 1943

PILOT	AIRPLANE #	T/O	CALL LETTERS	TARGET	ATTACK ALT	ATTACK TIME
					19500	0745 -1100

	PILOT	AIRPLANE #	T/O	CALL LETTERS
A	Alexandre			
A	Werden			
	Jolley			
B	Mason			
B	Friend			
B	Babo			
C	Batti			
C	Marshall			
C	Francis			
P	Byrd			
D	Popple			
B	Scott			

REMARKS:

SQUADRON ASSEMBLY:

ROUTE OUT:
ROUTE FORMATION:
PLAN OF ATTACK:

TARGET:
BOMB INTERVAL:

FREQUENCIES:

LIAISON:

STANDARD NAVY RESCUE CRAFT

AREA	CONTROL	BOAT CALL	FREQ.
	Quartz		6050
Munda-Rendova	Diamond	Pluto	6060
Barakoma	Sirius	Dick	6060
Russells	Y-59		6050
Dumbo at Munda		SOV28	6060

A.P.O. #709
16 November 1943.

424TH BOMBARDMENT SQUADRON (H), AAF
OFFICE OF THE Operations Officer

PILOT	SHIP	T/O'S	CALL LETTERS	TARGET	ATTACK TIME	ATTACK ALTITUDE
ALEXANDER	019	0810	13V27	Kahili		19,800' Ind.
HARPSTER	925	0812	14V27	"		19,800' Ind.
FRANCIS	107	0811	15V27	"		19,800' Ind.
WORBON	215	0813	16V27	"		19,800' Ind.
FRIEND	141	0815	17V27	"		19,800' Ind.
BISBEE	258	0814	18V27	"		19,800' Ind.
BYRD	145	0816	19V27	"		19,800' Ind.
PURYEE	260	0818	20V27	"		19,800' Ind.
SCOTT	266	0817	21V27	"		19,800' Ind.

REMARKS: Start engines 20 minutes prior to take-off. Lending new Squadron procedure.
SQUADRON ASSEMBLY: Over field at 2,000'. Assembly with 372nd over Save at 10,000'. Leave on course at 0910.
ROUTE OUT: Up Slot. Make left hand turn over Faure Island, then right hand turn over Alaising Island 5 in to target from the Sea.
ROUTE FORMATION: Echelon of 3's. Javelin down within Sqdns.
PLAN OF ATTACK: Right turn on to target. Let down 600'. 424th will be on left wing 500' below. Bombing by flights. Right turn away from target, leaving Bougainville Must north of Lake Lallule. Return to base by way of SLOT.

TARGET: Kahili Runway. Secondary: Ballale. Tertiary: Kara. Mt. FINIA
BOMB INTERVAL: 125' aim 1/3 way down runway. BOMB LOAD 12-500# GP 1/10 sec. Nose & Tail Fuze.

STANDARD NAVY RESCUE CRAFT

AREA	STATION	BOAT CALL	FREQ.
Segi	Gertz	Joe	6050 ;
Munda-Rendova	Diamond	Pluto	6050 ;
Barakora	Sirius	Lick	6060 ;
Russells	Y-69		6050 ;
Dumbe et blanc			6660 ;

FREQUENCIES: Stand by on 5620 KC and 6050 KC until beyond Russells and 6050 KC & 4500 KC from there on. Reverse on return.
LIAISON: 4576 KC continuous Secondary
3050 KC 1700 - 0800 Primary
7765 KC 0800 - 1700 Primary
Alternate Freq: 3560 KC 1700-0800 P. 7890 KC 0800-17.

CANCELLED

394th BOMBARDMENT SQUADRON (M)
Office of the Operations Officer

APO /700
14 November 1943

PILOT	SHIP	T/Pt	CALL LETTERS	TARGET	ATTACK TIME	ATTACK ALT.
Alexander	313	0700	2NBR	Rata Rummy	1940	12,000 Ind.
Kapuber	345	0715	KATYY	•	•	•
Friabik	107	0721	LATYY	•	•	•
Waten	313	0705	LOTYY			
Fried	143	0715	LITYY	•	•	•
Stahno	206	0731	LUTYY			
Dynd	145	0700	LPTYY			
Humphee	200	0715	LAMYY	•	•	•
Robb	214	0721	NITYY	•	•	•

Much of the remaining text is illegible due to the faded condition of the document.

STANDARD NAVY BEACON CRAFT

UNIT	CONTROL	BOAT CALL	FREQ
	Quartz	Jed	4450
	Diamond	Plato	4450
	Sirius	Dick	4450
	Y-10		
		ROTES	

FREQUENCIES:

LIAISON

ALTERNATE FREQ

424TH BOMBARDMENT SQUADRON (H) AAF
307TH BOMBARDMENT GROUP (H) AAF
Office of the Operations Officer

APO 4709
15 November 1943

FLIGHT SCHEDULE

PILOT	SHIP #	T/O	CALL LETTERS	TARGET	XXXXX ALT.	ATTACK TIME
Norban	315	0700	SVXY	SEARCH	1000'	--------
Batti	666	0702	SVXY)	SEARCH	1000'	--------
Pickos	107	0701	YXX7	SEARCH	1000'	--------

REMARKS : SEARCH FOR MISSING CREW. TAKE-OFF AND SEARCH IN FORMATION. ZUMBO AT MUNDA - CALL LETTERS

BOMB-LOAD : NONE. NOTES on 6050 FC.

STANDARD NAVY RESCUE RELAY

AREA	CONTROL	BOAT CALL	FREQ.
Segi	Quartz	Joe	8050
Munda-Rendova	Diamond	Pluto	8050
Burakosa	Sirius	Dick	6040
Russells	X-59		8040
Dumbo at Munda		NOVEB	6050

FREQUENCIES : Interplane 6050 KC
Munda Tower Call 6060
Toll Tower Call 6620
4575 KC Continous Secondary
5050 KC 1700 - 0800 Primary
7755 KC 0800 - 1700 Primary
STAND BY ON 5050 KC (for MESSAGES FROM GOVT.

LIAISON :

WILLIAM R. HARPSTER,
Captain, Air Corps

ONE TYPE K-20 CAMERA HAS BEEN PLACED IN EACH SHIP SCHEDULED FOR SEARCH AND ARE TO BE USED FOR OFFICIAL USE ONLY TO RECORD ANYTHING SIGHTED. CAMERAS ARE LOADED WITH FIFTY EXPOSURES AND LENS SPEED IS SET, CAMERA IS READY TO OPERATE.

SMITH
PHOTO

424th Bombardment Squadron (H), AAF
Office of the Operations Officer

A.P.O. # 709
7 December 1943.

PILOT	AP #	T/O	CALL LETTERS	TARGET	ATTACK AT.	ATTACK TIME
HANSEN	819	0710	1B27	1. Vunakanau	25,000' Ind.	1150
RATTI	157	0711	2B27	2. Rakanai	"	"
FRANCIS	200	0712	3B27	3. City of Rabaul	"	"
				4. Poporang 21000' I		
BYRD	146	0713	4B27	5. Kahili target "H"	"	"
MARSHALL	461	0714	5B27	21000 I	"	"
PUEPKE	266	0715	6B27			
→ JELLEY	144	0716	7B27		"	"
TAYLOR	809	0717	8B27		"	"
McCONNELL	216	0718	9B27			

SQUADRON ASSEMBLY: Over Field at 15,000.
GROUP ASSEMBLY: Over Field. #1 Sqdn. takes-off first makes two circles. Leave Koli at 0730.
ROUTE FORMATION: 424th Lead, 370th #2, 500' lower. Javelin down within sqdns. _____
ROUTE OUT: Direct to Torokina.- Rendezvous with fighters at 17,000' at 1000. Leave Torokina 1015. From there direct to 4° S
PLAN OF ATTACK: Right turn into target. Lose 1000' to bomb at 1200'. Right turn away going between Tobera and Rapope.
ATTACK FORMATION: Group Stagger. Bomb interval 100' Bomb Load: Max. Frag Clusters.
ALT. TARGETS: Rakanai, City of Rabaul, Poporang, Kahili target "H".
Bomb INTERVALS: 100'   60'   100'
REMARKS: 24 Fighters escorting. Start fuel transfer 0800. 25 Gal per engine at a time.

FREQUENCIES: Command   Primary   6050
                             Secondary   5620

STANDARD NAVY RESCUE CRAFT

AREA	CONTROL	BOAT CALL	FRE
Sogi	Quartz	Joe	605
Munda-Rendova	Shag	Plute	605
Barakoma	Sirius	Dick	605
Russells	Y-69		605
Dumbo at Munda		30B28	605

Liaison   4576 (Primary) Cont.
            7785 (Secondary) 0800-1700 L.
            3050 (Secondary) 1700-0800 L.

CALL LETTERS: GROUND STATION 13th BOMBCOM OOB1 GUARD AT ALL TIMES.

WILLIAM R. HARPSTER,
CAPTAIN, AIR CORPS,
OPERATIONS OFFICER.

Appendix B

COMBAT CREWS
424th Bomb Squadron (H)

Harold McNeese's Crew (178): Lost his first plane and part of crew on first mission from Guadalcanal up to Shortland Harbor on Feb. 13, 1943. Those who returned to fly again were Bill Adams, Wesley Caroll, Harvey Vanderslice, Don DeClerque. Losing plane and part of crew, they flew Man-O-War. Jelley flew as co-pilot and the rest of his crew flew with McNeese's crew until Shehasta was repaired and came up to Guadalcanal for takeover by Jelley's crew.

*McCloskey Crew (966) Dean Johnson, Bernard Banner, Frank Davis, John Delaney, Barnard Jennings, Jim McCloskey, Jim Grant, Earnest Ballou, William SanFranAndre, Edney Briggs.

*Worban's Crew (216) Vickers, Hulls, Boyer, Neal Daniel, Snow, Worban, Spikes, Roderer, McConnell, Longan.

*Bisbee's Crew (966 & 258) Flew with 371st and 424th. San Fillipo, Gaber, Buchanan, Cassedy, Loges, Bisbee, Stratton, Benson. Flew with 424th on fatal mission November 11, 1943.

*Hansen' Crew (221—Mammy Yokum) Morris, Donald C. Hansen, Mann, McConnel, Hornell, Scott, Horszko, Eason, "Red" McCarthy.

*Byrd's Crew (145) Ira Jackson, Mike Woyciesjes, Bob Ladd, Jack Morrison, Burns Downey, C. Walter Byrd, Steptoskie, McKinzie, Colangelslo, Cassidy.

Binder's Crew (Little Mick brought from U. S.) Robert Pringle, Ken Phelps, *Robert Toberski, *Richard Kruger, *Robert Brink, *Richard Haskin, Richard Birchfield, *Joe Slater, Joseph Binder, *Ralph Biornholm, (*all lost while flying with Willie Francis's Crew over Truk, 3/29/44)

* Puepoke's Crew (#260 Babe In Arms) Frederick L. Reed, R. LaMorita, N. H. Formwalt (other members not identified)

*Ratti's Crew (266 Jeannie C) Helmuth Schultz, Galen M. Milsap, George W. Moore, Harlan G. Simmons, Frank C. Hill, Warren E. Nelson, Tro E. Dahmer, Francis J. Murphy, Stanley T. Smith, Joe Markowentz, Salvadore Fatigato.

Vidmar's Crew (461) Donald Moore, Roy Rogerson, Bill Hulton, Chet Vaughn, Hubert Charboneau, Claude Becktell, Joe Fati, Ralph Lawrence, Frank Vidmar.

*Marshall's Crew (925 The Rattlet) Harper, John Coleman, C. Endy, K. D. Donavan (others not known) D. Marshall.

*Alexandre's Crew (137) Bud Lindahl, Peterson, Northcraft, Reineu-schnider, Woolverton, Alexandre, Bach, Keowen, Fisher.

*Francis's Crew (107) Barton, Bill Francis, Volstorff, Lauder. Some of crew lost on Truk mission, Refer to Binder's Crew. Others not known.

J. Rodwick's Crew (273 Rod's Rowdies) C. Buehl, J. Hepfer, C. Haglund, J. Rodwick, E. Anderson, J. Leffert, A. Corella, C. Wright, J. Brumfield, M. Hartdegeb.

(*) Crews listed above were on 424th Bomb Squadron's mission to Rabaul on November 11, 1943, when Shehasta was hit on its fatal mission. Crews changed planes at times based on availability. Scott's Crew and Friend's Crew were also on that mission. See Mission Sheet dated 10th and 11th November 1943. Based on mission sheets, plane numbers, and other information available to the Author.

About The Author

Lyman Austin "Ace" Clark, Jr.. was born in Weston, West Virginia. He served from September 1942 to September 1945 in the U.S. Army Air Corps and from July 1948 to December 1955 in the U.S. Air Force. He received an Honorable Discharge as Master Sergeant and was wounded on November 11, 1943 Solomon Islands. He was an Armorer-Aerial Gunner, Lower Ball Turret in the B-24 Liberator Shehasta. He was shot down over Rabaul, New Britain, bailed out and was rescued by the Destroyer U.S.S. Claxton. He flew 35 combat missions and is credited with 3 Zeros, 2 Haps and 4 probable enemy aircraft, achieving "Bomber Ace" status. He was a member of the 424th Bomb Squadron, 307th Bombardment Group (Heavy) and the 13th Air Force, USAFISPA. He was overseas three times; Guadalcanal, WWII, Guam, Korean War and Japan. He was awarded the Distinguished Flying Cross, Four Air Medals, Military Order of the Purple Heart, Asiatic-Pacific Theatre, four Bronze Battle Stars, American Campaign, American Defense, United Nations, Korean Service, Army and Air Force Good Conduct Medal, National Defense Service, WWII Victory, Medal of French Liberation, (New Hebrides Island). He served as Aerial Gunnery Instructor, MacDill Field 1944 in Tampa, Florida, on B-17 Flying Fortresses.

He has served in civilian life as an insurance agent, underwriter, superintendent, insurance company vice-president , real estate broker, G.R.I., and has A.A.S. B.A., LL.B. Degrees. He is commander, Military Order of the Purple Heart, Dept. of West Virginia 1991-92, 32°AASRFM, President, Sons of Revolution in West Virginia, 1992-93; Part-time instructor Fairmont State College; member WVU and FSC Alumni Associations; member VFW, MOPH, DAV, American Legion; Col. (Hon) W. Va. Militia.

Index

Index